50 0373918 3

AF749783

332.1
BHA

Financial Systems, Innovations and Development

Financial Systems, Innovations and Development

V. V. Bhatt

UWE, BRISTOL

-7 MAR 1996

Library Services

Sage Publications
New Delhi / Thousand Oaks / London

Copyright © V. V. Bhatt, 1995

All rights reserved. No part of this book may be reproduced or utilized in any form or by any means, electronic or mechanical, including photocopying, recording or by any information storage or retrieval system, without permission in writing from the publisher.

First published in 1995 by

Sage Publications India Pvt Ltd
M–32 Greater Kailash Market I
New Delhi 110 048

Sage Publications Inc
2455 Teller Road
Thousand Oaks, California 91320

Sage Publications Ltd
6 Bonhill Street
London EC2A 4 PU

Published by Tejeshwar Singh for Sage Publications India Pvt. Ltd., phototypeset by Line Arts, Pondicherry and printed at Chaman Enterprises, Delhi.

Library of Congress Cataloging-in-Publication Data

Bhatt, V. V. (Vinayak Vijayshanker)
Financial systems, innovations, and development / V. V. Bhatt.
p. cm.
Includes index.
1. Financial institutions—Technological innovations. 2. Financial institutions—Developing countries. 3. Banks and banking—Japan. 4. Banks and banking—India. 5. Development banks. I. Title.
HG173.B48 332. 1—dc20 1995 95–34215

ISBN: 0–8039–9268–8 (US-hb) 81–7036–501–5 (India-hb)
0–8039–9269–6 (US-pb) 81–7036–502–3 (India-pb)

Sage Production Editors: *Mehdi Arslan and Evellyn George*

For Swati, Gita and Shuchi

शिवाः ते पन्थानः सन्तु ।

Contents

Introduction 9

Chapter 1 *Financial Innovations and Credit Market Evolution* 13

Chapter 2 *Development Banks as Catalysts for Industrial and Financial Development* 40

Chapter 3 *The Main Bank System in Japan: Financial Innovation for Industrial Development* 66

Chapter 4 *Lead Bank Systems in India: Review of performance* 106

Chapter 5 *Financial Institutions and Technology Policy* 132

Chapter 6 *On Participating in the International Capital Market* 149

Chapter 7 *Relevance of a Development-Oriented Banking System for Developing and Transforming Economies* 175

Statistical Appendices

A. *Statistical Appendix Relating to the Main Bank System* 195

B. *Statistical Appendix: India—Structure and Efficiency of the Financial System* 207

Index 220

Introduction

The pace of economic development depends critically on the rate at which innovations are introduced by entrepreneurs; this entrepreneurial function has been performed historically by individuals or groups of individuals not only in the private sector but also in the government or financial institutions (whether government owned or strictly privately owned). However, the introduction of such innovations in the real productive sector has not been possible without a financial system that facilitates, stimulates or promotes the performance of the entrepreneurial function in the real sector; this strategic role of the banking or the financial system was first emphasized by Schumpeter, who considered credit creation as a 'monetary complement of the innovation process'.

The strategic role of the financial system depends on its capacity to introduce financial innovations—new financial instruments, new decision processes and criteria, cultivation of new markets for financial instruments, new organizational and managerial practices and new institutions. These innovations can reduce risk, and diffuse or spread inevitable risk, or transfer it to individuals/institutions that are willing to bear it because of their different subjective perceptions of risk and their ability to bear it. The nature and characteristics of financial innovations that stimulate economic development depend on the specific historical and socio-economic-political contexts of a given situation or a given country. A financial innovation that worked in one country cannot simply be imitated by another; as with technology, they need to be creatively adapted and improved to suit the specific context of the country concerned.

The nature and characteristics of financial innovations that have been responsible for the evolution and integration of credit and capital markets are discussed in Chapter 1, which also presents a case study of an innovative bank. This case study has current relevance and significance particularly for developing countries, as it indicates the type of financial innovations that are critical for tackling their problem of financing small enterprises—both farm and nonfarm—and mobilizing resources from low-income groups.

The broad theme of Chapter 2 relates to the financial innovation represented by the *credit mobilier* concept evolved by the Perreire Brothers in France during the middle of the nineteenth century. The ways in which it was adapted, improved and refined by various countries to suit their specific contexts for fostering, sustaining and stimulating the process of industrial and financial development are also discussed.

This concept was creatively adapted in Germany and other continental countries during the late nineteenth century and it gave rise to the universal banking system—the German investment banks—which, according to Gerschenkron, was a 'powerful invention comparable in economic effect to that of a steam engine'. The universal banking concept was adapted creatively in Japan while establishing the Industrial Bank of Japan in 1902, and in South Korea, when the Korea Development Finance Company (KDFC) deliberately adapted the concept and transformed itself into the Korea Long Term Credit Bank. This again was the concept or innovation which shaped the functioning of several development banks like the Industrial Development Bank of India, the Industrial Credit and Investment Corporation of India, the Industrial and Mining Development Bank of Iran (till 1979), and many other development banks started after the second world war.

Chapter 2 deals specifically with the role, which such successful development banks performed as catalysts for industrial and financial development. On the basis of their experience and performance, an attempt is made to generalize about the nature and characteristics of a development bank that can play such a role in other contexts, particularly in the developing countries. Further, the *differential* performance of these banks has been the result of *differential* institutional and policy frameworks; hence the nature and characteristics of the institutional and policy framework—the role of the State—that are consistent with the effective and efficient functioning of development banks are indicated in a general way.

After the second world war, Japan evolved a financial innovation—the main bank system—that was in several respects different from the universal banking system evolved in Germany. This main bank system was one of the strategic factors in the rapid industrial and economic development of Japan, particularly during the period 1951–73. The origin, nature and characteristics of the main bank system and the institutional and policy framework that made such a system effective are discussed in chapter 3. The relevance of this financial innovation for developing countries and the transforming socialist countries is also discussed in this chapter.

India began evolving the lead bank system in 1969—the theme of chapter 4—for performing functions similar to those of the main bank system in Japan. These lead bank systems represented a financial innovation, pregnant with great possibilities. However, unlike in Japan, the institutional and policy framework has not been conducive to the effective and efficient functioning of the lead bank system. Their performance, therefore, though quite significant, has not been similar to that of the main bank system in Japan. There is a potential for their functioning much more effectively given the radical changes in the policy framework since 1991–92, provided these systems are permitted to function according to their internal logic. The preconditions essential for their effective functioning are also indicated in this chapter.

The increasing store of scientific and technological knowledge in the world is a great asset for the developing countries, provided there is the know-how to absorb it. Such knowledge needs to be absorbed, adapted, improved and diffused, and the focal points or agencies in this process are the financial system and the technical consultancy centers; their role in this process is discussed in Chapter 5. The Universal Banks in Germany (in the late nineteenth century), the Industrial Bank of Japan, the Korea Long Term Credit Bank, and the Swedish banks did perform such a role. However, the Indian financial institutions—partly because of a lack of technology policy by the government—have failed to appreciate the significance of this role and have faltered even in utilizing effectively the agencies such as the Technical Consulting Organization (TCOs), specially promoted for the purpose. In the changed context of deregulation and liberalization policies, it is essential for rapid industrial and economic development to formulate and implement an appropriate technology policy and emphasize the critical role of the financial system for the purpose.

The international capital market, which was practically dormant since 1914, has been evolving vigorously since the sixties as a result of several financial innovations. However, the developing countries have not taken much advantage of this market so far. The preconditions for participation in this market are discussed, particularly in the context of India, in Chapter 6. Several policy measures have been taken recently for the purpose; however, two of the most essential conditions are still not operative: (*a*) macroeconomic stability and (*b*) investment banking competence to realize the benefits of import substitution and export promotion relating to financial services. The envisaged financial sector reforms still have not sufficiently emphasized the role of foreign banks, branches of Indian banks abroad and the acquisition of investment banking competence by the major Indian commercial and development banks for effective participation in the international capital market. A purposive policy on this is still to be formulated.

The concluding chapter (Chapter 7), emphasizes the urgency of evolving a sound, effective and efficient financial system in developing countries as well as the ex-socialist countries and the emerging market economies in China and Vietnam, as the financial system is one of the strategic institutional pre-requisites for generating rapid economic development. In the light of the evolution of various systems in historical perspective and the specific constraints and contexts of these countries, this chapter indicates the likely and desirable pattern of evolution of the financial system, provided they adopt a development-oriented institutional and policy framework. The nature and structure of such a financial system is likely to be a close *variant* of the Universal Banking System of Germany, the Main Bank System of Japan and the Lead Bank Systems of India; all these three systems have similarities in certain significant respects and are development-oriented—a characteristic that is highly relevant for the developing and transforming economies.

The theme of financial innovations and their impact on financial and economic development is still new. Its significance is not still adequately realized either in academic literature or in policy making particularly in the context of the developing countries. This book thus would be of interest to all those who deal with the relationship of the financial sector to socioeconomic development—policy makers and advisors, research and training institutes, top managements of banks and financial institutions in developing countries, as well as the transforming socialist countries like China, Russia and the East European countries, and international development banks like the World Bank and regional development banks in Asia, Africa, Latin America and Eastern Europe.

Chapter 1

Financial Innovations and Credit Market Evolution

I
INTRODUCTION

The role of innovation in the process of economic development has been well recognized in the literature since the seminal works of Marx, Schumpeter, and Kuznets. However, little attention has been paid to the significance of social innovations—in particular, financial and fiscal innovations. Financial innovations tend to reduce transaction costs and risk—both subjective and objective—and as a result bring about the widening, deepening, and integration of capital markets. Such financial development accelerates the pace of economic development through its favorable impact on saving, investment, and output.

The relationship between finance and development and the precise role of financial innovations is discussed in Section II, while Section III deals with the nature and characteristics of financial innovations. Section IV examines the role of policy intervention in quickening the pace of financial development in the developing countries. The nature and characteristics of financial innovations, essential for financing small farm and nonfarm enterprises and for mobilizing resources from middle- and low-income groups in the developing countries, are illustrated by a case study of an innovative bank in Section IV. Some concluding observations are made in the final section.

II
FINANCE AND DEVELOPMENT

The pace and pattern of economic development are a function, as Adam Smith perceptively observed two centuries ago, of the sequential and circular relationship between the growth of (*a*) division of labor and (*b*) extent of the market for real goods and services.[1] The innovations in the realm of money and finance tend to increase the size and the extent of exchange relationships or markets and thus promote division of labor, leading to increasing returns to scale and technical change.

Money as a unit of account and a medium of exchange reduces the transaction and search costs involved in barter transactions. Money as a store of value provides time for making purchase decisions, thus reducing the risk of ill-formed and hasty decisions.[2] Thus, through reduction of transaction costs and risk, money tends to enlarge the size of the market for real goods and services and hence the possibility of division of labor—the two interacting, mutually reinforcing forces that account for sustained economic development.

Just as money reduces transaction costs and risk for contemporary exchanges across space, credit or financial instruments reduce costs of transactions and risk for intertemporal exchanges of goods and services. It is thus that the existence of a credit or a capital market enlarges the market for real goods and services. The impact of money and capital markets on the market for real goods and services is similar to that of reduction of transport costs on trade or exchange across space.

Unlike the market for real goods and services, credit or capital markets are inherently imperfect in the sense that there is no certainty about the completion of a credit transaction. A credit transaction involves a relationship between a lender and a borrower in time (hence, in the context of uncertainty). A credit transaction is completed only when the borrower repays the amount borrowed, and there can be no certainty about this repayment.

First, there is the borrower's risk: the expected excess income required for repayment may or may not materialize. In addition, there is the lender's risk, which has two elements. One relates to the same risk facing the borrower, but the lender may have a different perception of it. The other element relates to the borrower's willingness to repay; even if he is able to repay, he may not. Both the lender's and the borrower's expectations with regard to the outcome in time—their perceptions of the riskiness of their ventures—are subjective, based as they are on the data available to each one of them and each one's ability to interpret them.[3]

Note that one part of the risk is double counted. The borrower has a certain perception of the risk he faces with regard to, say, his investment project. The lender, too, takes into account the same risk about which he may have a different perception or expectation. If the borrower's subjective risk premium is r_1, the lender's risk premium is $r_1 + ar_1$ (as the lender is likely to be more conservative in his expectations than the borrower) plus r_2 (his subjective risk with regard to the borrower's willingness to repay—the moral hazard problem.[4] The total risk premium, thus, would be

$$r_1 + ar_1 + r_2$$

This means that the borrower's expected rate of return or profit, *p*, on his investment should exceed the pure interest cost, *i*, by this magnitude, that is, $r_1\ (a + 1) + r_2$, plus t_1 (lender's transaction costs) plus t_b (borrower's transaction costs). For a credit transaction to take place the following condition should be satisfied:

$$P \geq r_1\ (a + 1) + r_2 + (t_1 + t_b) + i$$

Credit or capital markets come into being and evolve as a result of financial innovations that tend to reduce the total of r (representing $r_1\ [a + 1] + r_2$) and of transactions costs (representing $t_1 + t_b$) to a level that is mutually acceptable to both lenders and borrowers. The evolving nature and characteristics of these markets, of the dealers and the other participants, and of the credit or financial instruments are crucially shaped by the financial innovations that are feasible in a given socioeconomic context.

Financial innovations tend to reduce the lender's subjective risk to an extent much greater than they tend to increase transaction costs of lending and borrowing. Risk, of course, can be reduced with better and more accurate information, but this would involve an increase in transaction costs to the lender, the borrower, or both. Hence, to be effective an innovation should have a risk-reducing effect much greater than its cost-increasing effect.

UWE, BRISTOL LIBRARY SERVICES

III
THE NATURE AND CHARACTERISTICS OF FINANCIAL INNOVATIONS

The evolution and integration of capital markets through the introduction and diffusion of financial innovations are not possible without some occupational specialization in the field of credit and finance. Dealers and intermediaries are significant. Isolated and individualized financial transactions (lending and borrowing) among households and firms are quite important in certain sectors of the economy like agriculture and small enterprises, but for capital markets to evolve, it is essential to have dealers who specialize in financial claims or instruments.

A dealer need not be an intermediary; he need not borrow in order to lend. Even for a financial intermediary, his lending activity is crucial because his ability to borrow depends on the quality of his lending. A credit contract is completed only when the borrower repays his debt to the dealer in terms of the original contract. Hence, the lender's subjective risk and the innovations that reduce this risk assume critical significance. What, then, are the nature and characteristics of such innovations?

Nature and Characteristics

The degree of subjective risk depends on how well a lender knows the prospective borrower and can evaluate the borrower's ability and willingness to repay. Of course, the lender can demand information from the borrower and appraise it, but such information may be costly to collect and may not even be reliable.

The innovation of a *personal guarantee* reduces risk without at the same time increasing transaction costs. .Such a guarantee generally must be given by a person or a firm who has a well-known history and reputation for financial integrity, considerable assets, and a business that enables the lender to judge the character and nature of the prospective borrower. A well-established trader giving a personal guarantee for another trader, not known to the lender, illustrates the nature of this innovation. It is in this way that a dealer's market expands.

This device of a personal guarantee becomes feasible only when the market participants adhere to a common code of business ethics;

violations of this code lead to moral reprobation and excommunication from the market. Such codes and sanctions also provide the logic for the innovation of all types of cooperative credit arrangements among relatively homogeneous groups, who may not be considered creditworthy by other dealers and intermediaries. Lending by a dealer to individuals forming a homogeneous and cohesive group against individual as well as collective guarantees also belongs to this class of innovations.[5]

The innovation of short-term credit that is renewed or rolled over (provided repayments are made regularly and in time) is a very economical and effective way to select reliable and dependable borrowers and to avoid the risk relating to adverse selection. Short-term loans for working capital or liquidity requirements have this rationale: a regular borrower, who borrows as well as repays in time and who has the need to borrow at regular intervals for a known remunerative purpose, poses much less risk than does a new borrower without previous history. The loan size in these cases is a function of the degree of the lender's knowledge of the borrower; what might appear as credit rationing is merely a device for reducing risk to acceptable levels.

The innovation of interlinking credit transactions with trade transactions enables a trader to avoid the moral hazard problem. If a farmer regularly sells his output through a trader, the latter can deduct the principal and interest relating to his loan to the farmer from the sale proceeds due to the farmer. This interlinking of credit and goods markets to reduce the lender's risk is the device used by all types of cooperative credit and marketing societies. On the same principle, a landlord can provide credit to an agricultural laborer or tenant by interlinking credit market with the labor market.[6]

Short-term lending against personal or collective guarantees and/or to dependable and reliable borrowers is possible only when the dealers/lenders have fairly reliable personal knowledge and information about the borrowers and their occupations and assets. But the market for loans based on such personal contacts and on moral or social sanctions is limited. For enlarging and expanding the market, some objective substitute for personal guarantees (formal or informal) becomes essential—a substitute that has legal sanction. This is the logic of the innovation of collateral or security, comprising real or financial assets.

If the borrower deals in or possesses goods or assets that are easily marketable without much risk of capital loss, the loan size could be made a function of the value of such assets. The risk of capital loss can be reduced by having a loan size that is smaller than the market value of such assets, thus forcing the borrower to use his own money to finance this margin. This *security-cum-equity type of innovation* reduces the lender's subjective risk in two ways. First, the risk arising from the possible unwillingness of the borrower to repay virtually disappears. Second, the risk relating to the borrower's ability to pay is reduced as the borrower, because of his equity stake, is induced to manage his business as efficiently as he can.

This innovation, along with the *innovation of credit money*, creates conditions for the emergence of a bank with the capacity to create credit and thus to enlarge its scale of operations and take advantage of economies of scale, which tend to reduce transaction costs of both the bank as well as its borrowers. Further, the bank can reduce risk in a number of ways. With economies of scale, it can specialize in and standardize certain types of financial transactions and thus reduce risk through better expertise. Its scale enables it to pool and spread risks (the "Law of Large Numbers"), which is the basis of insurance.

The security-cum-equity type of innovation also creates the conditions for the emergence of securities markets—markets for financial instruments like all types of bills, bonds, and shares. This innovation of the securities markets reduces transaction costs for both lenders and borrowers. The lender's risk is reduced because of the information provided by the market dealers and brokers to the lenders and the negotiability and marketability of securities of all types. The borrower's risk is reduced as a result of the innovation of the joint stock company with limited liability; this enables the borrowing firm to spread its risk among a large number of equity holders. At the same time, it enables the firm to improve its profitability by making it possible for it to raise larger resources than it would have been able to do without this innovation (as the equity holder's risk is also reduced because of this innovation).

Where such securities markets do not evolve because of specific economic conditions, there emerges the innovation of a universal bank.[7] A universal bank finances both short-term and long-term credit requirements, specifically of industrial enterprises. The lender's risk with this innovation is reduced because of the security or collateral provision and also because of the active involvement of the universal bank in the entrepreneurial-managerial decisions of enterprises through its representation on the supervisory boards of these enterprises.[8] The main bank system that evolved in Japan since 1951 is in many respects a variant of the universal banking system of Germany—a system that evolved during the late nineteenth century in Germany. The nature and characteristics of these two systems are discussed in Chapters 2 and 3.

This management role of the bank has the same effect in reducing the lender's risk as the equity type of innovation. The innovation of the universal bank has lead to the evolution of refined techniques of cash flow analysis[9] and project evaluation. These techniques reduce the subjective risk of the lender by enabling him to make a reasonably accurate assessment of risk relating to the ability to pay of the borrowing enterprise.

It is somewhat difficult for one type of dealer to finance the acquisition of, and take as security, assets with which that type is not familiar. Hence, each class of dealers tends to specialize in one type of assets and thus in dealing with one class of borrowers; its technology for transactions and risk appraisal is in tune with this type of assets and the class of borrowers. It would increase both transaction costs and risk for a dealer with a technology suited for one type of transaction to undertake a different type, unrelated to the one in which he has specialized.

For example, a commercial bank that over time has acquired the technology for financing medium to large firms in industry and trade cannot finance agriculture or small enterprises without first acquiring a new type of technology suited to these transactions. Informal market dealers have a technology suited for financing small enterprises of all types, and if a commercial bank wants to expand its business in this type of transactions, it would be more economical and effective for it to lend to informal market dealers than to lend directly to the primary borrowers.[10]

A given technology is related to a certain class of transactions, comprising certain financial instruments, a certain class of borrowers, and certain assets as security. Dealers who have acquired a certain technology/expertise for historical reasons would find it more economical to undertake transactions related to their technology than to venture into fields that require a different type of technology. To deal with a different class of borrowers offering a different type of assets as security, therefore, is a function of a new type of dealer. Innovations that expand and deepen the scope of the capital markets are generally introduced by new entrepreneurs and a new type of dealer whose technology and expertise, as well as financial instruments, differ from those of the existing dealers. It is thus that new markets evolve.[11]

Since financial innovation leads to a variety of specialized dealers and markets, they create a diversity of financial instruments, each of them with unique characteristics and features. This diversity of financial products enables primary savers/borrowers to make a choice among instruments that is better suited to their special requirements. Such diversity stimulates saving in the form of financial assets as well as borrowing that promotes a more efficient allocation and use of resources. Further, the competition for mobilizing financial resources from the primary savers among this array of specialized dealers tends to integrate the various financial markets.

Once markets in specialized credit instruments evolve, a large intermediary—commercial or investment bank—can take advantage of economies of specialization along with economies of scale and scope.[12] Thus, this intermediary can deal in all types of credit or financial instruments, which lead to the emergence after 1960 of the so-called department store banking.[13] Because of technological externalities, inter-relationship among markets for various credit instruments, and technological revolution in the field of information gathering, processing, and transmission, this innovation tends to reduce transaction costs for both lenders and borrowers, and to reduce the lender's risk.[14] Commercial and investment banking tend to merge with each other, and loans and securities become close substitutes, giving rise to the so-called securitization of loans and, as a result, financial innovations like note issuance facilities, currency and interest rate swaps, options and futures.[15] (This is happening, for example, in the Euro-dollar market as well as in the credit markets of the United States.) All these innovations relate largely to global markets; separate institutions dealing in specialized credit or financial instruments particularly in local and national markets have their own distinct niches and are important for cultivating and nurturing new markets.[16]

Preconditions

What, then, are the preconditions for the emergence of such financial innovations, whose nature and characteristics have been described?

First, innovations require trust and confidence among the market participants. This general climate is reinforced by an effective and enforceable legal framework. If lenders and borrowers have to resort to legal safeguards for the greater part of their dealings, the transaction costs would be prohibitive. Without enforceable legal sanctions, the degree of risk in financial transactions would be inordinately high.

Second, there must be monetary stability. The uncertainty inherent in all credit transactions would be accentuated without some degree of monetary stability. Without it, the subjective risk of the market participants would increase and their confidence in the market would be shaken.

Finally, there should be no legal or customary obstacle to experimentation and innovation, particularly with regard to informal credit markets. Established formal dealers are reluctant to change over from one type of technology/expertise to another. To them, the subjective risk as well as transaction costs for the new untried technology appear much higher than those relating to existing technology.

Since informal market dealers operate largely on the basis of personal information and knowledge, they are in a much better position to identify new opportunities for financial transactions (that is, new markets requiring new products and processes). Moreover, their transaction costs and risk for such experimentation are relatively low. With the growth and expansion of formal markets, the informal dealers have a certain compulsion to innovate. Quite often new markets with new innovative products are created and nurtured by the informal market dealers. Once these new markets grow to a certain size, the formal markets with their scale economies are in a position to introduce the new products and thus compete effectively with the informal markets. This vital role of the informal markets in identifying new opportunities for financial transactions and in introducing innovations for creating and nurturing new markets is little appreciated in the literature as well as by the policymakers.[17]

The innovative ability of the informal capital market is demonstrated at the international level by the functioning of the Euro-dollar market. This Euro-market is quite similar to the informal credit markets in several developing countries—the markets that are out of reach of the national regulatory agencies. The former is relevant for large participants—large corporations, public entities, and sovereign governments—while the latter for small enterprises of all types. However, both the markets are characterized by relatively low transaction costs for borrowers partly because of this freedom from regulation.

This Euro-market has introduced several innovations or new financial instruments that have widened the choice with regard to instruments for both savers/investors and borrowers; investors now can choose instruments with characteristics (relating to yield, liquidity, risk and transaction costs) that they prefer, and similarly borrowers, too have a wider choice with regard to instruments with, different cost-risk combinations.

The major innovations introduced in this market tried to deal with the risks arising from the volatility of interest rates and exchange rates, resulting from the breakdown after 1973 of the Bretton Woods system of fixed exchange rates and the structural payment imbalances among the developed countries. These innovations are also relevant for the developing countries that are creditworthy. The preconditions for taking advantage of these innovations and participating in the international capital market are discussed in Chapter 6.

The most interesting innovation is the development of the swap market in both currency and interest rate swaps. This has been the most radical or revolutionary innovation that has been introduced in the international market in recent years, as it tends to reduce the risk to borrowers arising from the uncertainties relating to interest rate and exchange rate changes.

IV
THE ROLE OF PUBLIC POLICIES

Innovations are generally spontaneous, but they can also be induced by policy interventions. Innovations induced by policy interventions are of two types: one is cost and risk reducing, while the other relates to overcoming and offsetting the negative impact of general policy and it is cost and risk increasing.

Cost-risk Increasing Interventions

Interest rate ceilings and credit allocation quotas (for example, those prescribed for commercial banks by central bank/government authorities with a view to enlarging the flow of credit to small enterprises of all types, including those in the agricultural sector) are self-defeating and, in fact, raise the cost of credit to the very sector that the government intends to support.[18] The transactions costs and risks for dealing with small enterprises are higher for the banks than those for medium to large enterprises in the trade and industry sectors. The banks therefore would either not lend to the small sector or forestall the government directives by passing on a greater part of their costs and risks to the small sector through noninterest charges of various types.[19] If the banks did actually implement government directives, their financial viability would be adversely affected, and this would endanger the health of the financial system. This would result in undesirable consequences for economic development in general and for the development of the small sector in particular. Any way, it is meaningless to fix the price as well as the quantity; this would lead to credit rationing and queues and thus to considerable scope for corruption.

Arbitrary interest rate ceilings on lending by the banks lead to low interest rates on deposits. This has the effect of diverting private saving into commodities or private lending—both of which adversely affect the evolution of financial markets.

Another instance of negative policy intervention is the variety of restrictions placed on the functioning of the informal credit market. This market actually mobilizes resources from and purveys credit to sectors that are generally not within the purview of the formal market. Restrictions of its activity, therefore, either raise costs of credit or block credit to these sectors. Furthermore, the resources that this market mobilizes may be diverted to commodity hoarding and speculation.

Cost-risk Reducing Interventions

There are, however, types of interventions that have an impact similar to financial innovations or that may induce such innovations. For example, deposit insurance would reduce the subjective risk of primary savers and thus may increase the rate of financial saving. Viable credit guarantee schemes for agriculture and small enterprises may reduce the subjective risk of the dealers and may induce them to lend to these sectors. A deliberate policy of well-designed extension (through branch expansion) of the banking system along with credit allocation quotas (but without interest rate restrictions) and some fixed sum subsidy may induce banks to change their agenda and technology so as to reduce the overall transaction costs and risks to both lenders and borrowers. Effective and self-supporting crop insurance schemes may reduce the risk of lending to the farm sector and also may result in resource mobilization greater than would otherwise occur. Improving the access of farmers and small enterprises to financial and technical consultancy services can raise their productivity, thus reducing the risk of lending.[20]

By exempting saving in the form of financial assets from taxable income, the real rates of return on financial saving can be raised and thus the rate of financial saving could increase.[21] A fixed sum subsidy to, say, a commercial bank to cover the initial fixed cost of acquiring financial technology required for effective and economical lending to small enterprises, or to open a branch in an unbanked area, can make it possible for the bank to introduce financial instruments suited to the needs of the potential depositors and borrowers.[22]

Thus, the impact of policy intervention on the credit and capital markets should be judged on the basis of this simple criterion: does it reduce overall transaction costs and risks associated with financial transactions. If it does not have this cost-risk reducing effect, it would harm rather than help the evolution and integration of capital markets.[23]

The financial innovations essential for effective and viable financing of small enterprises (including small farms) and for mobilizing resources from small savers are illustrated by the following case study of an innovative commercial bank—the Syndicate Bank. This case study relates to the period 1925 to 1975—a period during which it had operational autonomy (which got eroded because of nationalization after 1969).

V
FINANCIAL INNOVATIONS: THE SYNDICATE EXPERIENCE

Until 1969, the large city-based banks in India concentrated on financing large industry and trade in the urban areas. Their transaction costs for these markets were quite low—well within the range of 1.5 percent to 2 percent of assets, which Keynes indicated many years back as the level below which interest rates cannot fall.[24] They did not enter the field of small to medium enterprises in the farm and nonfarm sectors. In these markets, their transaction costs would have been very high, and on the terms on which they could have lent, it was not possible to widen and deepen these markets.

It was difficult for a new bank to compete with these city banks in their markets. It had to enter a new field—a noncompetitive field—and this related to small to medium enterprises. This objective opportunity was there, but to seize it required an innovative approach to banking—introduction of new products and processes to reduce transaction costs. And this is precisely what the Syndicate Bank did since its origin in 1925.[25]

The Characteristics of the Syndicate

The Syndicate Bank was located in the small town of Manipal, India (the only bank with a head office in a rural area), and started with an initial paid-up capital of only 8,000 rupees. Its growth has been remarkable. From a negligible share in banking business till 1950, its share rose to about 1 percent in 1960 and 4 percent in 1975. Still, it was unlike the city-based banks, particularly till 1969, when it was nationalized along with the thirteen major banks. In 1968, 32 percent of its branches were in rural areas; for the entire banking system, the share of rural branches was only 22 percent. Its loans to agriculture and small enterprises constituted 30 percent of its total loans; for the other banks, such loans were less than 8 percent of their total loans. Ninety percent of its deposit accounts were small accounts (below Rs. 1,500) accounting for 50 percent of its deposits; and 50 percent of its borrowing accounts related to small to medium enterprises, their share in total borrowing being 30 percent.

Its average interest rate on loans was not much higher than that of the city banks; in the 1950s, it was about 2 percentage points higher than that of the State Bank of India—the largest commercial bank. Since the early 1970s, the rate has been more or less the same as that charged by the major city banks.

How did it, then, manage to grow so rapidly, even while concentrating on markets that the city banks found to be unremunerative? Obviously, its transaction costs must have been comparable to the costs of lending to large industry and trade by the city banks.

Transaction Costs and the Functional Cost Structure

Complete data on the cost structure of the city banks are not available. However, the data on establishment expenses are available; establishment expenses include a large part of administrative costs but do not include default risk (bad debt provision). The ratio of establishment expenses to total deposits for the Syndicate Bank was slightly higher than that for the banking system in 1951 and 1961. Since then, this ratio has been somewhat lower for the Syndicate Bank than that for the banking system as a whole. Quite surprisingly, the Syndicate Bank's ratio is comparable to that of the insured commercial banks in the United States.

Much more interesting, however, would be the comparison of the functional cost structure of the Syndicate Bank with the other city banks, who have been financing small to medium enterprises particularly since 1969. However, such data are not available for any bank in any country. Even for the Syndicate Bank, such data could be obtained only for 1975; they were compiled by the Syndicate Bank especially for our purposes. One other major commercial bank located in Bombay could give us these data again only for 1975.

The overall transaction costs of this city bank are lower than those of the Syndicate Bank. This was to be expected since this city bank's lending to small enterprises constituted only 25 percent to 30 percent of its total lending, while the share of small enterprise lending in the total lending by the Syndicate Bank is about 40 percent. However, the city bank's costs are more than three times those of the Syndicate Bank for lending to agricultural and small enterprises.

For deposit mobilization, the Syndicate Bank's administrative costs are much lower than those of the city bank. The interest costs of deposits are somewhat lower for the city bank as demand deposits constitute a much higher proportion of its total deposits.

But how has the Syndicate Bank been able to service a large number of small accounts—deposit as well as borrowing—and thus provide credit to the small enterprises at a cost that is much below that of the city banks? Briefly, the answer lies in its innovative approach to banking. The creative adaptation of the banking technology to suit local conditions seems to explain this phenomenon.

The Factors Accounting for Low Transaction Costs

New Entrepreneurs

This new style of banking was possible because of the characteristics of the leaders.[26] The promoters came from a lower-middle class background; they belonged to a community that respects learning. None of them came from an industrial house. The city banks were started by promoters who had close links with large industry. Of the three promoters, one was a medical doctor, one an engineer, and the third a trader dealing in handloom cloth.

All of them were participants in the movement for socioeconomic reform initiated by Mahatma Gandhi. They wanted to improve the socioeconomic status of the community and the region to which they belonged. Hard work, education, and thrift—these they considered crucial for socioeconomic reform. They had not only a passion for reform but also a hard-headed business sense. They considered banking as an instrument for the purpose of reform; to serve as an effective instrument, it had to be viable and gain vitality for growth.

They were responsible for establishing a school in each village in their district and an education complex, a type of university center at their village of Manipal. The bank management helped the process, but at the same time it was conscious of the deposit potential of these institutions. The bank provided employment opportunities for the educated members of the local community. This helped in terms of having a dependable and dedicated staff. The bank helped the farmers and small enterprises by providing technical assistance; such assistance also helped enlarge their business. The bank cultivated the habit of thrift in the community through a new deposit scheme called Pigmy Deposit, and this also enlarged the bank's resources.

Recruitment and Promotion Policies

The major factor responsible for the relatively high productivity of the staff was the Syndicate Bank's recruitment policy.[27] Relatively unsophisticated persons with local contact and rural or semi-urban background were selected. Unlike the city banks, the Syndicate Bank preferred high school graduates to graduates or post-graduates from universities. Their familiarity with the local scene and their contacts enabled them to expand the Syndicate Bank's business in a variety of ways; they inspired confidence in potential depositors, and they were able to appraise well the soundness of projects and the creditworthiness of borrowers and to assess the business potential of the area in which they functioned. The information costs thus were reduced; persons without this background would have had to collect more information and spend more effort and time in appraising the soundness of borrowers and their schemes.

Since they are high school graduates, they enter the banking business at a fairly young age and thus are more adaptable. Again, since they would not have gotten such a job in the city banks, they consider themselves fortunate and hence are more dedicated, dependable, and disciplined. They are prepared to do considerable field work, which is essential for attracting, maintaining and supervising small accounts. And, of course, their pay scales are lower than those for the graduates in the city banks. The Syndicate Bank's average salary per employee even now is 20 to 30 percent lower than that in the city banks. And the staff's academic qualifications are adequate for the banking business. Persons with university degrees are overqualified for many bank jobs. From the point of view of the institution, such persons are less adaptable, more ambitious, and less disciplined than those who have completed high school.

The promotion policy of the bank builds staff morale and attempts to avoid discontent and demoralization. Somewhat in the Japanese style, a person is promoted in terms of salary and grade on the basis of seniority, provided there are no consecutive adverse reports on his efficiency. But such a promotion does not mean that he would get a more responsible functional assignment. Seniority promotion in a salary grade is divorced from functional promotion. Responsible positions are assigned to bright persons without affecting adversely the salary promotion of others and without affecting favorably their own salary grades. Functional promotion thus is a type of reward for the really deserving; he wins recognition for his worth. The others are not discontented since their salary promotions are not affected.

This divorce of functional promotion from seniority promotion in a salary grade helps the bank in selecting persons for senior management positions. For the top few jobs, which are purely on a selection basis, the bank has a choice from among the persons who are really competent—those who are promoted to a higher function.

Another characteristic of the bank's recruitment policy is worth noting. When possible, the bank recruits married couples. These couples have proved to be more stable, reliable, and dedicated than other employees.

This recruitment and promotion policy is reflected in the productivity of the Syndicate Bank's employees. The deposit accounts handled per employee are 287 for the Syndicate Bank, while they are only 120 for the banking system as a whole. Again, the borrowing accounts per employee are 48 for the Syndicate Bank and only 14 for the banking system as a whole. The Syndicate Bank's productivity differential compared with the city banks' would be much greater than what these figures indicate, for the comparison is with the *average* for the banking system as a whole. If the wage differential is considered along with the physical productivity differential, the productivity differential in financial terms would be much more significant than the physical productivity differential.

Technical Assistance

The bank provides technical assistance to farmers as well as to small industrialists. It has a special staff for this purpose. The farm representatives are a special cadre of young officers recruited from the agricultural universities and specially trained for the banking business. Similarly, for the small industry sector, the bank has a cadre of industrial engineers and technicians.

Each one of these officers looks after about five to ten branches depending upon local conditions. The bank's policy of opening branches in clusters in a given region helps it to spread the costs of these special cadres over a number of geographically contiguous branches.

The technical assistance provided helps the borrowers; at the same time it enlarges the bank's business and reduces its risk. These special cadres are able to appraise credit proposals in the field. Their periodic field visits also provide an effective machinery for supervision as well as recovery of loans.

Decentralized Decision Making and Avoidance of Paper Work

The volume of work involved cannot be effectively handled without decentralized decision making. The loans to farmers and small enterprises are sanctioned by the branch managers with the advice of the technical cadre; there is no reference to the head office, and thus the head office costs for such loans are negligible.

The emphasis is on field work not desk work. Local decision making and initiative are valued. The branch and the branch manager are judged on the volume of deposits and the magnitude of loans and of their recovery. The bank thus exercises the utmost economy in the sphere of documenting information and its transmission to the head office. Such reporting procedures would increase costs and divert the attention of the branch manager from banking business to collecting and documenting information, which is hardly relevant for decision making either at the branch or at the head office.

Since its nationalization in 1969, information costs have increased because of the directives and requirements of the Reserve Bank of India. The management is attempting, however, to keep them within limits. The central banks and the international banks do have a craze for information and demand such information from the intermediary and final lending agencies—the type of information that may be enlightening for researchers but is irrelevant for real decision making. They still have to realize that there are costs involved—sometimes as large as 1 to 2 percent of the loan portfolio. Instead of reducing transaction costs, they raise them.[28]

Innovative Deposit Schemes

The bank introduced a variety of innovative deposit schemes linked to motives to save. One recent example is the Farmers' Protection Deposit Scheme. In times of dire necessity arising out of crop failure, the farmer is eligible for a loan equal to double the amount of deposits outstanding in his account. This deposit earns interest at 5 percent per year, and the loan is at a concessional rate of 9 percent per year—repayable over a period of three years. The small farmer does not save normally in the form of a financial asset; interest rate on deposits is not much of an attraction to him, particularly when his transaction costs are high. But he can be induced to save in the form of a deposit if it is linked with borrowing at a time of crop failure. In the absence of crop insurance, this is the type of saving that the farmers need.[29]

This principle of linking deposits with lending for a specific purpose has been applied by the bank in several cases. A farmer, for example, would get a loan for the purchase of a pump set if he has accumulated 25 percent of the cost as fixed or saving deposits. A small industrialist gets a loan for machinery purchase if he accumulates more than 20 percent of the cost as deposits. Such schemes help the bank to mobilize deposits as well as to judge the seriousness of purpose of the borrower. Because of the assurance of a loan, the borrower has inducement to save. Without such assurance in many cases there would not be saving enough for investment, and hence there would be a strong temptation to use up the funds for financing emergencies or social expenditures.

The bank is particularly known for its Pigmy Deposit, a scheme introduced in 1928 as part of its crusade to inculcate the habit of thrift among relatively poor people. The promoters regarded the Pigmy Deposit as a business opportunity. This opportunity was not seized upon by the other banks because of the transaction costs involved in collecting small deposits from a large number of relatively uneducated and poor customers.

The scheme, however, proved to be financially profitable for the Syndicate Bank and attractive to the depositors. The principle of the scheme was simple: door-to-door collection of a given amount of deposits (as low as 25 paise) at stated intervals. It was thought that many people—workers, petty shopkeepers, vegetable vendors, hawkers, small traders—could save these small amounts per day or week or month. But they do not have time to go to a bank and deposit this amount regularly. This potential saving was not realized since the poor had no semicontractual obligation to accumulate. With agents appointed to collect such deposits, this saving capacity and inclination could be tapped.

And thus Syndicate Bank introduced this Pigmy Deposit to be collected periodically from the doorsteps of the saver. The commission rate was linked with the amount of deposits collected, and it has not exceeded 3 percent per year. The interest was 3.13 percent per year if the saver did not withdraw from the scheme for seven years. A depositor saving Rs.0.12 daily could accumulate at the end of the seventh year Rs.350. Within the period, the saver could borrow from the bank against the security of his deposit.

Such was the original scheme. Its specific features have varied since 1969, but the broad principle remains the same.

On an average, the total cost to the bank of this long-term deposit has varied between 3 percent and 5 percent per year—significantly lower than the cost of a three- to five-year fixed deposit. Even in 1975, the total cost was only 5.52 percent compared with the cost of fixed deposits at 13 percent.

The bank thus seized a business opportunity without competition from other banks until 1960. The Pigmy Deposits constituted 14 to 15 percent of total deposits in 1946; this proportion rose to 21 percent in 1960. Since then, its relative significance has declined with the faster growth of the other deposits and competition from the other banks. But even in 1975 these deposits constituted 7 to 8 percent of the total deposits. In absolute terms, these Pigmy Deposits are currently more than ten times their amount in 1960.

Such a deposit enabled the saver to accumulate a fairly sizeable sum in seven years. Without this facility, he probably would not have saved or saved less. His motivation to save is the need to accumulate for an emergency or other anticipated expenditures rather than to earn interest. The deposit thus has been linked with this type of motive among the relatively poor.[30]

Even the commission paid to the agents has not been a net loss to the bank. The agent must keep a security deposit with the bank equal to 10 percent of his commission. This minimizes the danger of the agent disappearing with his collection.

The Central Bank's Response to the Syndicate Bank's Innovations

The Central Bank of the country, the Reserve Bank of India, has also been innovative.[31] But with regard to the unconventional practices of the Syndicate Bank, it took a negative attitude. Until 1965 the Syndicate Bank was considered an unsophisticated rural bank, and the Central Bank did not like some of its innovations. Central regulatory agencies—particularly when they try to imitate rather than adapt the technology of a developed country—can come in the way of creative adaptation of modern technology.

With regard to the Pigmy Deposits, the Syndicate Bank permitted its own employees to work as agents during their spare time. For the bank this was one of the ways of reducing its wage costs and increasing its business; for the employee, it was an incentive to earn more. But in 1962, the Reserve Bank found this practice to be objectionable on strict banking principles and prohibited the Syndicate Bank from engaging its own employees as agents.

The Syndicate Bank wanted to set up an agricultural demonstration farm in 1964 to enable it to promote the adoption of new high-yielding seeds by the farmers. The Reserve Bank considered such a venture in technical assistance inconsistent with healthy banking practices. Hence, the Syndicate Bank had to think of other ways. It induced the progressive farmers to set up a voluntary organization called the Syndicate Agricultural Foundation. The bank provides financial assistance to the foundation through annual grants.

In 1960, the bank pioneered a unique investment service through its Investor's Agency Department. This service enabled middle-income savers to invest in shares of reputable companies. The persons joining the scheme were assured a return of 9 to 10 percent per year on their saving; the bank, in turn, invested these sums in shares. This scheme became very popular with middle-income groups in semi-urban areas—persons who were not familiar with the stock market. It was a precursor to the Unit Trust of India sponsored by the Reserve Bank in 1964. The following year the Syndicate Bank's investment services ended because the Reserve Bank thought it could compete with the Unit Trust of India.

Since nationalization of 14 major banks in 1969, the Reserve Bank has induced the banks to expand their branches in rural areas so as to provide credit to small enterprises in both the farm and nonfarm sectors. With this emphasis on the widening and deepening of the geographical and functional scope of the banking system, the Syndicate Bank has come to be regarded by the Reserve Bank as a model bank.

VI
CONCLUSION

Credit or finance is one of the strategic factors that determine the pace and pattern of socioeconomic development. It facilitates as well as stimulates the development process.[32] Thus, the credit or financial system involves what economists call externality. Public or government intervention is essential to promote and develop a sound credit system. The public agency that must perform this function is obviously the central bank, which has to act as a leader, promoter, coordinator, and regulator of the entire financial system.

It is the function of the central bank to promote financial innovations that widen and deepen the credit or capital market through the introduction of new processes and products (credit instruments), cultivation and nurturing of new markets, and introduction of new institutional and organizational structures. The single most important criterion of the effectiveness of central bank action is the extent to which its policies reduce overall transaction costs and risks relating to all types of credit transactions, essential for accelerating the pace of development in the light of the country's development objectives and strategy. For this purpose, a central bank in a developing country has to have, a development orientation.[33]

A credit system can also distort and obstruct the development process because of what Keynes calls 'the inherent instability of credit'.[34] To quote Hicks:

> But on the other side there is the penalty that the credit system is an unstable system. It rests upon confidence and trust; when trust

> is absent, it can just shrivel up. It is unstable in the other direction too; when there is too much "confidence" or optimism it can explode in bursts of speculation. Thus, in order for a credit system to work smoothly, it needs an institutional framework which shall restrain it on the one hand, and shall support it on the other...it must be managed by a central bank, whose operations must be determined by judgement, and cannot be reduced to procedure by a mechanical rule.[35]

A central bank in developing countries can perform this regulatory function much more effectively when it also promotes a sound and healthy financial or credit system. Regulatory and promotional functions are vitally interrelated. To perform both these functions effectively, a central bank must have a certain degree of autonomy.[36] This autonomy has eroded, especially since 1965, in developing as well as developed countries because of the impact of fiscal policy on the credit or financial markets—national and international. The result has been instability of credit and international debt crisis, already affecting the development process particularly in some of the developing countries and the functioning of the international credit markets.

The autonomy of the central banks and the conditions for the emergence of an international central bank are complex issues; they are related to the discipline of political sociology—a type of inquiry that can analyze the casual factors responsible for the behavior of actors in the political field.

NOTES

1. See Adam Smith, *The Wealth of Nations* ed. Andres Skinner (London: Penguin Books, 1970), Bk. 1, Chs. 1–3. Allyn Young described the relationship between division of labor and extent of the market as 'one of the most illuminating and fruitful generalizations which can be found anywhere in the whole literature of economics'. See Allyn Young, *The Economic Journal*, Vol. 38, No. 152 (December 1928). For an elaboration of the theme, see Nicholas Kaldor, 'The Irrelevance of Equilibrium Economics', *The Economic Journal*, Vol. 82, No. 328 (December 1972).
2. See John Hicks, *The Crisis in Keynesian Economics* (Oxford: Basil Blackwell, 1974), pp. 53–57; and John Hicks, *Money, Interest and Wages* (Cambridge, Mass.: Harvard University Press, 1982), p. 258.
3. The asymmetry of information and expectations among different classes of lenders and borrowers accounts for unique characteristics of the credit or financial markets. First, supply and demand for credit are related not only to interest rates but also to other variables. Hence, supply and demand schedules for credit relate to the terms

of credit and not merely to interest rate. Second, supply and demand schedules for credit are interdependent. Third, if demand is related only to interest rate, there is the phenomenon of credit rationing. Fourth, the structure of credit markets can vary widely from monopoly to competition (oligopolistic-oligopsonistic, monopolistic-monopsonistic, competitive monopoly, etc.)

See J. E. Stiglitz, 'Information and Economic Analysis: A Perspective', in *Supplement to the Economic Journal*, Vol. 95; Arvind Virmani, *The Nature of Credit Markets in Developing Countries*, World Bank Staff Working Paper 564 (Washington, D.C.: World Bank, 1982); and V.V. Bhatt and Alan R. Roe, *Capital Market Imperfections and Economic Development*, World Bank Staff Working Paper 338 (Washington, D.C.: World Bank, 1979).

Mainstream economic theory tends to regard these unique features of the credit or financial markets as 'market imperfections', but actually they are inherent in the very functioning of credit markets. See George J. Stigler, 'Imperfections in the Capital Market', *Journal of Political Economy* (June 1967).

Sometimes the perceptions or expectations of both lenders and borrowers change in the same direction. Expectations tend to be based on what, according to Keynes, 'average opinion thinks about average opinion' or on what Pigou calls 'errors of optimism and pessimism'. This results in 'inherent instability of credit'. See John Maynard Keynes, *A Treatise on Money* (London: Macmillan and Co., 1930), Vol. 1, p. 27; John Hicks, *Money, Credit and Wages* (Cambridge, Mass.: Harvard University Press, 1982), p. 675; and R.G. Hawtrey, *Currency and Credit* (London: Longmans, Green and Co., 1919), p. 4.

4. On this, see John Maynard Keynes, *The General Theory of Employment Interest and Money* (New York: Harcourt, Brace and World, 1964). To quote:

> Two types of risk affect the volume of investment...The first is the entrepreneur's or borrower's risk...Now the first type of risk is, in a sense, a real social cost, though susceptible to diminution by averaging as well as by an increased accuracy of foresight. The second, however, is a pure addition to the cost of investment...Moreover, it involves in part a duplication of a proportion of the entrepreneur's risk, which is added twice to the pure rate of interest...This duplication of allowance for a portion of the risk has not hitherto been emphasized, so far as I am aware; but it may be important in certain circumstances (pp. 144–45).

5. For a historical account of financial innovations, see John Hicks, *A Theory of Economic History* (Oxford: Oxford University Press, 1969), Chs. 5 and 6.
6. A. Braverman and T. N. Srinivasan, *Interlinked Credit and Tenancy Markets in Rural Economies of Developing Countries*, World Bank Staff Working Paper 433 (Washington, D.C.: World Bank, October 1980).
7. See Alexander Gerschenkron, *Economic Backwardness in Historical Perspective* (Cambridge, Mass.: Harvard University Press, 1962), pp. 11–16.
8. See J. Cable, 'Capital Market Information and Industrial Performance: The Role of West German Banks', *The Economic Journal*, Vol. 95, No. 377 (March 1985). To quote:

> As is well known, German companies make little use of their relatively underdeveloped external capital market, and depend heavily on the banking system for

their external finance. Moreover, the banks not only supply or arrange access to investment funds, but are also extensively represented on the supervisory boards of companies, and in control of very large blocks of equity voting rights. The system of industrial financing which results can be viewed as one of 'quasi-internal capital markets', with potentially important informational and transaction costs implications...there is a significant positive relationship between the degree of bank involvement in lending to industrial companies and their financial performance (pp. 119 and 130).

9. For this and other financial innovations that emerged after 1960, see Janet Kelly, *Bankers and Borders* (Cambridge, Mass.: Ballinger Publishing Co., 1977), Ch. 6. The pure security approach is described as 'backward looking', while the cash flow approach as 'forward looking'. To quote:
   'While the British banks would make advances to Rolls-Royce because of the extensive assets of the company, American banks would assess the company's cash flow to see if the company would be able to service the loan over the necessary period' (p. 131).
10. Such a link is illustrated by the experience of rural banks and private development banks in the Philippines. See Katrine Anderson Saito and Dan P. Villanueva, *Transaction Costs of Credit to the Small-Scale Sector in the Philippines*, Domestic Finance Studies 53 (Washington, D.C.: World Bank, December 1978).
11. See Joseph A. Schumpeter, *Business Cycles* (New York: McGraw Hill Co., 1939), Vol. 1, pp. 93–97. Schumpeter emphasizes that innovation is generally introduced by the rise to leadership of new men, who set up a new firm with a new plant.
12. See John Hicks, *Capital and Growth* (Oxford: Clarendon Press, 1965), p. 292.
13. See R. W. Goldsmith, 'Some Reflections on the Past, Present and Future of Financial Institutions' (mimeograph, 1974). To quote:

There are two tendencies at work which have already operated since the early history of financial institutions, tendencies which you may call the specialty shop and the department store principles. A specialty shop in finance holds, essentially, one type of financial instrument and raises most of its funds also by one, though a different instrument. At certain times and in certain countries, the one or the other system has prevailed. England was, during most of its modern financial history, a financial specialty shop country, as was the United States. Germany, on the other hand, has always been more of a financial department store country, France being generally in the middle. In the last decade, however, there has been a definite tendency, in virtually all countries, for the department store model of finance to gain, particularly in the field of deposit banking... Finally, something happened during the fifties and the sixties. It probably became obvious to bankers that, if they continued to do business as before they would continue to lose in importance. This trend soon became worldwide, partly because it is much easier to transfer financial technology from one country to another than to do so in the case of industrial technology...This movement toward financial department store operations is, I think, one of the most important trends to watch in developed countries in the next generation...It has always been present to some extent and is particularly pronounced in less developed countries (pp. 82–84).

For the rationale of such a strategy in oligopolistic markets, see Swati Bhatt, 'Non-Price Competition in Oligopolistic Industries', Ph.D. Dissertation, Princeton University, 1986.

14. On technological changes in the electronics industry and their impact on structural changes in the financial institutions and markets, see C.A.E. Goodhart, *Monetary Theory and Practices* (London: Macmillan Press, 1984), Ch. 5.
15. See the survey on 'International Investment Banking' in *The Economist*, Vol. 294, No. 7385, 16 March 1985, pp. 44–84.
16. Ibid.
17 On the role of informal markets, see Yung Chul Park, *The Unorganized Financial Sector in Korea, 1945–75*, Domestic Finance Studies 18 (Washington, D.C.: World Bank, 1980); T. A. Timberg and C. V. Aiyar, *Informal Credit Markets* in Domestic Finance Studies 62 (Washington, D.C.: World Bank, 1980); and Juergen U. Holst, 'The Role of Informal Financial Institutions in the Mobilization of Saving', in *Saving and Development*, ed. Denis Kessler and Pierre-Antoine Ullmo, Economica (Paris, 1985).
18. See J. C. Sandesara, *Efficacy of Incentives for Small Industry* (Bombay: Industrial Development Bank of India, 1982); Shahid Yusuf, *The Commercial Banking Industry in Brazil, 1964–74*, Domestic Finance Studies 39 (Washington, D.C.: World Bank, 1977); and *Undermining Rural Development with Cheap Credit*, ed. Dale W. Adams, Douglas H. Graham, and J. B. von Pischke (London: Westview Press, 1984).
19. On the noninterest cost of borrowing, see Jerry R. Ladman, 'Loan-Transaction Costs, Credit Rationing, and Market Structure', in *Undermining Rural Development with Cheap Credit*, Ch. 8; and T. Riley, *Non-interest Costs of Lending and Borrowing*, Domestic Finance Studies 65 (Washington, D.C.: World Bank, 1980).
20. See V. G. Patel, *Innovations in Banking: The Gujarat Experiments*, Domestic Finance Studies 51 (Washington, D.C.: World Bank, 1978); and V. V. Bhatt, *Financial Institutions and Technical Consultancy Services: The Indian Experiment in Small Enterprise Promotion*, EDI Seminar Paper 24 (Washington, D.C.: World Bank, 1981).
21. See V. V. Bhatt, *Development Perspectives* (London: Pergamon Press, 1980), Ch. 15.
22. On this cost–risk reducing package of measures, implemented by a central bank, see C. Rangarajan, *Innovations in Banking: The Indian Experience*, Domestic Finance Studies 66 (Washington, D.C.: World Bank, 1980).
23. Mainstream economic theory and studies ignore these vital aspects of financial policies and emphasize the importance of unregulated markets and interest rate structure. This theory is congenitally incapable of analyzing the role and functioning of credit markets. For prescriptions based on this theory, see R. I. McKinnon, *Money and Capital in Economic Development* (Washington, D.C.: The Brookings Institution, 1973). See also V. V. Bhatt, *Development Perspectives*, Introduction (n. 21 above).
24. See Keynes, *The General Theory of Employment, Interest and Money* (n. 4 above), p. 208.
25. The following section is based on information specially obtained from the Syndicate Bank of India. Having been a member of the Board of Directors from 1969 to 1972, the author had the benefit of detailed discussions with the top management of the bank and access to confidential data. See also N. K. Thingalaya, *Innovations in Banking: The Syndicate's Experience*, Domestic Finance Studies 46 (Washington, D.C.: World Bank, 1978).

26. See Selden Menefee, *The Pais of Manipal* (New York: Asia Publishing House, 1969); and Schumpeter, *Business Cycles*, Vol. 1, pp. 93–97. The Syndicate Bank's experience supports Schumpeter's hypothesis that innovation is generally introduced by the rise to leadership of new men, setting up a new firm and with new plant (in this case, a new organization principle).
27. V. V. Bhatt, *Structure of Financial Institutions* (Bombay: Vora & Co., 1972), Ch. 2.
28. V. V. Bhatt, *Division of Public and Private Finance: Research Program and Its Rationale*, Domestic Finance Studies 43 (Washington, D.C.: World Bank, 1977), pp. 13–15.
29. V. V. Bhatt, *Structure of Financial Institutions*, Chapter 4.
30. Ibid., Chapter 4.
31. V. V. Bhatt, *Some Aspects of Financial Policies and Central Banking in Developing Countries*, EDI Seminar Paper 11 (Washington, D.C.: World Bank, 1974).
32. See Hicks, *Capital and Growth*, pp. 289–91. To quote:

> The beginning of a process of expansion might occur because of real factors (inventions and the like) raising the real prospective rate of profit. But it might also occur because of financial improvements, diminishing the size of our 'gap', thereby permitting access to funds, for improvements which could have been made earlier, if the necessary funds had been forthcoming. It is not savings only that are required, but a channel of communication between potential savings and potential real investment (p. 290).

See also Schumpeter, *Business Cycles*, Vol. 1, pp. 111–12; and John Hicks, *Economic Perspectives* (Oxford: Oxford University Press, 1977), pp. 78–79. What Schumpeter calls innovations and Hicks calls impulses require credit creation; the latter is, as Schumpeter observes, the 'monetary complement of innovation'.

33. V. V. Bhatt, *Some Aspects of Financial Policies and Central Banking in Developing Countries*, (n. 31 above).
34. Keynes, *A Treatise on Money* (London: Macmillan and Co., 1930), Vol. 1, p. 27.
35. John Hicks, *Critical Essays in Monetary Theory* (Oxford: Oxford University Press, 1967), pp. 158–59 and 164.

There is the same problem of the instability of credit at the international level as exemplied by the post–1975 functioning of the international credit markets and the recent international debt crisis. To quote Hicks again:

> There is the same problem of the instability of credit. There is the same need that international credit should be managed, in order to be secure...The remedy...would be an International Central Bank. An International Bank which would underpin the credit structure, but in order to underpin it must have some control over it. That was what Keynes, who understood this international aspect very clearly, wanted to get at Bretton Woods, but all he got was a Currency Board...the IMF. That, we are finding...is not enough (pp. 172–73).

36. Central banks do not have this autonomy either in the developing or most of the developed countries. This is indeed a political problem. In this connection, see Hicks, *Economic Perspectives*. To quote:

This perhaps is a dream; I do not claim to be a judge of political possibilities. But I am not afraid to draw the moral, which emerges rather clearly from the line of thought I have tried to follow out, that the issue with which we have been concerned is political—even constitutional—as well as economic. There is the technical economic problem of the Instrument; but it is tied up with the political problem of how to secure that it is used decisively. This is a problem which Keynesian economics, so it seems to me, has refused to face, while the monetarists, who have seen it, have to face the political implications. For myself, I would face it. I think we should say that monetary regulation is a major function of Government; but we should emphasize that if it is to be exercised decisively, it needs to be separated, in what is in fact the constitutional sense, from other functions. We need to remember the ancient doctrine of the Separation of Powers. The judicial function, in well-ordered States, is recognized to be a function of Government, but a function that is better *separated*. So it is with the monetary function (pp. 132–33, emphasis added).

Chapter 2

Development Banks as Catalysts for Industrial and Financial Development

INTRODUCTION

Industrialization has a strategic role[1] in accelerating the pace of socio-economic development for the simple reason that, as the classical economists emphasized, industry is subject to the law of increasing returns to scale, while the primary land based sector is subject to diminishing returns to scale. Rapid rate of growth in industrial output results, as Kaldor noted,[2] in quickening the pace of technological change in the industrial sector and in accelerating the process of technological change in all the other sectors like agriculture and services.

However, industrial growth depends critically on the extent of the market for industrial goods because of the circular cumulative interaction between the extent of the market and technical change. As Adam Smith[3] perceptively observed, increase in the size of the market leads to new opportunities for division of labor or technical change and the latter in turn tends to increase the size of the market; hence the phenomenon of increasing returns to scale.

Market size depends on the growth in agriculture and the exports of industrial goods and services. In many developing countries it may be difficult to accelerate the pace of change in the agricultural sector initially as decisions for technological change have to be made by a large number of farmers, while it may be easier to concentrate on raising the rate of growth of exports of industrial goods and services. A strategy of export promoting industrialization process leads to increasing the size of the market and thus accelerating the process of technical change and industrial development and employment; it also quickens the pace of technological change in agriculture by withdrawing labor from that sector for industrial employment and promoting innovations in agricultural processes and methods of operation.[4]

Export promoting process of industrialization also leads to greater capacity to import capital goods and technology and competitive pressures and stimulus to improve productivity and quality of industrial goods and services. Such has been the historical experience of Germany, Japan, South Korea, Taiwan and such other countries during their early stages of economic development.

It is not possible to initiate and sustain such an industrialization process without an active role of the state in developing and adapting an institutional and policy framework to evolving circumstances, environment and specific instruments of industrialization, suited to the stage of development of the country. One of the strategic instruments has been historically a development bank—called in different contexts by different names—which is distinguished from other financial institutions by its developmental orientation and emphasis on the spirit of enterprise.

Such a bank did play a momentous role in the industrialization of the relatively backward countries of Europe during the nineteenth century and functioned as a catalyst for the mutually interacting and reinforcing process of industrial and financial development.[5] The basic idea of a Credit Mobilier or Universal Bank or Industrial Bank as a specific instrument of industrialization was consciously borrowed and adapted by Japan, while promoting the Industrial Bank of Japan in 1902.[6]

In the post World War II period, the developing countries too adapted this idea in the form of the Development Finance Company or the development bank. There are now about 160 such banks, which are supported by the World Bank and many others, but which do not owe their existence to the World Bank. However, with the exception of a very few such banks, most of them have not performed the role of a catalyst for industrial and financial development; they have functioned largely as conduits for relending external resources obtained from international institutions and official agencies to industrial enterprises. Further, most of them are not financially viable and suffer from weak management and have been vulnerable to the tumultuous changes that have taken place in the international economic environment since 1973.[7] Their failure as specific instruments of industrialization is largely because of the lack of commitment by the state in these countries to *initiating* and *sustaining* an accelerated process of *viable* and widely diffused industrialization through a set of *well-co-ordinated* monetary, fiscal and trade policies. In countries, where the governments' commitment is the strongest, the development banks have performed very well as in South Korea or Botswana. In fact, in South Korea, the Korea Development Finance Company (KDFC) changed over consciously to a type of the Credit Mobilier or the Industrial Bank of Japan in 1980 and has been performing the role of the catalyst, mentioned earlier.[8]

The purpose of this chapter is to generalize about the nature and characteristics of a development bank that may serve as a catalyst for industrial development on the basis of the historical experience of successful development banks like the Universal Banks during the nineteenth century in Europe and particularly in Germany, the Industrial Bank of Japan (IBJ), the Industrial and Mining Development Bank of Iran (IMDBI till 1979), the Korea Development Finance Company (KDFC), the Botswana Development Corporation (BDC), the Industrial Credit and Investment Corporation of India (ICICI) and the Industrial Development Bank of India (IDBI).[9]

Section I deals with the role of the catalyst in industrial development while the role as a catalyst for financial development is discussed in Section II. These two roles are mutually reinforcing and the one cannot be performed without the other; their separate discussion is purely for analytic convenience. The role of the catalyst in ensuring sound performance of public enterprises is the theme of Section III, while the role of the state as a prior condition for the successful functioning of a development bank is discussed in Section IV. The concluding observations are made in the final section.

I
CATALYST FOR INDUSTRIAL DEVELOPMENT

Nucleus of Entrepreneurial Talents

A development bank cannot act like a normal commercial bank; it has no raison d'etre unless it seeks to promote a viable and widely diffused process of industrial development that is consistent with the country's development objectives. It is essential, therefore, that in view of the general shortage of entrepreneurial talents in the initial stages of development, the available talents should be harnessed by a development bank because of its strategic location with a large leverage for industrial development. In Japan, for example,...'the banking system was the locus of much of the early promotional and entrepreneurial talent, which initiated the industrial spurt.'[10] 'It should not occasion surprise, therefore, to discover that in successful cases of rapid industrialization truly creative entrepreneurs were to be found in such strategic sectors as the banking system, and that they used the leverage thus acquired for the promotion and finance of industrial undertakings.'[11] It has been historically the role of such entrepreneurs located in the banking system 'to activate the latent entrepreneurial talents and productive energies of hitherto tradition minded people'.[12]

However, it is not possible to attract such talents purely on the basis of the profit motive or the expected monetary rewards. It is the idea of a mission, a passionate urge for development, a motivating ideology that creates a sort of religious fervor that is essential for the purpose. 'Perhaps the most important of its contributions to economic development was the idea of development and the spirit of enterprise which was implicit in the conception of the Credit Mobilier...The source of these ideas in Western Civilization are manifold. As represented in the Credit Mobilier, however, they can be clearly traced to the doctrines of the Saint Simonions. One of the objectives of the "New Christianity" was "the amelioration of the moral, the intellectual and the physical existence of the most numerous and poorest classes." This dictum the Pereires adopted as their personal motto along with the more immediately practical tenets of Saint Simonians which guided their business activities...it can scarcely be doubted that it provided the philosophical basis which all men require as a rationalization of their behavior or that it remained a living creed for them to the end of their lives. In any event, the spirit of enterprise which they manifested and the idea of development which was represented by the Credit Mobilier long survived them both in the imaginations of Europeans everywhere.[13]

As Gerschenkron observes on the basis of the European experience during the nineteenth century:

> To break through the barriers of stagnation in a backward country, to ignite the imaginations of men, and to place their energies in the service of economic development, a stronger medicine is needed

than the promise of better allocation of resources or even of the lower price of bread. Under such conditions even the businessman, even the classical daring and innovative entrepreneur, needs a more powerful stimulus than the prospect of profits.[14]

Profitability as an Index of Success

This ideological fervor, however, has to be matched by good judgement, imagination and expertise that can ensure the profitability and growth with vitality of not only the enterprises supported but also of the development bank.

The bank, therefore, must have the ability to judge not only the worthwhileness of the project or enterprise but also the entrepreneurial-managerial calibre of the top management of the enterprise it seeks to finance. It should therefore devise appropriate mechanisms and criteria for the purpose.

A project, of course, has to be judged on the basis of its contribution to industrial development. That means that it should result into a profitable enterprise that has the potential of becoming internationally competitive; if that is not so, then it is not possible to generate a self-reinforcing and self-sustaining process of industrial development. There should not be a mechanical application of methods of project appraisal. Whatever criteria for project selection are adopted, they need to be taken merely as tools for decision making; they cannot be a substitute for decision making, which is not a purely analytic process.[15]

Most of the successful development banks did have in-house expertise and skills for decision making. For example, IBJ has over the years developed 'unparalleled technical knowledge and its capabilities to make proper judgement concerning the Japanese economy, industries and corporations—resources that the bank has accumulated since pre-war days...' The German Universal Bank did not 'ever get into serious straits, or even showed the scars of occasional wounds. This was due not only to their size and standing, but also to the fact that their business, however much at variance with English principles, was, or is during our period, became substantially sound in our sense; as a rule they financed reasonable propositions, which they carefully studied and which they were able to see through...'[16] 'To some extent at least, they were also successful in discouraging fraudulent or reckless promotion. And they could not have done this if they had kept aloof in the manner of English banks of deposit'[17]

The project and enterprise appraisals have been done very well by other successful banks also before taking a final decision to finance an enterprise. In cases where in-house expertise is inadequate, they did take help from other appropriate institutions; for example, KDFC used to approach Korea Institute of Science and Technology (KIST) for a sound technical appraisal of a project. The in-house resources of the IDBI are adequate but still to obtain expert opinion and judgement, the IDBI constitutes an Ad hoc Committee of Advisers for critical examination of its own project appraisal and invites this committee to discuss their comments with the project promoters. Such confrontation and dialogue gives IDBI an additional opportunity to test the managerial and technical competence of the project promoters; for, the manner in which they react to comments by the committee gives IDBI a good indication of their ability to understand and tackle problems, as they arise.

However, in addition to all such appraisals of the project or enterprise, what is most vital is the judgement of the ability and integrity of the top management of the enterprise. Such judgement is critical for the decision to finance an enterprise.[18]

Even if the decision to finance an enterprise or a project is sound initially, subsequent changes in internal and external environment could adversely affect its viability and international competitiveness. It is essential, therefore, to have vigilant supervision of the project or the enterprise even during its operational phases so that timely adaptive action can be taken to ensure its profitability and success. Such supervision requires a fairly close connection between a development bank and the enterprise. It is easier to have such supervision if a development bank also provides short-term finance and/or is represented at the board of directors of the enterprise as in Japan, India, Botswana, Iran and Germany; in such a case, a development bank would be in a position to identify emerging problems and suggest timely action to tackle them.

Such close connection, for example, was established in Germany.

> If a bank holds a controlling, or at all events, an important part of the capital stock of an industrial concern and acquires, as it then naturally will, all its current banking business, and if the fortunes of the concerns and the prices of its shares are associated with the bank's name and pecuniary interest, much closer supervision becomes of course necessary than would be the case if the bank was in a position to deal with every single transaction with the concern

> individually and simply on its merits...this supervision in many cases amounts to initiative and even to compulsion (such as enforcing mergers of, or at least understandings between competing enterprises, all customers of one bank)...The efficiency of that engine for the purpose of financing and supporting new enterprises is beyond question.[19]

Management and technical guidance were an integral part of this supervisory role.

In cases where public policy created highly protected domestic markets, development banks failed to emphasize the internationally competitive character of the enterprises they supported. In such cases, industrial development was much less rapid and self-sustaining and technological development lagged behind in comparison with the countries which were keen to take advantage of trade possibilities.

Such was the case, for example, in France and Austria before 1914 and in India, Iran and several other developing countries since World War II.

In France,

> ...the Bourgeois Monarchy was characterized by a most narrow-minded economic policy. The bourgeoisie was in power or at least stood close enough to the seat of power, but it was perfectly content to perpetuate in France a hot house atmosphere in which antiquated and inefficient enterprises were maintained at high cost, while new plants and enterprises lacked both the sting of competition and unobstructed communication with foreign countries for the importation of capital goods and know-how. Adam Smith knew well how short-sighted and detrimental the behavior of vested interests can be when they are using political power for economic purposes...It is by a standard of this sort that the capitalist development in France appear to have been disappointingly slow [till 1914].[20]

'In this connection, the French failure to reimport the French innovation in banking in the creatively adjusted form of the mixed bank may have deserved strong emphasis.'[21]

Similar was the case of Austria before 1914.

> Whereas in Prussia, the Zollverein and Reich followed liberal trade policies until 1878, and only moderately protective ones thereafter,

throughout the same period Austrian policy was consistently protectionist. That, together with a limited domestic market (low incomes, high transport costs) might well have engendered less aggressive behavior on the part of both bankers and industrial entrepreneurs. Whereas the Cartels created and serviced by the German bankers might have limited competition in the domestic market, they could nevertheless be aggressive and expansionist in foreign markets. The Austrian cartels, on the other hand, apparently remained content with a quieter, more sluggish domestic market.[22]

Dynamic Promotional Role

A development bank, to become an effective engine for rapid industrial development, has to grow in size and vitality by creating new markets for its products and services. It cannot remain passive and react merely to entrepreneurial developments in the industrial sector. Since the *latent* entrepreneurial talents have to be activated in a developing country, it is essential for expanding its clientele and market for a development bank to play along with the financing role also an active entrepreneurial role of identifying new opportunities and goading industrial promoters to seize them.

Such a promotional role was in fact undertaken by the Universal Banks in Germany, and by the IBJ in Japan and the IMDBI in Iran during the initial stages of their industrialization and the BDC in Botswana. In India and Korea, development banks have played this role to a much less significant extent, partly because of the existence of already developed entrepreneurial talents in the private sector.

The classic case, of course, is that of the German Universal Banks, which set the pattern for the other countries like Japan.

> In Germany, the various incompetencies of the individual entrepreneurs were offset by the device of splitting the entrepreneurial function; the German investment banks—a powerful invention, comparable in economic effect to that of steam engine—were in their capital-supplying functions a substitute for the insufficiency of the previously created wealth willingly placed at the disposal of entrepreneurs. But they were also a substitute for entrepreneurial deficiencies. From their central vantage points of control, the banks participated actively in shaping the major—and sometimes even not so major—decisions of individual enterprises. It was they who

very often mapped out a firm's paths of growth, conceived far-sighted plans, decided on major technological and locational innovations, and arranged for mergers and capital increases.[23]

These banks understood very well the vital role of technological change. They goaded the enterprises they supported to adopt, absorb, adapt, diffuse and improve upon the technology borrowed from advanced countries like England and in many cases emphasized the latest technology that was not even adopted elsewhere.

> If as an empirical fact many smaller areas, such as some European countries of the nineteenth century, did show a strong leaning towards rapidly increasing output of heavy industries, there was a specific reason: it was within the field of these industries that the contemporaneous technological progress had been most vehement, and backward countries often did tend to favor branches of industrial endeavors in which the most modern technology could be applied...This tendency was frequently strongly reinforced by state and banking policies...historical experience suggests a strong propensity on the part of backward countries to apply the most modern technological processes, not yet introduced in more advanced countries. That there are both exceptions and limits to this is another matter.[24]

> Under the conditions the statement may be hazarded that, to the extent that industrialization took place, it was largely by application of the most modern and efficient techniques that backward countries could hope to achieve success particularly if their industrialization proceeded in the face of the competition from the advanced country.[25]

This is also supported by the experience of Japan and South Korea.

The developing countries now have one asset: the increasing store of scientific and technological knowledge. But to take advantage of this asset they need to adopt, absorb, adapt, diffuse and improve upon the borrowed technology. For this purpose, the development banks need to play an active role in promoting technical consultancy services centers (TCSCs) that can help in this process and assist the development banks in properly evaluating the technological dimension of the projects either promoted or supported by them.[26] The KDFC's association with the KIST is for this purpose and, on the same logic, IDBI has sponsored and promoted the Technological Consultancy Organizations (TCOs) and supported in many ways the activities of private and public consultancy organizations.[27] Recently, the ICICI has taken the leadership in setting up the Technology Development and Information Corporation of India (TDICI). Its purpose is to provide, in addition to venture capital funding, information on sources of technology and assistance in assessing information on technological inputs with a view to accelerating the pace of technical change in the industrial sector. The technology problem and the role which financial institutions can play in tackling it are discussed at length in Chapter 5.

II
CATALYST FOR FINANCIAL DEVELOPMENT

For a development bank market expansion and the pace of industrial development are mutually related; the greater the increase in the market for its products and services, the more rapid would be the pace of industrial development. However, a development bank would not be able to expand its own market without introducing financial innovations—new products and services—that can induce industrial investment in new fields. Thus, for becoming an effective instrument for industrial development, it is essential for a development bank to enlarge and deepen its activities in the field of the progressive development of financial markets.

Financial Innovations and Risk of Lending

Its industrial promotion activities cannot bear fruit unless it is able to induce new promoters and entrepreneurs to undertake the new projects or enterprises it has identified, with its financial support. However, the cost of such finance depends on its own transaction costs, the risk provision essential for new activities and the interest cost at which it can mobilize its own resources. To this should be added its own margin of profit that it should have for its financial viability. The enterprise can borrow only if its expected rate of return exceeds this cost of industrial finance by a sufficient margin that should be greater than its own risk premium and transaction costs of borrowing.[28] The total cost of industrial finance to the enterprises would then be:

$$t_l + r_l + i + p_l + t_b$$

where,

t_l is the transaction cost of lending;

r_l is the risk premium that a lender has to provide for;

i is the interest cost of borrowing by the development bank;

p_l is the profit margin of the development bank;

and t_b is the transaction cost of the borrower.

It would be profitable for the new enterprise to borrow only if its own expected rate of return (P_b) exceeds this total cost of borrowing and the development bank, too, would not lend if it is not so. The financial innovations that the development bank should introduce, then, should be such as to reduce $t_l + r_l + i + p_l + t_b$.

The transaction costs ($t_l + t_b$) can be reduced to appropriate levels by sound management; t_b can be reduced by geographical spread, through branches, of a development bank (which would reduce the transport costs of the borrower) and shortening the administrative lag for sanctioning finance. These type of measures have been taken by successful development banks in varying degrees depending upon their specific context of operation.

However, the significant variables are: r_l, P_b and i. r_l and P_b are mutually related. There are several measures that can reduce r_l and simultaneously raise P_b. Entrepreneurial and technical assistance provided directly or indirectly through relevant institutions by a development bank for project formulation would reduce r_l and at the same time raise P_b; this would, of course, raise t_l but this cost can be passed on to the borrower as long as the increase in P_b is greater than the increase in t_b. In addition, management and technical assistance in project implementation as well during its operational stages would further reduce r_l and raise P_b. Again, these additional costs of management and technical guidance can be charged to the borrower as long as they are less than the increase in P_b.

Thus, it is essential for a development bank to provide entrepreneurial, managerial and technical assistance to new enterprises with a view to expanding its own market and accelerating the pace of industrial development. This was the logic for the promotional role of the Universal Bank in Germany, of the IBJ in Japan, of the IMDBI in Iran, of the BDC in Botswana, and the IDBI in India and for their vigilant supervision of the enterprises during their operation phase through the mechanism of short-term financing and/or their representation on the boards of the assisted enterprises. This has also been the logic of promoting training for new entrepreneurs through entrepreneurial development programmes by the IDBI and providing them with technical assistance through the TCOs and also for promoting management training institutions by the IMDBI, the KDFC and the ICICI.

If r_1 cannot be reduced further, it may be possible to diffuse this risk by risk transference and sharing with the other financial or relevant institutions. In the case of the German Universal Banks, this was done through the device of converting short-term assistance into long-term securities, which can be traded in the securities market. This method is similar to what is now called the process of securitization.

> The novelty about the practice of those French and German promotion banks consisted only in the directness with which the problem of financing innovation was faced and the energy with which regular banking business was made ancillary to it. While elsewhere this use of short-term credit, created ad hoc, led to a situation in which it was up to the entrepreneurs to look (unless receipts were coming in quickly) for some method of funding and thus consolidating their position, the 'industrial' or 'promoting' banks provided machinery to do this themselves. They took care of the necessary issues of stocks and bonds, thus helping the enterprise to redeem its short debt and providing it with additional means. In order to effect this they were ready to take those stocks or bonds for their own account not only if they were unable to place them, but also in the ordinary course of their business routine. They thus were able to await developments before making an offer to the public and even, in many cases, to keep a parcel for good. When eventually they placed the securities acquired, they again financed the private investors so that, temporarily at least, the transaction often meant no more than a shift in assets...All that is important to realize now is how short-term credit creation was thus made to dovetail with long-term investment in a way which almost perfectly expresses the economic nature of the process of financing innovation.[29]

Similar function of investment banking was performed by the IBJ in the domestic as well as the international markets. The IBJ assisted not only in the development of the capital market in Japan but also performed the role of obtaining foreign portfolio capital for the industrial firms in Japan. The Universal Banks and the IBJ, thus, performed the functions of commercial banking, development banking and investment banking and thus by diversifying their functions helped not only the enterprises they supported but also their own profitability—for they did charge the assisted enterprises for their financial services. This commission or fee business added to the profits of the banks without increasing their exposure to risk. The IMDBI in Iran also played a similar role. The ICICI in India provides merchant banking services, which helps not only the enterprises but also the ICICI in improving its earnings. The KDFC, converted into the Korea Long Term Credit Bank (KLTCB) in 1980, is seeking to perform similar investment banking functions.

The other method of reducing risk by diffusion and sharing is to involve other financial institutions in lending to a specific enterprise. In India, the IDBI has engaged in the function of refinancing and bills rediscounting of projects or bills of the state financial institutions and the banks. In these transactions, the risk is borne by the state financial institutions or the banks, while the IDBI merely provides risk-free refinancing. This method, of course, increases the IDBI's profitability as it is not vulnerable to risks associated with projects which are refinanced or whose bills are rediscounted. At the same time, the IDBI has become instrumental in promoting, somewhat in an indirect fashion, the development of small enterprises and new enterprises. A somewhat similar function was performed by the old KDFC and is being performed by the new KLTCB.

For medium to large projects, a development bank can diffuse or transfer risk by what is now called syndicated loans. This method has been operative with regard to the IDBI as well as the ICICI for quite some time (see Ch. 4). The IDBI has performed the leadership function in instituting what is known as Inter Institutional Group (IIG), whose meetings are held every month for taking decisions with regard to the financing of new projects; the institutions represented are: Industrial Finance Corporation of India (IFCI), the Life Insurance Corporation of India (LIC), General Insurance Corporation of India (GIC), the Unit Trust of India (UTI) and the ICICI. For projects worth financing, this IIG takes the decision about the financing package and the share of each institution; this method diffuses risk among several institutions and thus each one's risk is a small proportion of the total. Further, in case of large projects, the IIM induces the commercial banks to participate in the loans to industrial enterprises, thus diffusing the risk even further. The participation of banks in industrial financial services also serves the function of mobilization of resources by the development banks for long-term financing in an indirect fashion. This institution also helps in the functioning of the capital market as LIC, GIC and UTI generally subscribe to either equity or bonds. The underwriting commitment of the other institutions also provides in some sense a support for the evolution of the capital market.

The interest element in the lender's cost of providing finance depends on the interest rate at which the development bank can borrow. Thus the development bank's ability to lend at reasonable cost would also be determined by its ability to mobilize resources at minimum cost. Initially, concessional assistance in one form or another from the government and international institutions may be necessary as has happened in the case of all successful banks. However, a development bank cannot expand its activities without developing its capacity to mobilize resources on its own. This capacity, of course, is critically dependent on the financial viability and profitability of the supported enterprises, and as a result its own profitability. Hence, the enterprise, vigor, imagination and skill with which it can ensure the profitability of enterprises would determine its capacity to borrow and mobilize resources from institutions as well as the capital market. Successful development banks have been able to do so.

The IBJ, the KLTCB, the IMDBI, the ICICI and the IDBI—all of them have been able to borrow, through issuing bonds and debentures, from the capital market. The commercial banks have been the major subscribers to their bonds; the principal reason for this is their ability to mobilize resources through a variety of deposits at a very reasonable cost. The borrowing by the development banks was facilitated in some countries like Japan, Korea and India by their governments or their central banks by making the bonds of development banks eligible securities for borrowing from the central bank; this provided an additional incentive for commercial banks to subscribe to the bonds of the development banks. This provision made the bonds liquid and easily negotiable in the capital market. The commercial banks also gained in another way; the new enterprises supported by the development banks increased the demand for short-term finance and thus increased the business of the commercial banks. At the same time, because of their high credit rating, they were also able to tap the growing international capital market and even to take advantage of new financial innovations like currency and interest rate swaps (see Ch. 6).

Thus, the successful development banks were able to mobilize resources at reasonable cost, to reduce transaction costs and risk for both lenders and borrowers, and to diffuse the inevitable component of risk widely among various institutions and investors. All these efforts made it possible for them to expand their business. Those development banks which provided subsidized long-term credit to enterprises were unable to mobilize resources at market rates of interest and thus were unable to expand their business and become effective catalysts for industrial and financial development.

Promotion of New Financial Institutions

A development bank can strengthen its earnings and profitability and at the same time expand its activities by providing financial services to the savers and borrowers. It can do this by promoting specialized institutions that tend to strengthen and deepen the financial system. The IBJ has become an international investment banker; it has opened its offices in various financial centers and expanded its international network by tying up with leading financial institutions in countries around the world. It also took the initiative as a promoter in launching Japan Housing Loan Inc. in 1976. The KLTCB and the ICICI have entered the field of leasing and have also introduced venture capital instruments. The ICICI in addition has also promoted the Housing Development Finance Corporation (HDFC) and the Technology Development and Information Corporation of India (TDICI).

To ensure the sound functioning of the capital market, ICICI took the lead in promoting Credit Rating and Information Services of India Ltd. (CRISIL), to provide individual and institutional investors adequate information to make investment decisions. The IDBI took the lead in promoting the Stock Holding Corporation of India (SHCI) to modernize the post-trading operations related to securities transactions such as clearing house, safe custody and transfer register facilities. The IDBI and the ICICI participated actively in setting up, under the auspices of the Reserve Bank of India, the Discount and Finance House of India (DFHI) to deal in money market instruments in order to provide liquidity in the money market.

The KDFC (now KLTCB), similarly, promoted the Korea Investment and Finance Corporation (KIFC) to serve the short-term financing needs of corporations and to act as an underwriter in the bond and equity share markets. The KIFC is a major shareholder of Korea

Investment and Securities Co. Ltd., which is a broker-dealer of various types of securities, including equity shares and corporate bonds. The BDC promoted the Sechaba Investment Trust and Stock Brokers Botswana Ltd. to enable the BDC to start privatizing some of its portfolio companies and give citizens an opportunity to invest in private corporations. The IMDBI played an active role in setting up Tehran Stock Exchange with a view to developing the capital market.

The Critical Role of a Competitive Environment

As the financial system evolves and domestic and international capital market institutions develop, a development bank will face keen competition with regard to both resource mobilization and allocation. Such a competitive environment provides a powerful incentive to the development bank to adapt its functioning to the changing environment and assume innovative functions. Simultaneously, to induce creative experimentation and innovative behavior, it is also essential to have a plurality of development banks in a country. That is what the experience of countries like Japan, South Korea, and India indicates.[30]

III
DEVELOPMENT BANKS AND PUBLIC ENTERPRISE PERFORMANCE

One of the critical factors for the performance of industrial enterprises in general, and public enterprises in particular, as with development banks, is their exposure to a competitive environment which provides powerful incentives as well as pressures and compulsions for effective and efficient functioning. Apart from appropriate industrial and trade policies, development banks too can play an effective role. In fact, they can generate competitive impulses even in situations where it is not possible to create a competitive environment in the conventional sense, as may be the case with some public enterprises. They can establish norms of effectiveness and efficiency, based on some type of comparison and thus induce a *competitive spirit* in the management of some public enterprises to attain or even overreach such norms.[31]

The tasks of project evaluation, selection, financing and monitoring of public enterprises can be performed more efficiently and effectively when they are entrusted to a development bank rather than when they are performed by government ministries or departments. A development bank, because of its expertise, competence and culture, is better suited to accumulate experience and improve its competence in the fields of project evaluation, selection, financing and monitoring, provided it has competent management and has the required degree of operational autonomy for effective and efficient functioning.[32]

Such a bank can establish norms and monitor and evaluate the performance of enterprises in the light of these norms. Of course, the process of fixing norms is not a once and for all function; it has to be a continuous process in the light of the changing situation and circumstances. The basis for the norms can be (*a*) the potential of the enterprise as revealed at the project evaluation stage; (*b*) comparison of the performance of similar enterprises in the country as well as in other countries; and, (*c*) the bank's own intimate knowledge about the functioning of the enterprise.

The bank has sanctions in the sense that it can provide finance *only on certain conditions* and it has accumulated knowledge and expertise about the sector which it is financing. Thus, it is in a position to set norms and monitor the performance in the light of the norms, and thus generate a *competitive spirit or impulse* in the management of the enterprise to attain or over-reach these norms. The public enterprises, financed by the Industrial Development Bank of India, for example, have performed better than similar enterprises directly financed by the government.

The development bank has another advantage. It can insist on its representation on the Board of Directors of the enterprise so as to obtain a first-hand feel and knowledge about its functioning as well as to exert its influence and pressure on top management for performance improvement. This has been an effective device, adopted by the German Universal Banks,[33] the IBJ, the IDBI, and the ICICI and can as well be adopted by the National Development Banks.

Further, the development bank can insist, as part of its terms and conditions for financing, that a part of the financial requirement of an enterprise be secured by issuing equity and bonds through the capital market. Government ownership rights can be secured as long as a major part of equity (say more than 51 percent) is owned by the government; but the rest can be sold through the capital market to the general public, preferably with a proviso that no one individual or firm can have more than a certain percentage share in the equity. Such restriction need not apply to the purchase of bonds, issued by a public enterprise. Such provisions would induce the public enterprise due to the pressures exerted by the capital market, to improve financial performance to a level that is acceptable and attractive to the capital market. The pressures and compulsions for good performance would be even more intense if the public enterprise has to approach the international capital market for obtaining its foreign exchange requirements.

The development banks are thus in a position to judge the effectiveness and efficiency of the management of a public enterprise. If they find that the top management is not capable of attaining the norms of performance, they should be in a position to insist on a change in top management. One of the ways that they can suggest is competitive bidding for top management contracts. Ownership of an enterprise would be with the government but top management tasks could be assigned to any private business group that promises the best results. Such a device would encourage and stimulate competition for management contracts for a fixed period among the private business groups—indigenous or foreign—and whether there is the motive for pecuniary gain or not, these business houses would have a competitive urge to show results, if only for the sake of safeguarding and enhancing their reputation for managerial abilities. It may be noted that this device of management contracts can also be adopted by any regulatory and supervising agency other than a development bank; the management contract can even be directly with a public enterprise, as in the French system. However, these agencies, dependent as they are on the Ministry of Finance, do not have such sanctions or capabilities of generating pressures for performance as the development banks have.

It may be mentioned that neither the development banks nor the regulatory and supervising agencies can perform these functions without an effective institutional framework relating to project formulation and choice of technology. The relatively poor performance of public sector enterprises is largely due to defective and inadequate project formulation and the choice of inappropriate technology. Hence the significance of having a *plurality* of design engineering consultancy services or technical consultancy service centers (TCSCs) with vital links with the foreign TCSCs. Without such an institutional framework, it is not possible to formulate projects embodying the relevant technology. TCSCs and the financial system provide the vital links between modern technology and research institutions on the one hand, and the production system on the other. There is, thus, an urgent need for an appropriate technology policy and an institutional framework, relevant for the implementation of such a policy.[34]

IV
DEVELOPMENT BANKS AND THE ROLE OF THE STATE

It is possible for a development bank to perform the role of a catalyst for industrial and financial development only if industrial development is one of the overriding objectives of the state. The state, as a result, has certain important functions. Firstly, it has to create a climate favorable for the emergence and functioning of entrepreneurial talent in both the public and the private sectors by undertaking infrastructure development designed to create new opportunities for entrepreneurial exploitation. Further, it can try to improve the human resources in the economy through appropriate education and science and technology policy so as to strengthen its capacity to respond creatively to the new opportunities created in the economy. Secondly, it has to evolve an appropriate institutional and policy framework that would provide stimulus and incentives for effective and efficient functioning of industrial enterprises and ensure operational autonomy of functioning to development banks as well as the public enterprises. Thirdly, if private entrepreneurs are unable to promote industrial enterprises of strategic significance for industrial development because of their long gestation lag, requirement of large resources, technological sophistication or external economies, such enterprises may have to be initiated in the public sector. For the financing of such enterprises, it may be difficult for a development bank, if it is to be financially viable, to provide adequate resources. It may be necessary, therefore for the state to create a separate fund for the purpose, which should be managed by the development bank as has been done by the government in India with respect to the IDBI. (It is indeed ironic that the development function of such a fund is not appreciated in the current context in India; this very idea was scrapped by the government in 1992 and this fund no longer exists.)

The state did play such a role in Japan, South Korea, and India. However, in Japan and South Korea, administrative controls, or regulations and interventions, essential for accelerating the pace of development, were minimum, or were of strategic significance, selective, purposive and time bound; they were what Bhagwati calls 'prescriptive,' while in India, they were 'proscriptive.'[35] The 'Far Eastern governments, by and large, issue prescriptions rather than proscriptions...whereas countries such as India do the opposite. The government of 'dos' generally produce economic performance superior to that produced by government of 'don'ts.'[36] The former foster and promote entrepreneurial impulses, while the latter stifle them; the former establish a symbiotic partnership relationship with the private entrepreneurs, while the latter induce adversarial response and unproductive wasteful expenditure to overcome or to take advantage of restrictive measures without a positive rationale. Further, the industrial promotion and trade policies emphasized international competitiveness of industrial enterprises and were export promoting in Japan and South Korea, while India, by and large, emphasized import substitution. As a result, development banks in India could not generate a process of industrial development at the same rapid pace as in Japan or South Korea.

However, within the given institutional and policy framework, the relationship between development banks and the government has been close and participative in all these countries. The development banks have played a crucial role in assisting the governments in the formulation of policies for the development of the financial system and the markets. This has helped the development banks in the performance of their functions.

Before the Universal Banks came on the scene during the nineteenth century, the state in Germany had already begun to perform an entrepreneurial role with regard to industrial development. In Germany,

> the state—the Prince and his bureaucracy—not only meant more than, but also something different from, what they meant in the other countries, and that one of the consequences of this was not only regulation of industry that amounted to guidance, but also actual state enterprise. The social structure that supplied the personnel of public administration was ... much superior in intelligence, horizon, training and energy to the personnel of such private industry as there was; and this is one of the reasons why it would be as silly to condemn that public planning in the Germany of that time as it would be to hold it up as a model for societies of different structure. That the states build the canals and the roads which in England were created by private enterprise was natural under the circumstances....Much more interesting however is the entrepreneurial activity of the principalities in the field of mining and its technological neighbors...Here initiative as well as execution came almost entirely from the princes and their bureaucracy.

> Reorganization and the clearing away of obsolete legal structures...could in any case have been done only by the public authority. But the states went beyond forcing technological and commercial improvement on lethargic and impoverished owners. They actually undertook the development and operation of mines and embarked upon enterprise in the heavy industries...Mines and factories were operated for profit. Financing was largely on commercial lines. And the entrepreneurial function was as clearly present and as distinctly vested in individuals as it is in private industry. Those entrepreneurs were public servants and acted by virtue of official appointment, but both in type and behavior entirely conform to the idea of a 'captain of industry'. The central authority left them remarkably free to act, and in most cases ratified their plans as a matter of course.[37]

It is against this background that the universal banks were able to play what Gerschenkron calls the 'momentous' role in the industrial development of Germany during the late nineteenth century.

There is thus a strong similarity in the developmental experience of Japan since 1884 and South Korea since 1960 with that of Germany during an earlier period.

V
CONCLUDING OBSERVATIONS

As the experience of successful development banks indicates, it is possible for a development bank in a developing country to function as a catalyst for industrial and financial development. However, it can do so only if it (*a*) is financially viable and profitable, (*b*) adopts innovative policies and measures to grow in size and effectiveness, (*c*) emphasizes the widening and deepening of the market for its products and services by providing entrepreneurial, managerial and technical assistance to industrial enterprises and promotes the development of the financial system and markets and thus creates a competitive environment for its own functioning, (*d*) has the necessary operational autonomy to function effectively, and (*e*) functions in an environment created by the state that promotes entrepreneurial talents and competitive impulses for initiating and sustaining an industrial structure that is internationally competitive.[38]

In countries where there is no deliberate strategy to create such an environment, development banks cannot function as catalysts for either industrial or financial development. Hence international agencies like the World Bank that support and assist the development banks should emphasize the critical and strategic role of the institutional and policy framework that is appropriate for the creative and innovative functioning of the development banks. The crucial role of such a framework for the success of the main bank system in Japan and for the relatively poor performance of the lead bank system in India is discussed at length in Chapters 3 and 4 respectively.

NOTES

1. Nicholas Kaldor, *Strategic Factors in Economic Development* (New York: Cornell University, 1967).
2. Ibid., Ch. I. To quote:

   > To sum up, then, the dominant influence on the rate of economic growth seems to be the growth rate of manufacturing output (together with the ancillary activities, public utilities, and construction). This is so not only because the growth rate of productivity in the industrial sector itself rises but also because the growth rate will tend to increase the rate of productivity growth in other sectors. This may happen both in agriculture and in the distribution trades, partly on account of the absorption of surplus labor and partly because of a faster increase in the flow of goods into consumption. But, more generally, industrialization tends to accelerate the rate of change of technology, not just in one sector, but in the economy as a whole (p. 23).
   >
   > ...there can be little doubt that the kind of economic growth which involves the use of modern technology and which eventuates in high real income per capita, is inconceivable without industrialization. In that sense there are no alternative roads to economic development (p. 54).

3. See Adam Smith, *The Wealth of Nations Book I, Chapters 1 to 3*, ed. Andrew Skinner (Penguin Books, 1970). Allyn Young regarded the Smith relationship between division of labor and extent of the market as 'one of the most illuminating and fruitful generalization which can be found anywhere in the whole literature of economics.' See Allyn Young, 'Increasing Returns and Economic Progress' in *The Economic Journal*, Vol. 38, Number 152, December 1928; for an elaboration of this theme, see Nicholas Kaldor, 'The Irrelevance of Equilibrium Economics,' *The Economic Journal*, Vol. 82, Number 328, December 1972.
4. Nicholas Kaldor, *Strategic Factors in Economic Development* (n. 1 above), pp. 23 and 54.
5. See Alexander Gerschenkron, *Economic Backwardness in Historical Perspective* (Cambridge, Mass: Harvard University Press, 1962), pp. 11–16. To quote:

   > In particular, the story of the Credit Mobilizer of the brothers Pereires is often regarded as a dramatic but, on the whole, rather insignificant episode. ...It seems to be much better in accord with the facts to speak of a truly momentous role of

investment banking of the period of the economic history of France and of large portions of the continent. Occasional ventures of that sort had been in existence in Belgium, Germany, and France itself. But more important than their slavish imitations was the creative adaptation of the basic idea of the Pereires and its incorporation in the new type of banks, the Universal Bank, which in Germany, along with most of the countries on the Continent, became the dominant form of banking. The difference between banks of the Credit Mobilier type and commercial banks in the advanced industrial country of the time (England) was absolute. Between the English banks essentially designed to serve as a source of short-term capital and a bank designed to finance the long-run investment needs of the economy, there was a complete gulf. The German banks, which may be taken as a paragon of the type of Universal Bank, successfully continued the basic idea of the Credit Mobilier with the short-run activities of commercial banks.

But the German banks, and with them the Austrian and Italian banks, established the closest possible relations with industrial enterprises. A German bank, as the saying went, accompanied an industrial enterprises from the cradle to the grave, from establishment to liquidation through all the vicissitudes of its existence. Through the device of formally short-term but in reality long-term current account credits and through development of the institution of the supervisory boards to the position of most powerful organs within corporate organizations, the banks acquired a formidable degree of ascendancy over industrial enterprises, which extended far beyond the sphere of financial control into that of entrepreneurial and management decisions.

The Continental practices in the field of industrial investment banking must be conceived as specific instruments of industrialization in a backward country, (pp. 270–71).

6. See Hugh T. Patrick, 'Chapter VIII Japan 1868–1914,' in *Banking in the Early Stages of Industrialization*, ed. Rondo Cameron (New York: Oxford University Press, 1967). To quote:

The Industrial Bank, long proposed by the government on the model of the French Credit Mobilier, finally began operations in 1902. It had three major purposes: to provide long-term loans to modern industries, to promote the influx of foreign portfolio capital while avoiding foreign control of domestic industries, and to develop a market for corporate and local government bonds by creating the appropriate institutional arrangements...The Industrial Bank's major contributions prior to World War I lay in its successful development of a debenture-issuing market and in its attraction of foreign portfolio capital...its direct underwriting role for domestic corporations was limited... (pp. 270–71).

7. *World Development Report* (World Bank: Oxford University Press, June 1989), pp. 60–61.
8. See, *Staff Appraisal Report: The Korea Long-Term Credit Bank: The Korea Development Finance Corporation* (World Bank, Projects Department, East Asia and Pacific Regional Office, November 20, 1980).

9. The sources of information for these banks, unless otherwise indicated, are the following:

For Industrial Bank of Japan: 'History of the Industrial Bank of Japan' (The Industrial Bank of Japan Ltd.), a paper specially prepared by the bank at the request of the author.

For the Industrial and Mining Development Bank of Iran: A. Gasem Kheradjou, 'Banking for Development and Rapid Growth: IMDBI 1959–1979', *International Journal of Development Banking*, Vol. 2, No. 2, July 1984.

For Korea Development Finance Company:

(*i*) *Staff Appraisal Report: The Korea Long-Term Credit Bank* (World Bank: Projects Department, East Asia and Pacific Region Office, November 20, 1980).

(*ii*) 'Catalytic Role of Korea Long-Term Credit Bank', a paper specially prepared by the Bank at the author's request.

For Botswana Development Corporation: *World Development Report* (World Bank: Oxford University Press, June 1989), pp. 60–61.

For Industrial Credit and Investment Corporation of India and Industrial Development Bank of India:

(*i*) Annual Reports.

(*ii*) *Staff Appraisal Report: India, Industrial Finance and Technical Assistance Project* (World Bank, Industry and Finance Division, Asia Region, March 7, 1988.)

(*iii*) 'ICICI's Catalytic Role in the Development and Integration of Financial Markets', a paper specially prepared by the ICICI at the request of the author.

(*iv*) 'Emerging Role of Development Banking: Initiatives of IDBI', a paper specially prepared by the IDBI at the request of the author.

10. Hugh T. Patrick (n. 6 above), p. 278.
11. Rondo Cameron (ed.) *Banking in the Early Stages of Industrialization* (n. 6 above), Introduction, p. 12.
12. Hugh T. Patrick (n. 6 above), p. 318.
13. Rondo E. Cameron, 'The Credit Mobilier and the Economic Development of Europe,' *The Journal of Political Economy*, Vol. LXI, No. 6, December 1953.
14. Alexander Gerschenkron (n. 5 above), p. 24.
15. See V. V. Bhatt, *Development Perspectives* (London, Pergamon Press, 1980), Chs. 12 and 13.
16. Joseph A. Schumpeter, *Business Cycles*, Vol. I (New York: McGraw Hill Book Company, Inc., 1939), pp. 437–38.
17. Ibid. fn p. 438.
18. For the qualities and skills of development banks to exercise sound judgement, see Joseph A. Schumpeter, *Business Cycles* (n. 16 above) pp. 116–18. To quote:

> ...the banker should know, and be able to judge, what his credit is used for and that he should be an independent agent...to realize this is to understand what banking means...The banker must not only know what the transaction is which he is asked to finance and how it is likely to turn out, but he must also know the customers, his business, and even his private habits, and get by frequently 'talking things over with him,' a clear picture of his situation. But if banks, whether technically so called or not, finance innovation, all this becomes immeasurably more important. It has been denied that such knowledge is possible. The reply is that all bankers, who at all answer to type, have it and act upon

it...However, at the same time, it is clear that this is not only highly skilled work, proficiency in which cannot be acquired in any school except that of experience, but also work which requires intellectual and moral qualities not present in all people who take to the banker's profession...Not less important...is that banks should be independent agents...they must first be independent of the entrepreneurs whose plans they are to sanction or to refuse...But another kind of independence must be added to the list of requirements: banks must be independent of politics. Subservience to government or to public opinion would obviously paralyze a banking system. This fact is so serious because the banker's function is essentially a critical, checking, admonitory one (pp. 116–18).

19. Joseph A. Schumpeter (n. 16 above) p. 349.
20. Alexander Gerschenkron, *Continuity in History and Other Essays* (Cambridge, Mass: Harvard University Press, 1968), p. 268.
21. Ibid., p. 391.
22. Rondo Cameron (ed.), *Banking and Economic Development* (New York: Oxford University Press, 1972), Introduction, p. 17.
23. Alexander Gerschenkron (1968), *Continuity in History and Other Essays* (n. 20 above), pp. 137–38.
24. Ibid, pp. 403–4.
25. Alexander Gerschenkron, *Economic Backwardness in Historical Perspective* (n. 20 above), p. 89.
26. On technology policy and the role of development banks, see V. V. Bhatt, *Development Perspectives* (n. 15 above), Part II, Chs. 5 to 8.
27. V. V. Bhatt, *Financial Institutions and Technical Consultancy Services: The Indian Experiment in Small Enterprise Promotion, Journal of Development Planning* (United Nations, No. 18, 1988).
28. On these aspects of financial evolution, see V. V. Bhatt, 'Financial Innovations and Credit Market Evolution,' *Economic and Political Weekly* (Vol. XXII, No. 22, May 30, 1987); also as Economic Development Institute of the World Bank Informal Paper (1989).
29. Joseph A. Schumpeter (n. 16 above) pp. 348–49.
30. See V. V. Bhatt (1980), Development Perspectives (n. 15 above) Chapter 8.
31. V. V. Bhatt, 'On Competitive Impulses and Public Enterprise Performance,' *Economic and Political Weekly*, May 27, 1989.
32. V. V. Bhatt, *Development Perspectives* (n. 15 above), Ch. 8.
33. J. Cable, "Capital Market Information and Industrial Performance: The Role of West German Banks," *The Economic Journal*, Vol. 95, No. 377, March 1985.
34. V. V. Bhatt, *Development Perspectives* (n. 15 above), Chs. 7 and 8. Also, V. V. Bhatt, 'Decision Structure, Technology Choice and Public Enterprise Performance: A Case Study of Bagasse-based Newsprint Project,' *Economic and Political Weekly*, Vol. XXIII, No. 35, August 27, 1988.
35. Jagdish Bhagwati, *Protectionism* (Cambridge, Mass: The MIT Press, 1988), pp. 98–102.
36. Ibid., p. 98.
37. Joseph A. Schumpeter (n. 16 above), pp. 283–384.

38. For the role of development banks in the less developed countries, the classic book still is: William Diamond, *Development Banks* (Baltimore: Johns Hopkins Press, 1957). See also William Diamond and V. S. Raghavan (ed.), *Aspects of Development Bank Management* (Baltimore: Johns Hopkins Press, 1982), and Diamond's lecture at the Association of Development Finance Institutions of Asia and Pacific (ADFIAP) in 1989.

Chapter 3

The Main Bank System in Japan: Financial Innovation for Industrial Development

INTRODUCTION

The Industrial Bank of Japan (IBJ) played a critical role, as discussed in the previous chapter, in the industrial and financial development of Japan since its inception in 1902. However, after the second World War, Japan evolved the main bank system, which transformed the earlier banking system into a strategic instrument for industrial development and the IBJ became an integral part of this system. Just as the universal banking system in the late-nineteenth century in Germany—'a powerful innovation, comparable in economic effect to that of steam engine,'—was a creative adaptation of the Credit Mobilier concept in the German context, so was the main bank system in Japan in its specific context.

The main bank system differed from the universal banking system in several significant aspects. The latter was a spontaneous development, while in Japan, the role of the government—the Ministry of Finance, the Ministry of International Trade and Industry (MITI), and the Bank of Japan (the central bank)—was critical in the evolution of the main bank system since 1951. Further, unlike in Germany, the main bank system established cooperative partnership relations among banks, even in highly competitive financial markets, for evolving the system of syndicated loans or financial assistance to firms in order to provide the needed finances for long-term planning, thus extending the time horizon for decision making by the firms. Again, unlike in Germany, the government evolved, *consciously and deliberately*, an institutional and policy framework that was in tune with the effective functioning of the main bank system. Though India evolved the lead bank systems with more or less the same objectives as in Japan, the Indian systems faltered in the realization of those objectives because of the lack of an appropriate institutional and policy framework. India did not realize, as is discussed in the next chapter, the critical significance of such a framework.

The nature and characteristics of the main bank system in Japan are presented in this chapter not only for its historical significance in accelerating the pace of Japan's industrial development, but also for its relevance, *as a financial innovation*, for the developing and transforming socialist economies of ex-USSR, the East European countries like Poland, and China. Germany adapted the Credit Mobilier concept in evolving the universal banking system and Japan adapted the universal banking system in evolving the main bank system. Similarly the developing and transforming economies can creatively adapt the basic nature and characteristics of the main bank system to their own historical and specific socio-economic-political contexts to facilitate, promote and stimulate a self-reinforcing process of industrial and economic development.

Section 1 of this chapter seeks to present the origin, nature and characteristics of the main bank system in Japan in its 'stylized' form. The quantitative evidence is presented in section 2 and the appendix contains statistical tables. The institutional and policy framework, which appears to have molded the main bank system and its effectiveness and efficiency is discussed in section 3. Section 4 seeks to analyze the experience of Germany, South Korea, India and Mexico in the light of the main bank system. The concluding section discusses the relevance of the main bank system to developing and transforming economies.

I
THE ORIGIN, NATURE AND CHARACTERISTICS OF THE MAIN BANK SYSTEM

Origin

Though the system seems to have evolved spontaneously during 1950–55, the experience since 1935 was probably responsible for its adoption by the banking system.[1] During the late 1930s, the banks were forced to lend to newly established 'national policy firms' on which they had scant information, and as the dependence of the firms on external financing increased generally, the perceived risk to the banks tended to rise and their bargaining strength vis-à-vis the firms weakened. They tried to protect themselves by means of loan syndication, which also improved their capacity for strict monitoring of the firms. Loan syndicates emerged spontaneously among the private banks in 1936. As of the end of 1941, the number of such syndicates had risen to 127; 82 led by the Industrial Bank of Japan (IBJ), 17 by other banks and 22 by trust companies. In 1944, this system was formalized by introducing Designated Bank System for financing military production. Five specialized banks, including the IBJ, nine city banks and four local banks were designated to become leading banks in syndicated lending. In March 1945, this system was extended to cover all major firms including those not directly related to military production. But in this new system, each firm was related to one bank and not to a syndicate. It is not known whether the syndicates provided merely short-term loans or also long-term loans for fixed investment.

During the reconstruction period after the war, allocation of credit was controlled directly as well as indirectly. The financial institutions were required to provide investment and operating funds for strategic industries such as coal mining, iron and steel and fertilizers, and to invest in government bonds. The actual implementation and monitoring of this role, as during the war time, was assigned to the Bank of Japan (BOJ). The indirect methods of control involved making the bills, issued by industries like coal mining, fertilizers, textiles or other strategic industries, and export and import bills, eligible for the BOJ collateral needed for obtaining credit from the BOJ at favorable rates.

Loan syndication was used during this period too (1947–50) but under the leadership of the BOJ. While there is no doubt that the high degree of risk faced by the private sector banks necessitated such loan syndication, it is also true that, in the process, the position of the BOJ became extremely strong.[2] Thus, the strong links established between the lead or main bank and the syndicate partners on the one hand and between the lead or the main bank and the client firms on the other proved to be durable and resulted in the MB system after 1951.

Apart from that, the post-war reforms, despite the original intentions, did not touch the financial system and the anti-trust measures were not applied to the banks.[3] Banks, thus, were permitted to hold shares of client enterprises and as a result enterprise groups with banks at the core emerged to replace the Zaibatsu. Further, a dissolution of the Zaibatsu diminished the power of the holding companies (family owned) but did not affect significantly the enterprise structure. As a result, the old Zaibatsu group of companies got re-formed as what is now known as Keiretsu (business group);[4] Mitsui, Mitsubishi and Sumitomo Keiretsus are re-formed old Zaibatsu companies, but without the dominance of the old shareholders. And new Keiretsus got formed around banks; Fuyo, Sanwa and Ikkan are called 'bank–led groups'.[5] The post-war reforms, thus, increased the powers of the managers of firms on the one hand and of the banks over the firms on the other. The bank managers, of course, were subject to regulation by the Ministry of Finance and the BOJ.

The business firms, for their restructuring and expansion or for starting new enterprises, either by the business groups or new entrepreneurs like Sony, became dependent on bank finance as their demand for investible resources far exceeded what they could internally generate— or obtain directly from savers by issuing bonds and equity. The saving capacity of individuals was limited and they preferred assets like deposits, which were safe and liquid and did not involve much transaction costs. The saving was largely on account of transactions and precautionary motives. Further, the experience of savers with the bond market during the war was not very happy.

> Though most of the bonds were issued with government guarantee, the public was reluctant to hold these in their portfolio due to the paucity of information, apparent riskiness and also because these were without collateral. (The fact that the government failed to fulfill its loan guarantees after the defeat in the war, shows that peoples' expectations were probably 'rational'.)[6]

The post-war inflation and bottlenecks also created a climate of uncertainty, which deterred savers from investing in forms other than deposits. Similarly the public experience with the equity market, too, was not such as to inspire confidence in the market.

> A central problem immediately after the war was the complex web of debts between banks, the government and firms. In this environment without knowing how the debts were going to be handled, it was hard to establish the value of a typical firm...The situation in Japan was further complicated because most investors had only

> limited experience with a stock market. The pre-war market had been small. Thus the government and security industries had to educate the potential investors about the opportunities associated with stock ownership. Responding to this 'securities democratization' movement, many households put their savings into stocks. Other measures such as low interest loans for employees purchasing their own company's shares and permission to use freezed deposits to buy shares also helped to create the demand for shares. Although the stock exchange was closed, people actively traded shares at Shudan Torihiki (collective trading), where many security companies gathered to offer over-the-counter trades. When the stock exchange was reopened in 1949, it started in a boom, but soon began to sag, as the Dodge stabilization plan took hold and the economy slid into a recession...The Corporation Reconstruction and Reconstructuring Law declared that the war debts would be handled separately from post war claims, so that many of the new investors in the stock market lost their investments. The end result was that many individuals lost faith in the market.[7]

Thus, there was no alternative at the time for Japan but to develop a bank-oriented financial system; the situation was ripe for the main bank system to evolve as a result of all the experience during the war and the reconstruction period after the war. The banks had emerged as the focal point for mobilizing resources by way of deposits and making available the required finances to industry through the main bank. They developed the capacity to organize syndicated loans with the participation of other banks, thus assuming the role of a *delegated monitor* of the assisted firms on behalf of the participant banks.

Such a conjuncture in Japan during 1950–55 is not very different from that which prevails in many developing countries and the transforming socialist economies. Hence the relevance of its experience, particularly during 1951–73, to these countries.

The Nature and Characteristics of a Main Bank

Functions

There is no legal definition or *explicitly* stated characteristics of a main bank. One has to infer its nature and characteristics from the actual behavior of a bank via-à-vis its clients. From whatever anecdotal and other evidence (arising from interviews with the managers of banks as well as firms and press reports about financial markets) we have, it appears that the main bank is one which has a long-term relationship with a customer/firm (which involves mutual commitment to such a relationship), almost resulting in a *partnership* relationship between the bank and the firm, each one having a stake in the successful functioning of the other. Such a relationship can evolve only after the bank has repeated short-term transactions, particularly relating to payment settlement accounts and repayment in time of short-term loans and, as a result, is satisfied that it is not taking the risk of adverse selection or moral hazard. Thus, it is quite obvious that the bank would not establish a long-term relationship with a *new* firm, with which it had no dealings for a period of a few years. After once having established a long-term relationship, the main bank's functions vis-à-vis a client firm depend critically on the financial status and the accumulated human capital of the firm. For each type of firm, the main bank (*a*) normally provides financial services relating to payment settlement accounts; (*b*) holds a certain proportion of equity (10 percent or less before the seventies and 5 percent or less later as a result of government regulation), which makes it the top shareholder of the firm among banks; (*c*) is willing to provide information, and managerial, technical and financial assistance in various forms, whenever required by the firm, and particularly when the firm faces temporary financial problems; and, (*d*) is *willing to take responsibility* for restructuring or rescue operations by taking fairly drastic measures, like change in management, reduction in wage and salary levels, arranging for mergers and the like, and in extreme cases even taking over temporarily the management of the firm or arranging for its smooth and timely liquidation. In cases (*c*) and (*d*), the main bank is willing to bear a disproportionate burden of losses or of providing financial assistance to safeguard its *reputation* as a main bank, and a delegated monitor on behalf of the participating banks, so essential in highly competitive loan and deposit markets.

These functions of the main bank are common for all types of firms. In addition, for a growing firm requiring finances for expansion or new projects, it takes the responsibility of providing finance, essential for *long-term planning*, by arranging syndicated loans in partnership with other banks. In such cases, it is normally the largest lender and the sole monitor of the firm's performance on behalf of the other banks (performing the delegated monitoring function, as it is known in literature). This was its major function during the high growth era and continues to be its function with respect to small and medium size firms as well as other large firms that do not have adequate internal resources or have no access to outside finance, directly from the bond and equity market. The delegated monitoring function does involve appointing bank directors on the Boards of the firm as well as deputation of bank officers (including retired bank officers) to occupy responsible positions in the firm.

When a firm is able to raise finances in the bond market—as has been happening since 1985—more cheaply than resorting to bank finance, the main bank performs the legally required trustee administration for bond holders. The trustee administration involves the assessment and custody of collateral, and when necessary, calling, chairing and setting the agenda of the creditors' meeting. The position of the main bank as the bond issue administrator means not only that it is able to earn significant income in commission fees, but it is also placed in a strong position to intervene in the firm's management should the firm get into financial distress.

In the case of overseas bond issues, an overseas subsidiary of the main bank acts as the co-manager of bond issues. As well as commission income on the bond issue, the main bank earns fees on the associated foreign exchange transactions.

The bank, till early 1993, was not allowed to underwrite bond issues in the domestic market or act as a lead manager for overseas bond issues; these regulations were lifted in April 1993, giving more scope to the banks *as main banks* to provide the lucrative and essential financial services.

Sound Entrepreneur and Enterprise Appraisal

In performing these functions, the main bank assumes the critical monitoring function—what has been called ex-ante monitoring. In view of the competitive conditions in the loan market, each bank has an incentive and a compulsion to attract and to retain good creditworthy customers. Hence, the main bank chooses its customers carefully on the basis of their character, integrity and competence of the top management of the firm or enterprise, and the soundness of their projects and of their existing operations to avoid the risk of adverse selection and moral hazard. The soundness of its judgement regarding entrepreneurs or enterprises depends on the possibility of close direct contact with them; hence it establishes main bank relationship only in those centers where it has a good network of branches or with firms with which it has cross shareholding relationships and historical ties.

The Provision of Information and Arranging Syndicated Loans

Once the customer firm is carefully selected, the main bank helps the firm in a variety of ways. It provides information relating to technology, markets, suppliers, etc. based on its experience with a large number of enterprises and industries (economics of scope), its contact with specialized financial institutions like the Industrial Bank of Japan and other channels like the Ministry of International Trade and Industry (MITI).

The main bank is generally able to appraise the competence of the firm to formulate and implement investment projects because of its intimate relationship with it. However, it generally lacks the technological expertise to evaluate a radically new technology. Hence it often relies on the expertise of the Industrial Bank of Japan (IBJ), which has acquired such expertise over its long period of existence, and in such cases, quite often takes the IBJ as a critical member of its loan syndicate. Since the 1980s when high technology became increasingly important, the formation and financing of R&D oriented small firms have been led by large firms, having better technological assessment, and even when main bank lending is involved, it relies on the assessment of large firms.

In addition to enterprise or project appraisal (ex-ante monitoring), it organizes, when necessary, adequate finance for its customers by arranging a financing package, with the help of other participant banks, suited to the needs and requirements of the client enterprises. It manages the collateral on behalf of the participant banks for appropriate fees. Because of their confidence and trust in the judgement of the main bank, the subordinate or participant banks have no need to appraise the enterprise they are assisting, nor have they the need to manage the collateral; they are thus able to reduce their transaction costs and risk. Since relationships are *reciprocal* as each bank functions as the main bank for some enterprises and the subordinate or participant bank for others, *the main bank has a compulsive need and incentive to establish its reputation as a responsible bank*, which can be trusted by the participant banks in the syndicated loan package.

In a highly competitive loan market, this *reputation angle* is extremely important; this is the reason why the main bank is willing to bear a disproportionate burden in cases of restructuring or rescue or liquidation of enterprises, financed with syndicated loans. Of course, as a main bank, it is able to attract the business of the subsidiaries or affiliates of assisted enterprises, the lucrative fee business of its customers, and the deposits of the enterprise group's employees as well as firms (and these fees and related businesses provide an incentive to the main bank to bear disproportionately the burden of monitoring costs as well as insurance risk involved in rescue or rehabilitation tasks). Such *competitive impulses* tend to maintain stability in the business shares of the main bank and the participant banks in the customer firm—a sort of a competitive equilibrium. For, otherwise, the markets are contestable, and once the main bank loses its reputation as a responsible bank, any member of the core group of participant banks can take over the functions of the main bank. Thus, there is an incentive as well as a compulsion for the main bank to behave in a responsible fashion; otherwise it not only may lose its main bank business but also the business which other main banks can give it as a participant bank in their syndicate operations. This reciprocal relationship—reciprocal delegated monitoring relationship—ensures the stability of the system. (The current events—the asset deflation with regard to shares and real estate—are upsetting the delicate equilibrium and stability of the system).[8]

Monitoring and Guidance

To reduce the risk of the moral hazard (because of the asymmetry of information) as well as to improve the functioning of the client enterprise, the main bank establishes formal and informal mechanisms to obtain accurate information about their functioning, identify and anticipate performance problems, and suggest timely action to solve them. Such monitoring devices or mechanisms include representation on the boards of client enterprises, deputation of its senior officers to work for them, and intimate contact in a variety of informal ways with their top managements (including the *Enterprise Group banks* as well as for their participation in Enterprise Group's Presidents' Club—started by Mitsubishi in 1955, by Sumitomo in 1951 and by Mitsui in 1961).[9] Since they seek to establish partnership relations with their client enterprises, the latter have an incentive to provide accurate information, thus eliminating the problems involved as a result of information asymmetry between the bank and the customer firm. This implies not merely control; it also involves management guidance for the sound functioning of the enterprises.

Risk Sharing

If the client enterprises are not doing well because of causes beyond their control, the main bank shares their risk by modifying the terms of the contract relating to interest payments and repayment of the principal; these terms are closely related to the profit performance of the enterprises. Risk sharing is done in other ways also. The main bank invests in the equity of the client enterprises and the latter are also induced to invest in the equity of their main banks. Such cross shareholding mechanism cements and nurtures the long-term relationship and mutual commitment of the bank and the client enterprise. Each has a stake in the sound functioning of the other.

Pro-active Role in Rehabilitation and Rescue

Owing to its monitoring mechanisms, the main bank is in a position to accurately evaluate enterprise performance. If it deteriorates because of managerial failure, the main bank takes timely action to improve the management; and if that is not possible, then to change the management of the client enterprise or even take over its management temporarily or induce a merger with other sound client firms or, in extreme cases, arrange for liquidation without resorting to legal remedies or waiting until the firm actually becomes bankrupt. Thus the assurance of rehabilitation and rescue is coupled with potential punishment of the management and even labor (their wages and salaries may be reduced). Since there is no managerial market in Japan because of lifetime employment and firm-specific human skills and expertise, such punishment is perceived as quite severe. Hence the assurance of rehabilitation and rescue does not lead to perverse incentives and motivation of the firm management.

Further, takeover or legal bankruptcy is quite inefficient. The firms which want to take over another one in distress do not have the inside information, which the main bank does; further, they may behave in an opportunistic manner, thus cheating the existing and the new shareholders. The main bank is in a much better position because of

UWE, BRISTOL LIBRARY SERVICES

its information to restructure or rehabilitate the distressed firm effectively, and to the advantage of all the stakeholders—shareholders, creditors, workers, suppliers, etc.

Legal bankruptcies as in the United States are very costly to all the shareholders and particularly to creditors and workers, and the judge or the liquidator can hardly have sufficient expert knowledge to arrange for the takeover or merger or disposal of assets.[10]

The Japanese main bank function of reconstruction and rescue is in a way a *more effective substitute* for 'the missing external markets for corporate control and monitoring services'; it conserves the firm-specific resources, avoids waste, and tends to make the firm financially viable much earlier than an alternative arrangement would.[11]

The main bank bears a disproportionately large share of any losses incurred or of additional financial assistance provided. If it did not bear such cost, its credibility as a main bank and delegated monitor would suffer and further it will not be able to induce other participant banks to provide additional assistance, if necessary. Because of the reciprocal relationship between the main bank and the syndicate partners, and the competition in the financial markets, the disproportionate cost is the price which the main bank pays for maintaining and improving its share of banking business in a competitive environment, as argued earlier.

The Major Function of the Main Bank System

The major function of the main bank system appears to be the establishment of an environment of trust and confidence relating to the relationship between (*a*) the main bank and its clients, (*b*) the main bank and subordinate or participant banks, and (*c*) the main bank and specialized financial institutions, like the Industrial Bank of Japan and the Japan Development Bank, and government institutions like the MITI, and the Ministry of Finance and the Bank of Japan. It is this partnership or cooperative relationship that ensures the soundness of the financial institutions as well as of the assisted entrepreneurs or enterprises through the reduction of transaction costs arising out of information asymmetry and opportunistic behavior. Such trust and confidence has externalities, which the other types of financial system are unable to capture; the main bank system captures these externalities and internalizes them.[12]

The Main Bank System as Financial Innovation

The main bank system can be regarded as a financial innovation relating to the decision making process in the bank as well as the client firm. As with all sound financial innovations, this innovation reduces the overall transaction costs and the risk of all the participants in the banking system *taken together*; thus the banking system tends to provide a stimulus for an increase in financial saving and overall investment and for improvement in investment and productive efficiency of enterprises.[13]

The Main Banks

The transaction or administrative costs of the main banks tend to increase as a result of project appraisal, monitoring and control devices involved. However, these costs are more than offset by the reduction in risk relating to adverse selection and the moral hazard. Further, the main bank is able to secure all the business relating to financial services (mostly fee earning services) of the client enterprise as well as its subsidiaries, suppliers, etc., and the deposits not only of these institutions but also of the employees of the enterprises. Thus, the marginal cost of retaining creditworthy clients declines substantially. It is also able to improve the profitability of the client enterprise by arranging for adequate finance through syndicated loans and the provision of relevant information; this improves the ability to repay of the client enterprises and thus further reduces the credit risk of the bank. The establishment of partnership relations with subordinate or participant banks in syndicated loan transactions enables it to secure a part of their loan business, relating to their customers, with whom they have a main bank relationship, at nominal transaction cost and risk. Thus, the overall cost and risk relating *its total loan transactions*—as a main bank as well as a subordinate or participant bank—tend to be lower than they otherwise would be.

The Subordinate or Participant Banks

The subordinate or participant banks in their syndicated loan transactions with a main bank's client do not have to incur appraisal, monitoring and control costs—these functions are performed by the main bank. Because of the *reciprocal* relationship, the main bank has an incentive to perform these functions effectively and efficiently. Further, it would not be able to arrange syndicated loans for its client enterprises and thus improve their profitability and reduce its own credit risk, if it did not perform its tasks in a manner so as to inspire trust and confidence about its functioning in the participant banks.

Client Enterprises

Because of the mutual commitment to a long-term relationship, the client enterprises are able to formulate projects or schemes from a long-term perspective and thus improve their long–term profitability. Further, the information and guidance which they obtain from the main bank help them in improving their projects or schemes.

Their transaction costs *in the initial stages of their relationship* could be high; however, once this relationship matures, the costs tend to decline because of the mutual trust and confidence. Further, these costs are offset to some extent by the main bank's readiness to modify the terms and conditions of its loans in times of financial distress of the client enterprises and provide additional assistance for reconstruction and rehabilitation. The risk of failure thus diminishes, and the inevitable risks are shared by the main bank.

The Depositors

Since the main bank system tends to improve the quality of portfolio of the banking system and thus ensure financial viability and soundness of banks, and because of strict prudential regulation of banks by the Bank of Japan and the Ministry of Finance, the depositors do not face the risk of default by the banks. Thus the agency costs between the main bank and its depositors are eliminated. Apart from this risk elimination, the system itself introduces competitive incentives and pressures on each bank to improve its deposit mobilization performance with a view to expanding its loan business and improving its profitability. This is because, under the prevailing regulatory system, profitability depends critically on the extent of deposit mobilization. Each bank thus tends to introduce mechanisms (including branch expansion) to reduce the transaction costs of depositors and thus to improve their real noninterest yield [represented by interest minus (transaction costs + risk)]. The banks promote financial saving in the form of deposits through various forms of non-price competition such as gifts to depositors, door-to-door solicitation, facilities for special purpose saving, and the revival of the old system of lottery deposits.

The interest rates on deposits and loans have been regulated; but they were positive in real terms and quite high (deposit rates were 1 to 3 percent and loan rates were 6 to 8 percent in real terms), particularly up to 1973. Further, for several savings instruments like deposits, the interest income was tax-exempt up to 1988 and 58 percent of personal savings in 1986 were in tax-exempt instruments. However, this tax-exemption does not seem to be responsible for the high rate of saving; saving in Japan does not seem to be sensitive to changes in interest rates; such changes merely change the pattern of saving rather than its overall rate.[14]

The interest rate regulation has thus been quite effective in preventing price competition for financial resources among banks. Such competition would have merely raised deposit rates without much impact on financial saving and as a result would have induced the banks to lend to risky enterprises which could pay high rates on loan. The strict monitoring function of the main bank system would therefore have been ignored and would have adversely affected the growth of the Japanese economy. What the interest rate regulation has done so far is to pass on the rents which savers would have earned to the entrepreneurs—resulting in gains to the economy in terms of real incomes and employment. Since the loan market for small and medium firms is oligopolistic, some of the rents also accrued to the banks, who used them for higher wages to their employees—higher than in the industry.

The Overall Impact of the Main Banks System

The bank-oriented financial system with the main bank relationship as its characteristic trait has been able to reduce the *overall* transaction costs and risk (agency costs) in financial transactions. It has been able to improve investment and productive efficiency of enterprises and reduce waste of invested resources through a pro-active role in identifying financial and managerial problems. It has also been able to tackle them through financial and technical reconstruction, change in management or, as a last resort, merger with client enterprises or liquidation which does not rely on legal means but which is at the same time fair to participant banks as well as the enterprises.

II
THE EMPIRICAL EVIDENCE RELATING TO THE MAIN BANK SYSTEM

Most of the empirical research on the functioning of the main bank system began only in the early eighties, and most of it after 1985. Whatever empirical evidence is available so far is presented in this section.

The Origin

The inference that the main bank system evolved as a result of the introduction of the Designated Financial Institution System for Munitions Company Financing in 1944 appears to be substantiated by current research. Each munition company was assigned one or two banks, one of them being a manager bank, and these banks were allowed to organize consortiums which included several other banks. Recent research shows that the bank-firm relationships that emerged as a result of these forced marriages seemed to have been long lasting. A comparison of a firm's main bank in 1962 with its *designated* lender during the war shows that the designated lender was both the largest lender and one of the ten largest shareholders in 1962 in 37 cases (67 percent) out of 55 identified cases. If one includes another 6 cases, where the designated lender was the largest lender but not one of the top ten shareholders, 78 percent of firms in 1962 had the same main bank as the designated lender as in 1944. Thus the main bank relations in 1962 seem to have been strongly influenced by the designated financial institution system introduced during the war. This also shows that the main bank relationship is indeed a long-term relationship. Of course, even the 1944 relationships were *probably* based on the relationships established in the 1930s between Zaibatsu banks and the Zaibatsu firms—and these relationships got reflected in the 1944 and 1962 patterns.[15]

Existence and Characteristics

The Large Firms

However, one of the earliest research (of which the results are published in English) to identify the main bank relationships was by

Horiuchi, Packer and Fukuda[16] and Sheard[17]. Of course, the Japanese scholars had started their research earlier (early eighties), but their results were published in Japanese; this research helped the outside researchers. Sheard identified the main banks of 873 large firms in 1982 and found that in 1980, the main bank was the largest shareholder in 16.4 percent of the cases and was among the top five shareholders in 72 percent of the cases. The main bank was also the largest lender in 67.3 percent of the cases and was among the top two largest lenders in 84.5 percent of cases in 1971. The average loan share was estimated by him at 25 percent (Appendix A, Tables 1 and 2).

There were also directors from the main bank on the boards of the customer firms. In 1985 there were 1820 listed firms in Japan and these firms had a total of 1721 directors who were formerly or concurrently executives of banks (about 5 percent of total directorship). About half the listed firms that had bank borrowings in 1980 had at least one representative on their board from the main bank (Appendix A, Table 3). Further, the six major bank-centered industrial groups have a regular forum at which the top level executives meet and about 150 leading financial and industrial firms participate. The main bank, being a part of these groups, is represented at these meetings (called the presidents' club) and thus has access to inside information in addition to what it obtains as a result of its representation on the boards of the client firms.

Sheard also showed that the Industrial Bank of Japan, *though it is not a commercial bank providing payment settlement services*, was the seventh largest main bank in 1980 (Appendix A, Table 1). Its rank was fifth in 1967, and even in 1990, it was sixth and, by way of shareholding of client firms, its rank was fifth (Appendix A, Table 4).

The Small and Medium Firms

Sheard identified the main bank relationship with respect to large firms. However, Horiuchi showed on the basis of a survey by Small Business Finance Corporation in 1984, that small and medium size firms too have a main bank.[18] However, in their case, the main bank does not have any shareholding in the client firms nor does it have representation on their boards. It also does not offer all the services that it offers to large firms. The small and medium firms' dependence on main banks is quite high and the degree of their dependence depends on their size and history. Because of competitive environment, the small and medium firms do have a flexible policy with regard to their main banks. Initially, the choice of their main bank depends on their *location*, but they do tend to shift, as they mature, their main bank relationship to city banks, who can offer more *diversified* services and greater credibility to them in the financial markets (Appendix A, Tables 5 and 6). This survey also showed that the small and medium firms, as they mature and grow in size, reduce their dependence on the main bank in order to obtain better terms for their business transactions with other banks.

The Main Bank Relationship Across the Entire Spectrum of Banks

So far the major emphasis in research was on the city banks (which are the major banks), as the surveys were based only on a limited number of firms. In 1988, a weekly journal—Diamond (which is published with the help of a credit research agency responsible for surveying firms' creditworthiness) carried out a survey based on the annual reports of 110,823 firms with an annual capital turnover greater than 1 billion yen. These firms generally have loan relationships with many banks, the names of which are shown in their reports; the main banks are also identified in these reports. The total number of their loan relationships was 347,320 at the end of March 1987; this total is larger than the number of firms because of their multi-bank relationships.

This survey shows that smaller regional banks have higher main bank shares than do city banks because of their having many more branches concentrated in specific business areas than the city banks, whose activities stretch throughout Japan as well as into international markets. Further, among the city banks, the main bank share is determined on the basis of cross-shareholding; the Mitsubishi bank has a larger main bank share than the Dai-Ichi Kangyo Bank (which has more customers) because of its heavier cross-shareholding relationship. Similarly, the Industrial Bank of Japan has a larger lending volume and stronger cross-shareholding relationship than the Long-Term Credit Bank of Japan; hence its main bank share is higher than that of Long-Term Credit Bank (Appendix A, Table 7).[19] This survey also shows that the main bank relationship with respect to the City Banks, the Regional Banks and the IBJ relates only to 20 to 40 percent of their customers, while their non-main bank relationship is quite significant. This fact shows the significance of *reciprocal relationship between the main banks*; main banks of 20 to 40 percent of their customers are also participant banks (with respect to other main banks) with regard to their non-main bank customers. Thus, in a *competitive environment*, to retain the status of a main bank (with all its advantages) and be a participant bank (involving much lower transaction costs), the main bank has to establish credibility about its responsible functioning, as argued in section I.

The Current State of Bank-firm Relationship

To find out the current state of the bank-firm relationship, a detailed survey was undertaken by the Kyoto Institute of Economic Research under the leadership of Toshihiro Horiuchi, with the assistance of the Japan Center for Economic Research. The firms were classified into four categories: I) unlisted firms with less than 300 employees; II) unlisted firms with more than 300 employees; III) listed firms with less than 300 employees; and, IV) listed firms with more than 300 employees.

The analysis of the survey results show that the majority of firms have one bank as the main bank; but they also have relationships with about 6 other banks—a core bank relationship. Any one of these core banks is competent to take over the function of the main bank. On an average, the firms rely on about 20 to 21 banks, including the main and the core banks.

Given the competitive environment in which banks seek better reputation and firms seek cost minimization, the firms, as they grow in size, reduce their dependence on the main bank, and this is particularly true about large firms (Category IV). However, whatever the extent of dependence of their main bank, the relative shares of main banks as well as core banks (in a certain ranking order) are *relatively stable* as a result of the competitive impulses and their bargaining strength in the market. There are three major reasons for this: (*a*) Reliability of main and core banks; (*b*) Long-run relationship; and (*c*) Cross-holding of shares.

However, with regard to project finance, the firms depart from this rule of *stability of shares* without considerable negative effects on their relationship with the main banks. Also, this possibility probably works as a threat to get better bargaining power in routine finance even within the framework of the stable share allocation among banks.

Further, the long-term relationship with the main banks has not resulted in less competition among banks. There is nothing rigid or inflexible about this relationship. About one third of the sample firms have in fact changed the relative shares of the set of their main banks.

Monitoring of Enterprises

None of these surveys has advanced our knowledge about the *actual delegated monitoring* function performed by the main banks. The main instruments for their monitoring role are already indicated in Section I: Behavior of Payment Settlement Accounts, Directorship on Boards and deputation of officers (current or retired) in strategic positions in the firm, participation in Presidents' Club, experience with regard to repeated transactions that enables the banks to eliminate the risk of adverse selection and moral hazard, and cross shareholding. All these formal and informal mechanisms of monitoring do provide effective instruments for judging the firm's performance. However, most of these relate to what is called interim monitoring; ex-ante monitoring—appraisal of projects or schemes for expansion, or new enterprises—ability of the main banks appears to be limited and generally related to the avoidance or appraisal of risk related to adverse selection or moral hazard.

The Role of the IBJ

The real effective ex-ante monitoring function relating to project appraisal and technology choice does not seem to be performed by the main banks. It appears to be performed by the Industrial Bank of Japan either as a main bank or as a participant bank because of the expertise and human capital accumulated by it over a long period of years since its establishment in 1902; or probably by the large industrial groups (Keiretsu), who have acquired such competence, and on which the main banks rely for their judgement. The Japan Development Bank also has developed competence in evaluating projects in some selected industries.

It is quite significant to observe that the Industrial Bank of Japan has maintained its position as a main bank even up to 1990 as indicated earlier. This position appears to be the result of the expertise and skills which the IBJ has acquired over the years and its critical strategic relationship with the MITI and the government. The recent surveys also showed that for project financing, the firms do not rely so much on the main or core banks; they probably rely on long-term credit banks like the IBJ and the Japan Development Bank (JDB).

This is confirmed by the evidence gathered by Packer. He shows that in 1956, more than 75 percent of loans for plant and equipment financing was arranged by the long-term credit banks and the JDB; even in 1966 it was a little less than 50 percent; and even by 1974, it was about 40 percent. The city banks provided only about 15 percent of such assistance until 1966 and only about 30 percent in 1974 and 1988 (Appendix A, Table 8).

This shows that the critical function of project appraisal (ex-ante monitoring) and the related function of interim monitoring (during the implementation and operation stages of the projects) were performed by the long-term credit banks and in particular the IBJ. The IBJ was able to do this because of its freedom from political pressures as well as its neutral position vis-à-vis business groups; this autonomy of functioning as well as its capacity to raise resources in various ways account for the strategic role of the IBJ.

Even with respect to what is called ex-post monitoring—rescue, rehabilitation, and liquidation of firms in financial distress—the role of the IBJ has been quite significant. The cases of such ex-post monitoring cited by Packer are extremely important cases and most of them occurred before 1973. These cases relate to: Nippon Yakin Kogdyo (a specialist steel manufacturer, 1953), Nittoku Metal Industry (1964), Ikegaio Tekko (1984), Merger of Nissan and Prince in the automobile industry (1965), Merger of Yawata and Fuji Steel to form New Japan Steel in 1969, the Yamaichi Securities (1965) and the Japan Airlines (1988–1989). In the case studies made by Sheard, out of the 17 cases of rescue, the IBJ was responsible for 5 cases, and the cases of structural changes (related to rescue), out of 10 cases, the IBJ was responsible for 3.

Thus, the IBJ, modelled explicitly in 1902 on the Credit Mobilier concept,[20] performed a key role in monitoring (ex-ante, interim and ex-post) of enterprises in Japan; since its establishment in 1902 till the early post-war period, it was a semi-government bank and had developed over the years considerable expertise and skills in project appraisal and evaluation. The Long-Term Credit Bank of Korea, and even the Korean Development Bank and the Industrial Development Bank of India were inspired by the Credit Mobilier concept and tried to perform the role which the Universal Banks in Germany or the IBJ in Japan performed. These development banks in South Korea (the Korea Development Bank and the Korea Long-Term Credit Bank) and in India (the Industrial Development Bank of India, the Industrial Credit and Investment Corporation of India and the Industrial Finance Corporation of India) are indeed performing the roles played by the Credit Mobilier and the IBJ in a different context. They have been, given the constraints, quite successful in performing this role, somewhat akin to the main bank system in Japan. Hence, it appears that the *IBJ concept* may be more relevant to the developing economies, including the transforming socialist economies. This IBJ concept can indeed be related to the functioning of the banking system (the development banks working in close cooperation with the commercial banks) both for finance as well as monitoring—the concept which was visualized in the evolution of the Indian banking system but not implemented fully because of a variety of reasons, as indicated in Chapter 4.

The Relevance of the IBJ Concept to the Developing and Transforming Economies

Thus, more than the main bank system in Japan, what appears to be much more relevant to the developing and transforming economies is the concept of a development bank, free from all sorts of inhibitions and regulations about the role it can play—that is not restricted by law and practice to the conditions laid down for the development finance institutions. A development bank of the type of the Universal Bank in the late nineteenth century, or of the IBJ type or of the IDBI (India) type would perform much better in financing an industrial spurt (of the kind described by Gerschenkron), *given the appropriate institutional and policy framework*, than the Main Bank System of Japan. It is difficult to establish the latter kind of system in these countries as they do not have the requisite banking competence developed in Japan over a long period beginning from the 1880s. After the war World War II, the Japanese financial system did not develop in a vacuum; it had more than 60 years of experience, during which it developed the human capital and skills which are lacking in the developing or the transforming economies. To have a well functioning main bank system, one first needs to have the *competence and skills essential for sound banking*.

Hence the appropriate course of action for the developing and transforming economies would be to concentrate their scarce entrepreneurial and managerial talents in establishing a plurality of development banks with monitoring competence—appraisal of projects, monitoring and supervision of projects during implementation and operation phase and playing a pro-active role in reconstruction, rehabilitation or rescue of enterprises in financial distress; and linking them organically with the banking system—the commercial banks. This was the type of approach adopted in India but it was not as effective as anticipated because of macroeconomic instability and the institutional and policy framework. *After such a system evolves, it may be possible to adapt and improve upon the financial innovation of the Main Bank System in Japan.*

The Role of the Main Bank When Borrowing Firms are in Financial Distress

One of the significant advantages of the long-run mutual commitment and relationship between the main bank and the firm is the *implicit* commitment of the main bank to assist the client enterprise, when it faces temporary or acute financial problems. This relationship enables the firm to plan its activities within a longer time horizon and thus improve its economic and technical competence from a long-run point of view.

Hoshi et al. examined the evidence relating to 125 firms in financial distress (immediate cash-flow crisis) during the period 1978 to 1985; of this sample of firms, 45 were group firms and 80 were non-group firms. Their analysis of the performance led them to conclude that the firms with strong ties to a main bank invest and sell more than firms without such strong ties.[21] Sheard has collected detailed evidence about the manner in which the main banks assist firms in financial distress. In his study, such evidence relates to 29 cases: 19 cases of financial-technical assistance and 10 cases of structural change along with financial technical assistance during the period 1975 to 84.

> The assistance packages typically involve the provision of emergency finance in the first instance and thus reductions or exemptions of interest payments for anything up to a three or five-year specified adjustment period. Intervention of the main bank in such cases is often subtle in nature in that the bank will require a recovery plan to be devised and submitted to it for approval and in the course of agreeing to this plan, the bank will typically require measures such

as labor-force reductions and asset disposals to be implemented. The plan is usually drawn up in close consultation with the main bank, again reflecting its role in monitoring. In some cases, it is no exaggeration to say that the bank devises the plan itself.[22]

In other cases, the intervention is much more direct and dramatic. It involves the bank sending in its own executives to supervise the rationalization from within the firm or to take control of the management of the firm...Japanese businessmen refer to this as being placed under 'bank management'; Pascale and Rohlen..., in a case study of the car-maker Toyo Kogyo, accurately describe it as a process whereby (the bank puts) the company in quasi-receivership status, but without any involvement from courts or lawyers'.[23]

In the course of intervening in and managing the reorganization of the firm, a number of things are commonly observed. First, the bank may oust the president or other key managers, whose intransigence or incompetence it is that has often precipitated the crisis. The bank will overhaul the management structures and implement major asset disposals and changes to the corporate organization, extending to and often centering on the affiliate network. Third, the bank will often arrange some kind of tie-up or merger with another firm, which is commonly a firm also having this bank as its main bank. Such an arrangement will typically signal the withdrawal of the bank from direct management in the firm.[24]

In Japan, there is a virtual absence of an active external takeover market; in particular, hostile takeovers of the kind prevalent in the United States and elsewhere are almost unheard of in Japan. And this is closely related to the nature of intercorporate shareholdings in Japan. Appendix A, Table 9 presents the cross-holdings ratio during 1962 to 1974 for the six large business groups; in all these groups, the ratio has tended to increase over the period 1962 to 1974. For example, for the Mitsubishi group, it rose from 17.30 percent to 26.57 percent, while even for Sanwa Group, it rose from 7.58 percent to 13.01 percent.

Cross-shareholding prevailed in the 1950s also; however, the ratio tended to rise only during the 1960s. The major reason till the mid-1970s was to defend against forced takeovers from abroad.[25] Such threats diminished after 1970; however, the rationale for cross-shareholding changed. For, cross-shareholding came to be seen as:

> a potential disciplinary device in a cooperative long-term relationship, either between a parts maker and a big auto company or between a bank and a manufacturer. The holding of shares facilitates close monitoring, and in the event of financial distress the big auto company (or the bank) may send executives to the parts supplier (or the manufacturer)...Recently another round of increases in cross-holding has become evident. More active capital markets in Japan have prompted more merger and acquisition (M&A) activity...It seems that the original motivation for cross-holding—to defend against hostile M&A activity—seems to have reappeared in the Japanese capital market.[26]

This, together with the system of interlocking shareholdings (in which the main bank itself plays a pivotal role), the main bank performs a role that closely parallels in its effect the external takeover market. What characterizes the Japanese case is not that there is no market for corporate control but rather the form that the 'market' takes on in Japan...In effect, the main bank substitutes for the missing markets for corporate control and monitoring services much more effectively and with much less transaction, information and agency costs. And it is able to do this because it is prepared to bear a disproportionately large share of the burden—either by way of losses or additional financial assistance. If it did not do this, it would lose its credibility as a main bank.[27]

Of course, the main bank performs this role of 'rescue' only for large firms with which it has a long-term relationship. For the small to medium firms, it does not perform this role. What it does is to provide consulting services directly or indirectly or induce trading houses or purchaser firms to provide the necessary technical or financial assistance. Of course, if the small or medium firm is a part of a keiretsu—vertical business group—it may obtain assistance from the large firms, belonging to that group. Independent small or medium firms cannot obtain 'rescue' assistance from any source; they have to face liquidation.

Financial Liberalization Since 1975: Its Impact on the Main Bank System

Till 1975 interest rates and bond markets were strictly regulated in Japan. However, since 1975, there has been a gradual process of financial liberalization.[28] First, the secondary market for Government bonds expanded at an extremely rapid pace. This expansion was based on the large flotations of Government bonds after 1975, and was spurred in particular by the easing of regulations on banks concerning the sales of such bonds in 1977. The expansion of the secondary market in Government bonds meant an expansion of an open market in long-term instruments with free interest rates, and also promoted expansion of short-term open markets and the relaxation or abolition of interest rate controls.

Second, short-term open markets developed considerably after 1975. An example is the market for repurchases (also known as gensaki), which had existed on a small scale since around 1950 and expanded along with the growth of the secondary market in Government bonds. A market for negotiable certificates of deposits (CDs) was established in May 1979 partly as a reaction to the growth of gensaki market. Further, with the revision of the Foreign Exchange and Foreign Trade Control Law that took effect in December 1980, cross-border movement of funds became more active.

Third, interest rate arbitrage rose substantially, not only among markets within Japan but also between Japanese and foreign markets. The growth of arbitrage occurred after 1978, with the adoption of a series of liberalization measures that expanded and diversified the open markets in both long- and short-term assets, and abolished controls on who might participate in the markets.

Thus, after 1975 the organic connection among markets strengthened and this resulted in further liberalization measures. In the 1970s, the money market mutual funds (MMMF) grew very rapidly and started to take customers away from the banks, as there have been no interest rate restrictions on the MMMFs. Hence the Depository Institutions Deregulation and Monetary Act was passed in 1980; this created the Money Market Deposit Accounts, which are not subject to regulation of their interest yield. Further, the interest rate for large amount time deposits were deregulated in 1985. Thus, while on large-time deposits with the banks, interest rate restrictions were removed, the interest rate on consumer deposits is still regulated.

However, the significant measure that affected the loan market of the banks was the deregulation of the corporate bond market. Till the early 1980s a firm desiring to issue corporate bonds was first required to comply with certain regulations—for example, the bonds had to be collateralized. Since these requirements were deregulated in 1985, many convertible bonds and bonds with warrants have been issued, particularly for the 'Euro-Market'. Thus, the large firms reduced their reliance on the loans from the main banks and the banking system.[29]

However, the evolving market-oriented system in Japan since 1985 does not seem to have supplanted, even for large firms, the main bank system. And that is because even large firms still value the main bank relationship for three reasons: the function of main bank as (*a*) manager of payment settlement accounts; (*b*) organizer of funds either through loan syndication or through assisting the issue of bonds; and (*c*) a lender of early resort in case of financial distress.

Some researchers at the Japanese banks feel that bond financing would soon be replaced by domestic loan financing (particularly with respect to issue of bonds in the Euro-dollar market) as a result of the recent collapse in the share prices and its impact on the demand for bonds with warrants issued by the Japanese firms in the Euro-dollar market. They also feel that the large firms value the *lender of early resort function* of the main bank system and in the current economic situation, are renewing or revitalizing their main bank relationships.

Further, because of a variety of reasons, the issue of bonds by the large firms depends critically on the reputation established by the firms with the main banks and requires active assistance of the main banks. Out of 109 cases of domestic convertible bond issues in the six-month period October 1988 through March 1989, the main bank was the number one trustee in 84 cases (77 percent) and number one, two or three in 105 cases (96 percent). In the case of overseas bond issues (straight bonds, convertible bonds, and warrant bonds), an overseas subsidiary of the main bank has been able to act as the co-manager of bond issues, although it has been 'administratively guided' by the 1975 agreement not to act as a lead manager. In 84 cases of overseas dollar warrant bond issues by Japanese firms between October 1988 and March 1989, there were 5.3 co-managers per issue and the firm's No. 1 transacting bank was involved as a co-manager in 71 cases (84.5 percent).

Thus so far the main bank system is still relevant in Japan, though it performs different functions in the light of the emerging economic situation. Still, the system—the long-term relationship between the main bank and the firm—continues to operate and is still relevant even for large financially sound firms as it is, and would be for a long time to come. The growing small to medium firms also require for their long-term planning such a long-term commitment between them and their main banks. Of course, the future is uncertain and how a market-oriented system and the main bank oriented banking system will co-exist and reinforce each other is a question which nobody can answer (excepting the astrologers).

III
THE INSTITUTIONAL AND POLICY FRAMEWORK IN JAPAN

The main bank system's success in Japan, particularly during its high growth period (1951 to 73), in promoting a rapid pace of industrialization appears to be mainly due to certain aspects of Japan's institutional and policy frameworks. The major objectives which governed the institutional and policy framework, are related to the establishment of macroeconomic stability, rational price structure, a sound and healthy financial system, and orientation of the industrial structure toward *viable* import substitution and export promotion.

Macroeconomic Stability and Rational Price Structure

Balanced budgets and effective monetary credit policies of the Bank of Japan have been the major instruments for establishing macroeconomic stability. The price structure initially was rationalized with a view to anchor it to relative prices as prevailed during a normal period of 1934 to 36, which was the last peaceful and prosperous period before the war; and the nominal prices were fixed as a certain multiple of the prices that prevailed during that period. Subsequently, the price controls were removed. Further, the exchange rate was fixed at a single rate in 1949, thus relating domestic prices to international prices. These measures, taken before 1950, resulted in an undistorted price structure; and this structure provided an instrument for rational cost-benefit analysis to the enterprises as well as the banks. Of course, import controls in the early 1950s did distort the price structure; however, gradual relaxation of import controls in the 1960s linked domestic prices to international prices very closely (except for agricultural products).[30]

Macroeconomic Policies for Stimulating Viable Import Substitution and Export Promotion

Once the signalling function of the price-system was rationally devised, the macroeconomic policies have been such as to stimulate a process of rational import substitution and export promotion. For this purpose, the long-term credit banks (like the IBJ) helped the banks in evaluating project proposals and technology choices by enterprises at least until 1973. Further, the desired resource allocation was brought about by creating specialized public sector financial institutions for various sectors like agriculture, small and medium industries, housing and foreign trade and long-term finance to industries. Private sector financial institutions for specific sectors like agriculture and small–medium enterprises were established and promoted since 1951. The public sector financial institutions were more or less complementary to the private financial institutions. Thus, while the growing heavy and chemical industry was financed mainly by the private financial institutions, the public sector financial institutions provided finance mainly for infrastructure and industrial adjustment in industries like mining, agriculture, marine transportation and small- and medium-sized firms.[31]

Further, the government gave

> subsidies and import protection to certain targeted industries. Infant industries are protected by import restrictions until domestic manufacturers are able to compete with foreign ones. The import restrictions were lifted only after domestic manufacturers became strong and competitive. For example, the restrictions on buses and trucks were lifted in 1961, those on color TVs in 1964, those on passenger automobiles in 1965, those on color film in 1971, those on cash registers in 1973, those on large-memory integrated circuits in 1974, and those on computers in 1975. It would be interesting to know whether the Japanese manufacturers that now dominate the markets for these items could have achieved their dominance without import protection during their infancies.[32]
>
> In the 1950s, 'rationalization'...plans became the center of policy. The main tools at this stage were special tax provisions and the use of the Fiscal Investments and Loans Program for the purchase of labor-saving machinery and modern plants. In particular, the government adopted accelerated depreciation and tariff exemptions for imported machines in targeted industries. Policies at this point were conducted within the framework of a market economy with tax incentives. The policies can be interpreted as a plan to share the large risk associated with building costly modern machines and

plants. The industries targeted for rationalization included steel, coal, ship-building, electric power, synthetic fibers, chemical fertilizers, and in the late 1950s, petrochemicals, machine tools and parts, and electronics.[33]

The business firms, which had an overhang of debt, and which were adversely affected by the suspension of various types of compensation after 1946, were allowed to operate on new accounts, the old sunk costs being offset by reduction in capital, retained earnings and the like. Thus the firms' capital structure was reconstituted and their functioning was protected from the debt-overhang problem. This restructuring of the capital base of firms was extremely important in inducing them to improve their efficiency.[34] Such reconstruction of the capital structure of firms has relevance to the problems of state enterprises in the developing countries and more particularly in the transforming economies.

Another aspect of Japanese policy also seems to be relevant to the developing and transforming economies and that pertains to linking stabilization with growth in output. Despite the severe damage during the war, most of the production equipment was unimpaired.

> The ratio of production capacity available in 1945 to the maximum capacity attained before 1994 was 78 percent in electricity, 100.2 percent for steel, 89 percent for non-ferrous metals, 52.2 percent for machinery, 68.9 percent for chemicals and 31.2 percent for textiles...Thus the decline in production after the war was primarily the result of raw material and energy shortages...[35]

The priority production system (PPS) aimed at breaking this bottleneck by concentrating scarce materials, energy and manpower into key industries. These industries were financed at subsidized interest rates by the Reconstruction Finance Corporation (RFC); and the commercial banks were compelled to use 50 percent of their new funds for such financing. (The RFC was active during 1947 and 1948 and was dismantled in March 1949 with the Dodge plan and the control on commercial banks' loans was abolished in August 1949.) Both the RFC and the commercial banks relied heavily on the Bank of Japan for their resources; as much as 70 percent of RFC funds were raised via the BOJ credit.

This PPS system was accompanied by subsidies to enterprises. They were constituted in such a manner as to improve their capacity utilization; subsidies declined as output increased. The subsidies represented the difference between the final product prices as determined on the basis of international prices and the producer's cost at the level of its capacity utilization. These subsidies according to Teranishi played an important part in production recovery after the war. The PPS system was linked with credit creation and though it increased output, it also created severe inflation. However, 'the pricing and anchoring systems were extremely important in bringing down the rate of inflation and raising the level of production simultaneously.'[36]

It is argued that these measures owed their success to the following four factors. First, the price anchoring was aimed not only at stabilizing nominal price levels but also establishing or attaining a return to the relative price system suited to 'normal' times. Second, price subsidies were closely linked to the level of capacity utilization and were used to guide production levels. Third, the price subsidies were determined at a level sufficient for the production units to retain idle resources with firm-specific skills in anticipation of higher activity levels in the future. Fourth multiple anchoring was adopted to retain integrity of control and avoid spillover effects. Although the wage rates were left to be determined by the market, the standard wage for each industry was linked closely to price subsidies and after April 1949, fixation of exchange rates served as a powerful anchor for tradable prices.

It may be discerned that the control and anchoring system summarized above is strongly geared to recovery of and efficiency in production. We believe that this growth or production oriented policy was the key to the Japanese experience of stabilization with growth.

[Thus] the Japanese economy showed a strong upward movement in the level of production or real economic activity not only after the successful implementation of the stabilization program but also during the period of implementation. It is suggested here that this, rather exceptional, performance of the Japanese economy during the 1945–50 period was due to the growth-oriented nature of stabilization measures.[37]

Of course, the Dodge plan involving balanced budget, single exchange rate and suspension of RFC activities finally eliminated inflationary pressures. The balance of payments constraint and the effective demand constraint were removed by the spurt in Japanese exports as a result of the Korean war and indeed put Japan on the growth path earlier than would have been possible otherwise.

Regulatory Framework for the Financial System and Resource Allocation

The regulatory framework for the financial system till at least 1975 had two objectives: one was to ensure the safety and soundness of the system and the other was resource allocation to priority sectors.[38]

The viability of the financial system was ensured by administrative determination of interest rates—both on deposits and loans—by the Bank of Japan until at least 1980 and in a diluted form thereafter. The entry and branch expansion require approval of the Ministry of Finance. Further, the Bank of Japan's financial assistance to the banks is discretionary and depends on its judgement relating to the soundness of the portfolio of the banks.

The administrative fixing of deposit rates prevents price competition among banks relating to interest rates on deposits. It induces the banks, as argued earlier, to lower the transaction costs and the risk of depositors and thus to improve their noninterest yield as also to mobilize a greater part of household saving in the form of bank deposits. Of course, this represents a tax on savers, while the rents are passed on to the entrepreneurs and the banks. Since no substitutes were available, the savers have been denied access to other financial instruments as a result of regulations.

The lending rates are fixed in such a manner as to provide an adequate margin to the banks for their transaction costs and minimum profit. Of course, the operative rates could be changed by the banks through the mechanism of compensatory balances by the assisted enterprises. The banks thus circumvent the interest rate regulations. The public sector financial institutions could not do this; hence the regulated rates are effective for them. Because of the oligopolistic loan market vis-à-vis the small and medium firms, the banks here do charge higher effective rates to them. In any case, the banks are induced to enlarge their profits by supporting sound projects and enterprises, rather than merely through charging higher interest rates on loans.

Thus, the banks' main objectives center around deposit mobilization through lowering of transaction cost and risk of depositors, and enlarging the loan business on the basis of main bank relationship and participatory relationships with other banks with respect to syndicated loans. The banks are thus motivated to support sound projects and enterprises, as their profits depend on the volume of their loan business. Banks could improve their returns by equity participation relating to assisted enterprises, but such returns again depend on the viability and profitability of the assisted enterprises.

The banks can enlarge their business by increasing their deposit business; however, this depends on branch expansion and their branch expansion plans have to be approved by the Ministry of Finance, which also has the power to examine their income-expenditure accounts and regulate their dividend policies. Thus, unless their portfolio were sound, they could not obtain the approval of the Ministry of Finance for branch expansion and dividend distribution. The restriction on dividend distribution is aimed at enlarging the reserves of the banks so as to enable them to provide for default risk on their loans.

The entry of new banks also requires the approval of the Ministry of Finance; this regulatory device is aimed at ensuring the soundness of the new entrants and thus of the banking system. During this period (upto 1980) no new domestic banks were allowed entry.

The Bank of Japan, at its discretion, provides credit to the banks; they help the banks in enlarging their business by keeping very low excess reserves. However, this makes them—the city banks in particular—dependent on the Bank of Japan; thus the Bank of Japan acquired the power to evaluate the bank's performance and their soundness before taking a decision to assist them. This was an important informal method of ensuring bank compliance with Central Bank guidance, since these central bank loans were at low (subsidized) interest rates.

Thus, the Ministry of Finance and the Bank of Japan have the power under the regulatory framework to ensure the soundness of their functioning as well as the consistency of their credit allocation decisions with the national priorities, particularly with respect to export orientation and viable import substitution. However, there are no formal rigid credit allocation requirements; the banks have autonomy in deciding their credit allocation patterns.

The other device for resource allocation is the regulation with respect to the issue of bonds by the enterprises and the public financial institutions. The government appointed committee decides on the prices as well as the size of the bond issues. These bonds are rationed to syndicate banks, at prices exceeding the market price. While banks suffer from low interest rates on bonds, these bonds are eligible securities for the Bank of Japan credits that carries a lower rate of interest than the market rate (call rate). The electricity industry and, to a *lesser* extent, the steel industry were the main beneficiaries till 1974.

This bond regulation, however, has been particularly important for long-term credit banks like the Industrial Bank of Japan; they have been able to secure the required finance at lower interest rates and they are able to *transform* short-term savings into long-term credit instruments. The interest rates and bond market regulation have been progressively relaxed since 1975.

Capital Restructuring of Banks

The banks had given government loans to munition companies till 1945; after the war, the government repudiated these guarantees, and this created a serious bad debts problem for the banks. To tackle this, the government divided the balance sheet of the banks *into old and new accounts*. The assets of the new account included cash and government bonds, and the liabilities included tax liabilities and a limited amount of deposits, which were protected from write-offs. The assets of the old account included all government guaranteed loans, and the liabilities included the unprotected deposits and capital. The financial institutions were allowed to continue their business using the new account, while the losses due to the repudiation were financed by cancelling the liabilities and reducing the capital in the old account. This process was started in late 1946 and was completed in early 1948. Most banks were forced to reduce significantly their capital to cover the losses. For example, 55 out of 61 ordinary banks reduced their capital by more than 90 percent and 6 lost all their capital. The capital was subsequently replenished by issuing new shares; however, the big old shareholders were not allowed to buy these shares.[39] This balance sheet cleansing increased the power of the bank management and reduced that of the shareholders.

This Japanese reform after the war is very relevant for the developing economies with a financial system burdened with high non–performing loans largely to public enterprises, as well as for the transforming economies, which have the same problem but in a more serious form as the state enterprises there are the dominant enterprises. Unless the restructuring of capital of both banks and firms is done somewhat in the manner of Japan during 1946 to 48, the banks and the firms would not be able to function in a financially viable way.

IV
THE BANKING SYSTEMS IN GERMANY, SOUTH KOREA, INDIA AND MEXICO

The banking systems in these countries have some elements of the main bank system of Japan but differ from it in some important respects.

Germany

In Germany, the large banks (eleven in all but three dominating banks) have dealings with large firms (principally the top 100). However, the firms have no exclusive main bank relationship with any one bank, unlike in Japan. Because of a highly competitive environment, the large firms have multi-bank relationships. The house bank relationship is no longer typical for German corporate finance, as it was during the late nineteenth century and possibly till 1970.

However, there are some similarities between the main bank system and the German banking system. Since banks own equity in firms, have proxy voting rights in shareholders meetings on behalf of their client shareholders and have representation on the Supervisory Board, they have a degree of control on the management board of the firms. (Germany has a system of two boards—the Supervisory board and the Management board. The supervisory board members are elected by the shareholders and the workers; this board does not—cannot—interfere in the day-to-day functions of the management board but can change it in case of financial problems.)

Thus in *ex-post* monitoring—or rescue operations of financially distressed firms—the large German banks taken together—or a bank singly if it acquires a dominant position by way of shareholding and/or proxy votes and representation on the supervisory board—can and do perform the role which the main bank system has been playing in Japan with respect to large firms.

Further, because of the management control over banks, the bureaucratic control over bank management and the nature of the regulatory framework, bankruptcy laws and the general environment, the rescue operations are undertaken in the interests of all the stakeholders (creditors, shareholders, workers and even suppliers). In Germany too, there is representation on the supervisory board not only of the shareholders but also of the banks (as shareholders and creditors) and the workers. Hence as in Japan, in Germany too the rescue or reconstruction or merger, etc., operations are conducted in such a way as is fair to all stakeholders including the workers and there are no hostile takeovers or externally induced takeovers of firms in financial distress. The banks do change management and thus perform the function of the takeover market.

The German banks, unlike in Japan, are universal banks, that is, they combine the functions of commercial as well as investment banking and thus can provide all types of financial services.[40] The German banking system that is much more relevant to the developing and transforming economies is the one that prevailed during the late nineteenth century. The Universal Bank during the period performed much more effectively all the main bank functions and, in addition, also performed the entrepreneurial role, that is so relevant for the developing and transforming economies.

To quote Gerschenkron:

> In Germany, the various incompetencies of the individual entrepreneurs were offset by the device of splitting the entrepreneurial function; the German investment banks—a powerful invention, comparable in economic effect to that of steam engine—were in their capital-supplying function a substitute for the insufficiency of the previously created wealth willingly placed at the disposal of entrepreneurs. But they were also a substitute for entrepreneurial deficiencies. From their central vantage points of control, the banks participated actively in shaping the major—and sometimes not so major—decisions of individual enterprises. It was they who very often mapped out a firm's path of growth, conceived far-sighted plans, decided on major technological and locational innovations and arranged for mergers and capital increases.[41]

South Korea

In South Korea, the credit allocation decisions at least until recently were taken largely by the government; the banks were owned by the government and carried out the credit allocation decisions of the government. They did not perform any role usually performed by a main bank in Japan.

However, after 1974, the main bank system was introduced by the government particularly with a view to *control* credit to large business groups. It was the *explicit* result of government intervention. The main banks, however, did not own equity in enterprises nor did they perform any monitoring function. This system was controlled by the Board of Supervisors and was introduced largely to facilitate their role of controlling credit to the large business groups.

The lead commercial bank system in India had a similar purpose and was introduced by the regulatory bodies to control credit to the large business houses (see Chapter 4).

Both systems have not found favor with banks or the firms as their main role has been to control and restrict credit to large business groups rather than that of a main bank in Japan.

In Korea, however, the Korea Development Bank and the Korea Long-Term Credit Bank do perform some of the main bank functions—particularly related to ex-ante, interim and ex-post monitoring of firms, to which they provide project financing. The KLTCB is in fact modeled on the Industrial Bank of Japan concept—in fact explicitly on the concept of the Credit Mobilier as is mentioned in Chapter 2.

India

India has three national development banks and several state level development banks. Two of the development banks are owned by the government. They evolved spontaneously the lead development bank concept in the late sixties. The lead development bank performs all the functions of the main bank in Japan; it appraises projects critically, performs the function of monitoring and supervision of assisted projects and plays the lead role in arranging for reorganization or restructuring of assisted enterprises, which face financial problems. It arranges for syndicated loans as well as syndicated participation in bond-equity financing. The participant institutions are not only the other development banks but also commercial banks, the Life Insurance Corporation of India, the General Insurance Corporation of India and the Unit Trust of India. The lead bank performs the delegated monitoring function on behalf of all the participating institutions. Thus it reduces transaction costs and risk, not only for the participating institutions but also for the borrowers.

The system has functioned well so far and its inefficiencies have largely been the result of macroeconomic instability, the rigid and inflexible control system—investment and import licensing—and the political-bureaucratic intervention in decision making (see Chapter 4 for details relating to the institutional and policy framework in India).

Mexico

Mexico, until 1982, had a banking system controlled by the Industry. Until 1970, this system performed quite well, particularly with respect to its monitoring function. However, after 1970, the resources of the system were pre-empted by the government and there was serious macroeconomic instability and government interference with the result that the banking system had hardly incentive to perform the monitoring functions. The banks were nationalized in 1982; this improved their efficiency but because of government pre-emption of its resources, they did not grow in size until 1990. Recently they have been privatized; again the owners of the financial holding companies are represented by the industrial groups. It is yet to be seen how this privatized system will function.

V
THE RELEVANCE TO THE DEVELOPING AND THE TRANSFORMING ECONOMIES OF THE MAIN BANK SYSTEM OF JAPAN

As in Japan after the war and until 1951, many of the developing countries and particularly the transforming economies face similar problems: (*a*) Structural Adjustment and Stabilization; (*b*) Restructuring and privatization of State Enterprises (particularly those that make losses); and (*c*) Restructuring of the banking system, ridden with bad debt, and functioning without any operational autonomy. In Japan, the banking system's capital was restructured and hence it was in a position to play an effective role in financing restructured enterprises and improving their efficiency as a result of its monitoring function.

Because of the similarities of the initial conditions (Japan during 1945 to 51) in the developing and the transforming economies now, the main bank system is extremely relevant for these countries. These countries require restructuring and privatization of state enterprises and active support—financial and technical—by the banking system to restructured state enterprises as well as the potential new small and medium enterprises. The various monitoring functions—ex-ante, interim and ex-post—thus assume critical significance and only a system like the main bank system can perform effectively and efficiently this monitoring role as well as the delegated monitoring function on behalf of the participating financial institutions. As in Japan up to 1970, so also in most of these countries, the equity and bond markets are underdeveloped and, in any case, even when they do develop and function, they would provide financial resources only to very large mature firms with a good track record. Hence the financial system has to be bank-oriented rather than market-oriented—at least with regard to its relative roles and priorities.

However, it is worth emphasizing the significance of the *banks, like the development banks* (of the Industrial Bank of Japan type or the Universal Banks of Germany during the late nineteenth century, on the basis of which the IBJ was conceived). The Universal Banks in Germany during the late nineteenth century, the Industrial Bank of Japan (conceived on the Credit Mobilier concept) and the development banks in South Korea and India have performed a very critical role with regard to (*a*) providing entrepreneurial assistance to new firms; (*b*) appraisal of new projects (ex-ante monitoring); (*c*) arranging the required financing through syndicated arrangements with other financial institutions; (*d*) monitoring of assisted projects on behalf of all participating financial institutions (delegated monitoring function); and (*e*) rescue or rehabilitation of firms in financial distress.

In view of the *scarcity* of skills, expertise and human capital accumulation in these countries, it may be more effective and operationally more practical to create and support such development banks that can play a catalytic role in not only the industrial development but also the financial development of these countries. If such banks are established *without restriction* in their role in providing financial services as may be required, and are ensured *operational autonomy*, they may turn out to be the *focal point* for further financial development of these countries along the lines of the MB system in Japan. The MB system is quite relevant for the countries because of its monitoring functions—which tend to reduce or eliminate risk arising from adverse selection or the moral hazard; hence, the initial emphasis on the establishment of development banks could be aimed at evolving the MB type of system.

NOTES

1. Juro Teranishi, *Financial Sector Reform After the War* (Tokyo: The Institute of Economic Research, Hitotusabashi University, Discussion Paper, Series A, No. 244, 1991).
2. Ibid.
3. Takatoshi Ito, *The Japanese Economy* (Cambridge, Mass.: The MIT Press, 1992), pp. 178–82.
4. There are two kinds of Keitetsus. First type of group relates to horizontal integration—a set of firms in different industries—through cross holding of stocks and reliance on a main bank; there are six largest groups of this kind, but other banks also have developed their own groups. The second type of Keiretsu represents vertical integration—through long-term relationship as well as cross holding of stocks—of manufacturers with suppliers, distributors and the like; large manufacturing companies such as Toyota, Hitachi and Matsushita have also formed such groups. See Ito (n. 3 above), p. 178.
5. Ito (n. 3 above), p. 180.
6. Juro Teranishi, 1991 (n. 1 above).
7. Takeo Hoshi, Anil Kashyap and Gary Loveman, *Lessons from the Japanese Main Bank System for Financial System Reform in Poland* (Mimeo. 1993).
8. *'The Japanese Banks: Overburdened', The Economist* (London: July 25–31, 1992) pp. 77–78.
9. Ito, (n. 3 above), pp. 180–89, for details.
10. Bankruptcy *The Economist*, (London: August 1–7, 1992), pp.63–5.
11. Paul Sheard, 'The Main Bank System and Corporate Monitoring and Control in Japan,' *Journal of Economic Behavior and Organization*, 1989.
12. Kenneth J. Arrow, *The Limits of Organization* (New York: W.W. Norton and Co., 1979), pp. 23–24.
13. V.V. Bhatt, *Financial Innovations and Credit Market Evolution* (World Bank: Economic Development Institute, Informal Paper, 1989).
14. Ito. (n. 3 above), p. 273.
15. Hoshi et al (n. 7 above).
16. A. Horiuchi, F. Packer and Shin'ichi Fukuda, 'What Role has the Main Bank Played in Japan,' *Journal of the Japanese and International Economies* (1988).
17. Sheard, 1989 (n. 11 above).
18. Toshihiro Horiuchi, *'Cross-Section Empirical Analysis on the Japanese Firms' Terms of Loan by Bargaining Approach'* (Japan, Kyoto: Kyoto Institute of Economic Research, Draft Preliminary Paper, 1992).
19. Toshihiro Horiuchi, *Management Structure of Japanese Banks and Their Optimal Relationship with Firms as 'Main Banks'* (Japan, Kyoto: Kyoto Institute of Economic Research, Discussion Paper No. 309, 1990).
20. Toshihiro Horiuchi, *Comparisons of Main Bank Relationship by Firm Size* (Mimeo, 1993); Toshihiro Horiuchi, *The Corporate Loan Syndication Process: The Respective*

Role of Main Bank and the Corporate Clients (Mimeo, 1993); and Horiuchi, 1990, (n. 19 above), and 1992, (n. 18 above).

21. Hoshi et al. (n. 7 above).
22. Sheard. (n. 11 above).
23. Ibid.
24. Ibid.
25. Ito, (n. 3 above), pp. 191–92.
26. Ibid, pp. 191–92.
27. Sheard (n. 11 above).
28. Yoshio Suzuki, *The Japanese Financial System* (Oxford: Clarendon Press, 1987), pp. 5–7.
29. Ito. (n. 3 above), pp. 105 and 124–25.
30. Juro Teranishi, *Inflation Stabilization with Growth: Japanese Experience During 1945–50* (Tokyo: The Institute of Economic Research, Hitotsubashi University, Discussion Paper A No. 243, 1990).
31. Ibid.
32. Ito. (n. 3 above), pp. 197–98.
33. Ibid, pp. 198–99.
34. Teranishi. (n. 1 above).
35. Ibid.
36. Ibid.
37. Ibid.
38. Juro Teranishi, 'Financial System and the Industrialization of Japan: 1900–1970,' *Banca Nazionale del Lavoro Quarterly Review*, No. 174, September, 1990.
39. Hoshi et al. (n. 7 above).
40. Theodor Baums, *Banks and Corporate Control* (University of Osnabruck, Working Paper No. 91–1), 1991, and Christian Harm, *The Relationship Between German Banks and large German Firms*, (Washington, D. C.: World Bank, Policy Research Working Paper Series No. 900, 1992).
41. Alexander Gerschenkron, *Continuity in History and Other Essays* (Cambridge, Mass.: Harvard University Press, 1968), pp. 137–38; and Joseph A. Schumpeter, *Business Cycles*, Vol. I (New York: McGraw Hill Book Co. Inc., 1939), pp. 437–78 and 348–49.

Chapter 4

Lead Bank Systems in India: Review of Performance

INTRODUCTION

In both Japan and India, the financial system was used after the Second World War as an instrument for rapid economic development particularly through the accelerated pace of industrialization. The systems in both the countries—in Japan till 1970 and in India till 1985—were largely bank-oriented as both had to finance new projects and enterprises which had no track record to facilitate financing through a market-oriented system, which can function only on the basis of detailed information about the actual performance of entrepreneurs and enterprises; such information for obvious reasons was not available for new projects or enterprises. Further, in the initial years, the saving rates were low and because of considerable uncertainty, savers were unwilling to assume the risk attached to market instruments; and in Japan the policy environment also was not favorable for the functioning of the capital market. Hence, one of the mechanisms for making adequate finance available to new entrepreneurs and enterprises was the Main Bank System in Japan and the Lead Bank Systems in India. The main bank relationship in Japan was with respect only to large firms with which the banks had long historical and Zaibatsu ties.

The objective of this chapter is to give a brief account of the lead bank systems in India and review their performance. These systems are in the nature of financial innovations, somewhat similar to the universal banking system in Germany during the late nineteenth century and the main bank system in Japan, with regard to their objectives.

The plan of this chapter is as follows. A synoptic overview of the financial system in India is presented in section I. The Indian lead bank systems and their characteristics are presented in section II and the reasons for their relative ineffectiveness are indicated in section III. The preconditions for the effective and efficient implementation of the financial innovations represented by the lead bank systems are discussed in the final section.

I
A SYNOPTIC OVERVIEW OF THE FINANCIAL SYSTEM IN INDIA

The Indian financial system as it has evolved is comparable in many respects with the financial systems of the most advanced developing countries as well as some of the developed countries. It has a well-diversified structure of financial institutions and instruments and in fact financial development has outpaced economic development.[1]

Growth and Diversification

The financial system has developed at a fairly rapid pace since 1950–51 and its growth rate has exceeded the growth rate of gross domestic product or gross capital formation. The ratio of financial assets of the system to gross domestic product has increased from 62 percent in 1981 to 94 percent in 1990 and the financial interrelations ratio (net increase in financial assets to net capital formation) has risen from 0.98 in 1965–66 to 2.50 in 1990; this *marginal* financial interrelation ratio is comparable with the *average* financial interrelations ratio in the U.S.A.[2] The household sector's gross saving in the form of financial assets has increased from 5.5 percent of net domestic product in 1965–66 to 12.2 percent in 1990. The population per bank branch has declined from 65,000 in 1969 to 11,000 in 1990. The various indicators of financial development are given in Appendix B, Table 1. India's financial development is comparable to that of South Korea and the network of financial institutions as it functions at present does not appear to be having a parallel in any other part of the world.[3]

Financial Institutions: The Central Bank

The Reserve Bank of India (RBI) is India's Central Bank. The RBI performs the traditional central banking roles of note issue and banker to the government and commercial banks. It formulates and manages monetary and credit policy by setting deposit and lending rates, and lending targets. It also manages the foreign exchange market and the exchange control system. The RBI regulates and supervises all commercial banks and manages the public sector commercial banks. It provides deposit insurance and credit guarantees for some bank loans through a subsidiary (the Deposit Insurance and Credit Guarantee Corporation). In the money market, the RBI established the Discount and Finance House of India (DFHI) in 1988 to encourage secondary trading in treasury and commercial bills and to facilitate open market operations. Finally, the RBI has played a developmental role by providing refinance lines. Two of them have been spun off into separate development finance institutions for industry (the Industrial Development Bank of India) and agriculture (the National Bank for Agriculture and Rural Development). The RBI's largest remaining refinance lines are for agriculture and exports.

Financial Institutions: Deposit Institutions

Commercial banks still dominate the financial system. Their widespread network of nearly 59,000 branches enables them to raise deposits countrywide. The large banks effectively operate as universal banks, taking in all types of deposits and offering many kinds of loans; in addition, some banks have established subsidiaries for leasing, underwriting, mutual funds, merchant banking and other corporate services.

Commercial banking is dominated by 20 public sector banks (nationalized in 1969 and 1980) and the 196 Regional Rural Banks. Public banks account for over 90 percent of commercial bank assets and deposits. The RBI controls the operations of all public sector banks through directives and guidelines and a comprehensive annual financial review.

The private commercial banks consist of 29 Indian scheduled banks, 21 foreign banks and 3 small non-scheduled banks (Scheduled banks have a minimum asset size, are limited companies and must abide by the RBI and the Central Government regulations. They are eligible for the RBI's refinance and licenses to deal in foreign exchange).

The Post Office Savings Bank also mobilizes deposits. Operating through post offices throughout the country, it caters mainly to lower income groups and raises over 35 percent of its deposits from rural areas. Traditional Post Office Savings deposits are equivalent to less than 2 percent of broad money. Other Post Office deposits and small saving instruments have been more successful because of their attractive interest rates and benefits. These other Post Office deposits amount to about 4.5 percent of broad money and almost 7 percent of the time deposit component of broad money. All of the resources mobilized by the Post Office Savings Bank go to the government.

Company deposits, which are term deposits with nonbank companies, are another important financial asset. Company deposits are equivalent to about 15 percent of broad money. About 75 percent of these deposits are in nonfinancial companies. One-half of all company deposits are with government companies, representing security deposits for service and deposits of profitable public sector firms with unprofitable firms. Interest rates on these deposits are 13 to 14 percent, making them both a low cost source of funds for firms and more attractive than bank deposits for individuals. Large firms are allowed to take deposits up to 35 percent of their capital.

The Financial Institutions: Term Lending and Apex

Three important all-India Industrial Development Finance Institutions (DFIs) provide term finance to industry: the Industrial Development Bank of India (IDBI), the Industrial Credit and Investment Corporation of India (ICICI) and the Industrial Finance Corporation of India (IFCI). In addition, the Industrial Reconstruction Bank of India (IRBI) assists in restructuring of firms experiencing operational and financial difficulties. At the state level there are the State Finance Corporations (SFCs) and the State Industrial Development Corporations (SIDCs). There is also a Small Scale Industry Bank, providing refinance to financial institutions, which provide credit to small industry. The IDBI (established in 1964) acts as an apex and coordinating institution; about 30 percent of its disbursements represent refinance. It also holds equity positions in the IFCI, the IRBI, the Unit Trust of India (UTI) and the SFCs. The IDBI has taken a major role in promoting consortium finance for industrial projects, which currently governs about 90 percent of all direct lending by the DFIs. The IDBI, the IFCI and the SFCs are all government-owned institutions, while the ICICI is a semi-private institution.

The National Bank for Agriculture and Rural Development (NABARD) is the apex body for agricultural finance funded by the

Reserve Bank of India and international agencies and owned by the central government. Its main responsibilities include extending loans and refinance assistance to the commercial banks, the Regional Rural Banks (RRBs) and the State Corporative Banks. It also coordinates the financing activities of constituent institutions and invests in their share capital and securities. In the last few years, the NABARD has assumed additional tasks, including the rehabilitation of weak RRBs and cooperative banks.

The National Housing Bank (NHB) was established by the RBI in 1988 to regulate and supervise housing finance. While the NHB's role is still evolving, it already sets interest rates for deposits and mortgage loans and provides refinance for small new houses.

The Life Insurance Corporation of India (LIC) and the General Insurance Corporation of India (GIC) were formed when the Government nationalized the life insurance companies in 1956 and took over the general insurance companies in 1972. Both are required to invest a substantial proportion of their portfolios in Government securities or other approved instruments. Both institutions also invest part of their 'free' funds in industry, through the capital market, where they are important net buyers as well as underwriters. Moreover, some of the investment in industry consists of obligations of the DFIs. The LIC and the GIC also purchase bonds issued by housing agencies and have recently established subsidiaries to finance housing directly.

Industrial exports are financed by the commercial banks and the Export-Import Bank (EXIM). The EXIM Bank was formed in 1982, taking over many of the IDBI's functions as a supplier of credit to exporters and is owned by the Government. Despite the EXIM Bank's growth, commercial banks still supply a significant portion of export credit.

The Financial Institutions: Capital and Money Markets

India's capital market is among the largest in the developing world. The market is composed of 15 regional exchanges selling long-term government debt, debentures and shares. Nearly 6000 firms are listed on the Indian Stock Exchanges, more than any country other than the U.S.A.. Market capitalization of listed firms in 1987 was similar to Brazil, Malaysia, Singapore, and Denmark, but much smaller than Korea. Until recently, the government security market was the largest segment of the capital market. In the 1980s, however, private issues have grown dramatically. Large companies now raise about 20 percent of their new funding in the market; for them it has become a viable, low cost source of funds and a way around the limits on credit and its high cost.

The Unit Trust of India (UTI), owned by the government, raises resources from sales of small denomination 'units' to households and invests the proceeds in the stock market and in private placements. In recent years, the UTI has become a dominant player in the capital market. Recently, several banks have established mutual funds, as their subsidiaries; so far there are seven such mutual funds, competing with the UTI.

The Indian money market is composed of transactions between financial intermediaries (call money, interbank funds and rediscounting of bills), treasury bills and the intercorporate market. The RBI has taken a major role in stimulating the development of the money market.

The RBI has also actively sponsored new instruments. In 1988, to help banks even out liquidity, the RBI reintroduced participation certificates. In 1989, the RBI introduced two new instruments: commercial paper and certificate of deposits. These new instruments are likely to represent a major source of competition for banks.

The Financial Institutions: Finance for Agriculture

Institutional finance for agriculture is provided to farmers by the Primary Agricultural Cooperative Credit Societies (PACs), which extend short- and medium-term credit to members; branches of cooperative Land Development Banks (LDBs) provide term loans; and branches of commercial banks and the RRBs provide credit of all maturities. Other credit, largely short-term, comes from money lenders, input dealers, relatives and so forth; these informal market transactions are an extremely important aspect of agricultural finance as well as finance for all types of small enterprises.[4]

II
THE NATURE AND CHARACTERISTICS OF THE LEAD BANK SYSTEM

In the late sixties, India devised three types of lead banks with the explicit objective of raising the rate of financial saving, allocating financial resources on the basis of sound criteria to various sectors of the economy and improving investment and productive efficiency of assisted enterprises by providing entrepreneurial, managerial and technical assistance. The financial system since then has been expected to play a catalytic role in stimulating the process of rapid industrial and economic development. The lead bank systems had, hence, some of the characteristics of the main bank system in Japan; however, the institutional and policy frameworks have been quite different from that in Japan during 1950 to 70 and these differential characteristics in this framework in India seem to have affected adversely the functioning of the lead bank systems.

There are three types of lead bank systems, *each with a different function*: (*a*) the Lead Development Bank for *investment financing*; (*b*) the Lead Commercial Bank for *working capital finance*; and (*c*) the Lead Commercial Bank in a District or simply the Lead Bank with the function of providing access to bank finance to small enterprises of all types in a district and promoting such enterprises through entrepreneurial, managerial and technical assistance.

The Lead Development Bank

There are three all India development banks: the Industrial Development Bank of India (IDBI), the Industrial Finance Corporation of India (IFCI), and the Industrial Credit and Investment Corporation of India (ICICI). At the state level, practically each state has a State Financial Corporation (SFC) and a State Industrial Development Corporation (SIDC); there are eighteen SFCs and twenty-six SIDCs.

The IDBI is an apex Development Bank with the function of coordinating the activities of the Development Banking System; its charter is broad and flexible and it can finance, directly or indirectly, any sound project, irrespective of its ownership, organization and size.

Inter-Institutional Meeting (IIM)

For coordinating the functions of all India development banks, the IDBI has devised an informal institution called Inter-Institutional Meeting (IIM), comprising as members the IDBI, the IFCI, the ICICI, the Life Insurance Corporation of India (LIC), the General Insurance Corporation (GIC), and the Unit Trust of India (UTI). The latter three are significant resource mobilizers; the LIC and the GIC account for about 8 to 9 percent of household sector's gross financial saving and the UTI for about 3 percent. Since they are long-term investors, they also have an interest in providing finance to sound new enterprises by way of loans, purchase of bonds or equity; hence their participation in the IIM. The lead development bank function, however, is performed only by the development banks—the IDBI, the ICICI, and the IFCI.

Till about 1970, the IIM was held every month with the specific objective of (*a*) sharing and exchanging information on projects requiring finance, (*b*) forming a *collective* judgement about the soundness of the projects, presented to each of them for financial assistance, and (*c*) arranging for the required finance for each large project, above a certain size, through syndicated financial assistance.

This system reduced the risk relating to adverse selection by pooling information on enterprises and projects available with each institution, mobilized adequate finance for new sound projects and reduced each lender's risk by risk sharing. However, each enterprise had to submit a separate application form to each institution; and each of them appraised and evaluated the applications and also managed the legal formalities with respect to collateral separately. This process involved transaction costs to each of them as also to the borrowers.

To reduce these transaction costs, the institutions devised a common application form and a system of a lead development bank. The institution, which is expected to be the largest lender, functions as the lead bank in this new system devised after 1970. It is at the IIM that a decision is taken as to the specific institution which is to function as the lead bank with respect to investment finance, provided on a syndicated basis.

The Functions of the Lead Bank

The functions of the lead bank are the following: (*a*) it is responsible for appraising and evaluating the soundness of the enterprise or project on the basis of criteria commonly devised by the institutions and its appraisal is accepted by the other institutions in deciding about their share of assistance to the project, the lead bank's share being the largest; (*b*) it secures the required financial resources from the participating institutions by issuing to them participation certificates and is solely responsible for providing the financial package to the borrower; (*c*) it manages the collateral on behalf of all the institutions and is thus responsible for all legal formalities required for the purpose; (*d*) it is responsible for collecting interest payments and repayment of principal from the borrower; and paying to each institution its respective share; (*e*) it is responsible for monitoring the project or enterprise and for this purpose, it deputes its own staff member to the Board of the assisted enterprise and in addition obtains information about the enterprise functioning by way of quarterly reports and periodical visits by its staff to the enterprise; (*f*) it is responsible also for identifying financial and technical problems facing the enterprise, for taking anticipatory action to solve them, if necessary by changing the management, or in any other way with the help of the other institutions; and (*g*) it presents the action program to the IIM for reconstructing or restructuring of enterprises or projects that have become sick and have accumulated arrears relating to interest and repayment of principal.

The Impact on Transaction Costs and Risk

As in the case of the Japanese Main Bank System, the lead development bank system reduces the transaction costs of the borrower, as the borrower enterprise has to deal with only one institution for all matters relating to appraisal, sanction, documentation, disbursement and repayment. The transaction costs of participant banks have been reduced though the lead bank's transaction costs have increased. However, overall transaction costs of lenders and borrowers taken together have been reduced; the risk of adverse selection is reduced as a result of pooling of information and critical appraisal of the enterprises or projects and the moral hazard risk is reduced because of lead bank's monitoring role and its representation on the Board of the assisted enterprises.

The incentives for becoming a lead bank relate to (*a*) expansion of one's own business—a portfolio of sound projects formulated by reliable and dependable firms; (*b*) the prestige attached to being a lead bank—which is essential for expanding one's business and (*c*) the building of reputation as a sound development bank for creating a favorable impression on government authorities—essential for securing several privileges.

Efficiency of the Lead Bank System

This lead bank system has ensured adequate long-term finance for sound industrial projects and has been responsible for the diversification of the industrial structure. Practically, all medium to large new projects and all major expansion and diversification projects have been financed to a significant extent by the development banking system. As a result, substantial production capacities have been built up in a large number of industries—not merely in the traditional ones like textiles and food processing but also in modern industries like chemicals, fertilizers, cement, industrial machinery, commercial vehicles, rubber, paper, and metal products. This deliberate diversification of the industrial sector has contributed towards the structural transformation that is taking place in the manufacturing sector. The system has been financing about 35 to 40 percent of the project cost of assisted enterprises, and holds about 25 percent of the equity and 62 percent of debentures issued by the assisted private sector companies. It is partly because of the development banking system that the annual growth rate of industrial output during 1950–51 to 1989–90 was about 6 percent, which was much lower than in Japan but still higher than the growth rate attained before 1950–51.

However, this lead bank system's performance in improving the investment and productive efficiency of assisted enterprises and thus in reducing the risk inherent in long-term financing was not as good as in the case of Japan during 1950 to 70. For example, in the case of the ICICI, which is the most efficient development bank in India, only less than 50 percent of the projects were completed in time, less than 60 percent were completed without any cost overrun and less than 50 percent were able to earn the anticipated return of 12 percent or more (Appendix B, Table 11). The performance of the Korea Development Bank has been better in all these respects; of the assisted projects, 50 percent were completed in time, 72 percent had actual cost saving (that is their costs were below the anticipated costs), only 16 percent made losses and 90 percent of the projects earned more than 15 percent return (Appendix B, Table 14) at constant prices (prices relevant at the project appraisal stage).

When judged in terms of the economic rate of return or exports to sale ratio of assisted projects, the performance of the Korea Development Bank has been much better than that of the development banks in India (Appendix B, Tables 11 and 14). This shows that the lead bank system has not performed well its functions of promoting viable import substitution and export promotion—the basic indicators of investment and productive efficiency and efficient use of resources.

This is also reflected in the poor performance of the private corporate sector as a whole. The ratio of gross profits to sale of selected companies (most of them assisted by the development banking system) was only 10 percent in 1981–82 and has since been declining (Appendix B, Table 12). The incremental capital-output ratio in the manufacturing sector is high and has been rising from 2.8 in 1950 to 6.2 in the 1970s. The growth rate of total factor productivity in the manufacturing sector during 1965 to 80 has been only one percent per annum in contrast to the rate of 2 to 5 percent in several developed and advanced developing countries; and manufacturing exports constitute only about 5 percent of manufacturing output.

As a result, though the ICICI's administrative cost as a proportion of total assets was only 0.33 percent in 1988–89 as compared to about 0.59 percent of the Korea Development Bank in 1987 and 0.96 percent of the Korea Long-Term Credit Bank in 1989, its default risk provision as a proportion of total assets has increased from 0.87 percent in 1981 to 1.79 percent in 1988–89; while this was only 0.53 percent for the Korea Development Bank in 1987 and 0.30 percent for the Korea Long-Term Credit Bank in 1989 (Appendix B, Tables 9 and 13). This was largely the result of the ICICI's loan recovery performance; it could recover only 70 to 75 percent of repayment due in 1987–88 (Appendix B, Table 10).

Causes of Low Efficiency

This relatively poor performance reflects deficiencies in (*a*) project appraisal and evaluation, (*b*) monitoring and supervision of projects, and (*c*) mechanisms to anticipate problems and take a pro-active role in tackling them through managerial, technical and/or financial assistance in time to projects and enterprises which did not perform as well as anticipated at the time of project appraisal. In particular, in spite of the lead bank's representation on the Boards of assisted companies and its holding of their equity, the monitoring and control mechanisms were not such as to identify in time the problems that emerged in the implementation of projects as well as in the functioning of assisted enterprises. Hence corrective action was delayed till the enterprise actually became 'sick', and even then the rehabilitation and reconstruction measures were not formulated well and their liquidation was hardly even thought of (of course because of the complicated legal procedures and the unwillingness of the government to let enterprises die).

One of the reasons for the lack of adequate monitoring of enterprises was the failure of the lead bank to evolve mechanisms of coordination with the commercial banks. In India, the development banks provide term finance for investment, while working capital finance is provided by the commercial banks. The commercial banks are in a position to identify the problems of the enterprise in time, as they are dealing with the enterprises on a day-to-day basis and the performance of the enterprise is reflected in their transactions with the commercial banks. The lead bank could have, therefore, improved its monitoring functions if it had forged a dependable relationship with the commercial banks for exchange and sharing of information relating to the performance of the enterprise.

> Although both the term lending institutions and the commercial banks broadly look for the same aspects as a part of follow-up, they monitor the performance separately without sharing the information systematically on an ongoing basis. This sometimes leads to duplication of efforts and results in the institutions working at cross purposes.[5]

This was the finding of the Inter-Institutional Group appointed by the Reserve Bank of India. Thus, the relationship based on mutual trust and confidence among the participating institutions that was established in Japan did not evolve in India with respect to the lead development bank and the concerned commercial banks.

Of course, the lead bank and the assisted enterprises in India face a greater degree of uncertainty and have much less freedom to adapt to changing circumstances than in Japan because of the direct controls regime and institutional and policy framework that have been, to use the felicitous expression of Jagdish Bhagwati, 'proscriptive' rather than 'prescriptive'.[6]

The Lead Commercial Bank System

Origin

In order to prevent large borrowers, mostly twenty and more large business houses—which are similar to the business conglomerates in Japan and South Korea—from resorting to excessive bank credit and using it for purposes other than working capital finance, the Reserve

Bank of India (the Central Bank of the country) instituted a Credit Authorization Scheme (CAS), which was introduced in 1965. Under the CAS, banks are expected to obtain prior authorization of the RBI before fresh or additional credit limits to large clients are sanctioned. However, since large borrowers borrowed from several banks (called the multiple banking system), it became difficult for the RBI to enforce adequate credit discipline on large borrowers. Further, the transaction costs of borrowers increased as they had to submit information to each bank on their total credit requirements and the banks' transaction costs also increased as each had to collect such information. The RBI's transaction costs also increased as it had to collect information from each bank, consolidate it and then appraise the credit proposed.

The Functions and Performance

To reduce the overall transaction costs, the RBI introduced in 1974 a scheme for consortium financing by banks to large borrowers. Under this scheme, the Reserve Bank directed the banks that if the credit limits enjoyed by a single borrower from any bank exceeded 1.5 percent of that bank's deposits, formation of a consortium was obligatory in order also to reduce the credit risk of each bank. Under the consortium arrangement, the largest lender has to act as a lead bank and the lead bank's functions are the following: (*a*) it is responsible for credit appraisal, monitoring and supervision, legal formalities with respect to collateral, sanctioning and disbursement of consortium finance to the borrower on uniform terms and conditions, and collecting payment of interest and repayment of principal by the borrower on behalf of all participant banks; (*b*) it has to share other banking business of the borrower with the participant banks in agreed proportions; (*c*) it has to take the lead in arranging for reconstruction or rehabilitation of assisted enterprises facing managerial, technical and financial problems.

The RBI also directed that in case of disagreement among the consortium members on the quantum of permissible bank finance, terms and conditions to be imposed, etc., the view of the lead bank shall prevail; the dissenting members have to fall in line with the lead bank's decision and have no option to walk out of the consortium. The basic objective of the RBI is to make the 'banks move towards a "single window" concept regarding delivery of credit, execution of documents, submission of data, and recoveries,'[7] in order to reduce transaction costs of the RBI, the participant banks and the borrowers, and to reduce the credit risk of each participant bank. Thus this lead commercial bank system, in its objectives, is similar to the lead development bank system.

In practice, this system has not attained its objectives for several reasons: (*a*) The banks did not devise a mechanism, like the IIM of the lead development bank system, for taking decisions at the highest levels. This has led to delays in sanctioning assistance to the borrowers and avoidable transaction costs to participant banks because of frequent meetings at various levels, none of which has the final authority to take decisions—the final authority resting with the Bank's Boards. (*b*) The participating banks had no incentive to share and exchange information relating to a large borrower as each was interested in not losing the other fee business of a creditworthy customer. The lead bank too has not been sharing such business of the customer with the participating banks. (*c*) Since each bank's share in that credit is small—in practice much less than 1.5 percent of deposits—none of them takes the responsibility of monitoring the client's accounts.

> The lead bank does not enjoy the de facto status of a consortium leader and the observations, suggestions, and discussions of the consortium leader are not taken seriously by other banks. When an account gets into problems it becomes difficult to adopt a common approach vis-à-vis erring borrowers. Sometimes interests of an individual bank tend to gain precedence over common interests of all the involved banks.[8]

Since the system is in fact *imposed* by the RBI on the banks, the necessary trust and confidence among the participant banks are not established and each one tries to exploit the situation to its advantage. (*d*) The large borrower has not liked the CAS of the Reserve Bank, as it causes delays in obtaining credit and makes it difficult for him to obtain credit limits, which he thinks are necessary for his purpose. Hence he has an incentive to deal with several banks and thus obtain credit in a manner that avoids the discipline of the CAS. Therefore, he is not willing to divulge full information about his credit needs and dealings with banks to any single bank and the banks too have no incentive to share information with others since they are reluctant to lose good profitable business. Because of the various credit allocation controls, only the business with large borrowers is profitable for the banks.

The failure of the system to attain its objectives is clearly brought out in a letter issued by the RBI to the commercial banks in 1987. To quote:

> ...we regret to point out that even after the lapse of several years, we continue to get reports of non-implementation of the related guidelines by banks either in letter or in spirit. A quick study recently carried out by us has revealed that such deviations have been in various areas such as entering the formal consortium arrangements, joint appraisal, exchange of information, holding of meetings and the level of representation thereat, sharing of business (including ancillary business) and stipulation of uniform terms and conditions. The non-compliance with our guidelines has resulted in inordinate delays and uncoordinated approach which have adversely affected the borrowers concerned. At times, borrowers have taken advantage of the lack of coordination amongst banks by obtaining additional credit facilities and/or concessions in terms and conditions for various facilities, affecting the overall health of the advances made to such borrowers.[9]

In 1988, the RBI moved over from prior authorization of credit to large borrowers to post-sanction scrutiny in order to reduce delay in credit disbursement to large borrowers. It has, however, cautioned banks that if any bank is not enforcing the basic disciplines under the CAS, the RBI will instruct such banks to refer large cases to it for prior authorization. However, there does not seem to be much improvement in the implementation of the lead bank concept under consortium financing arrangements. The recent official committee, appointed by the Ministry of Finance, has recommended that the *mandatory* nature of the system should be given up and the system should evolve on the basis of *voluntary* agreements among the banks.

The Lead Bank for District Development

Origin

From experience gained till 1969, it was found that a bank with nationwide branches is unlikely to develop the intimate knowledge and feel of the local situation in a district (unit of local government like a county in the U.S.A.) so necessary for district development. A small district bank could have served the purpose. However, given the structure and evolution of commercial banking, it was not practical to develop small district banks. To meet this situation, the function of district development was assigned in 1969, after the nationalization of fourteen commercial banks, to a commercial bank which was prominent in the concerned district or region. Some districts were thus assigned to a lead bank and it is the function of such a lead bank to coordinate the policies of the other banks and the financial institutions operating in a district. Such a lead bank was expected to be much more financially viable because of its nationwide operations and, for the same reason, it would have at its disposal much larger resources than a small district bank.[10]

Functions

The main functions of a lead bank are: (*a*) identify places in a district for branch expansion; (*b*) prepare a phased program for branch expansion in the district so as to bring banking services within the reach of farmers and potential small enterprises in the entire area; (*c*) estimate the current requirement of credit and prepare a phased program to meet it; (*d*) devise such schemes of deposits and financial instruments as would prove attractive to the local people and effective for the purpose of mobilizing financial resources; (*e*) identify the potential areas of agricultural and small enterprise development and induce local entrepreneurs to undertake such development; (*f*) identify the major bottlenecks in the development of the district and induce appropriate agencies to take corrective action; and (*g*) goad the local entrepreneur in agriculture and small enterprise sector to improve progressively his productive efficiency.

Performance

This lead bank scheme has succeeded in its branch expansion program as well as in providing access to credit to farmers and small enterprises. The population per bank branch has declined from 65,000 in 1969 to 11,000 in 1990. The bank branches in rural areas now form 58 percent of total branches as against 23 percent in 1969. The bank credit to agriculture and small enterprises of all types now form about

40 percent of the total bank credit as against 3 to 4 percent in 1969 (Appendix B, Table 1).

The system has also succeeded in mobilizing financial resources. The proportion of rural deposits to total deposits has increased from 3 percent in 1969 to 15 percent in 1990 and aggregate deposits of banks now form about 37 percent of GNP (Appendix B, Table 1).

However, the portfolio quality of the banks has deteriorated. In the farm sector, the proportion of loan recovery was only 57 percent in 1988. The proportion of advances to sick small-scale industry to total advances to the small-scale industry sector had reached the level of more than 15 percent in 1990 (Appendix B, Table 8).

The lead bank system, thus, has performed poorly with regard to the appraisal, monitoring, and supervision of assisted small enterprises in the farm and the nonfarm sectors. The system devised entrepreneur development programs and also established Technical Consultancy Organizations to promote the development of nonfarm small enterprises and improve their investment and productive efficiency; however, these mechanisms have not been effectively used for this purpose.[11]

The major reason for this failure in promoting sound enterprises has been the institutional and policy framework. The banks have been given targets for branch expansion and credit allocation to agriculture and small enterprises by the Reserve Bank of India and hence their principal effort has been concentrated on meeting these *quantitative targets* rather than in promoting sound schemes of farm and small enterprise development. The credit allocation and subsidized interest rates through *directives* have weakened the top managements of the banks, and government ownership of banks has also led to political and bureaucratic intervention with regard to credit decisions and as a result corrupt practices.

III
THE INSTITUTIONAL AND POLICY FRAMEWORK IN INDIA

In contrast to the Japanese institutional and policy framework, the Indian framework has several characteristics which adversely affect the functioning of the banking system.

Macroeconomic Imbalances

There have been growing fiscal deficits, which have been financed by credit creation by the Reserve Bank and this has led to inflationary pressures as well as payment imbalance. The wholesale prices increased at an annual rate of more than 7 percent during 1960–61 to 1990–91 and are currently rising at about 7 to 8 percent. The monetary and fiscal imbalances and the resulting inflationary pressures increased uncertainty and made it difficult for the lead development banking system and the enterprises to appraise investment projects and monitor their performance. Further, the relative prices have got distorted because of price controls and import controls; the price mechanism thus has got distorted and cannot perform the signalling function for resource allocation. In contrast, Japan had relative macroeconomic stability during its high growth period—1950 to 1973.

Regulation and Control of the Banking System

The twenty major commercial banks are under government ownership as are the development banks. The commercial banks are closely controlled by the Reserve Bank. The cash reserve and liquidity requirements take 50 percent of deposits and priority sector lending to agriculture and small enterprises absorbs another 20 percent. In addition, the banks are also compelled to finance special programs. Thus, the banks have discretion in allocating only 20 percent of resources freely across the sectors. Even the free lending category is highly regulated. The RBI establishes credit limits for every significant borrower and prescribes norms for working capital loans by industrial sub-sector and firm location. The RBI also sets virtually all deposit and lending rates. The government and the RBI are responsible for banks' top management decisions.

Thus, the commercial banks have hardly any operational autonomy.[12] Their position has been further weakened by political intervention in credit and recovery decisions. Management accountability, as a result, has been diluted, loan appraisal standards lowered, and collection efforts eased. Commercial banks' bad debts have increased and their profitability has declined.

The lead commercial banking system, devised by the RBI, failed in attaining its objectives as banks have no incentive to implement it. Their discretionary allocation of resources relates only to large borrowers and only such loans are profitable as the interest rates on them were the highest. Hence each bank has an interest to woo these large borrowers and thus no incentive to impose credit discipline on them and the borrowers too stand to gain from this inter-bank rivalry.

The system involves centralized decision making through directives and direct controls on credit allocation; this does not leave adequate scope for experimentation, innovation and full use of widely dispersed information. The Bank managements hence are more concerned with their dealings with the RBI and the government rather than with good customer service and sound decision making relating to credit transactions. In Japan, the financial institutions have operational autonomy and the Bank of Japan and the Ministry of Finance have adequate sanctions to ensure the soundness of the banking system.

The Control Regime

An enterprise has to have an investment license, import and foreign exchange license and technology import license, if it wants to undertake a new investment project or new expansion or diversification projects. If these licenses are not granted, it cannot undertake such projects. Because of this uncertainty, the enterprise has no incentive to formulate its project in detail at the time of applying for these licenses. Thus the licensing system has to take decisions on the basis of inadequate information furnished by the enterprise. Further, the system has not the competence to estimate the precise requirements for investment, imports and foreign exchange. However, once such licenses are approved, the main parameters of the project are already determined. It is at this stage that the lead development bank comes into the picture for appraising the project for financing.

However good its appraisal, the lead bank has no discretion to alter the parameters of the project even if such a course would improve the project and its financial and economic viability. Its only option is not to finance the project; but that too cannot be done lightly as the enterprise has obtained the required licenses. Thus both the lead bank and the enterprises have to function within these constraints.

Apart from constraints on project appraisal, both the enterprises and the lead bank do not have the freedom to alter the design of the project at the implementation or the operation stage with a view to adapting it to the emerging situation. Thus when the project faces adaptation problems, the licensing system does not permit the lead bank or the enterprise to undertake the adaptations that may be necessary to improve the viability of the project.

The licensing system, thus, does not permit the lead bank to perform well its major functions of appraisal, monitoring and supervision, and reconstruction or alteration of the project. In Japan, there are no such constraints.

The Import Substitution Strategy

The main focus of the licensing system is import substitution. Such a strategy does not permit domestic competition or international competition. Thus the discipline that competition and particularly international competition imposes on the enterprise and the lead bank is lacking because of the import substitution strategy. As a result the lead bank and the enterprise have neither the incentive nor the compulsion to improve investment and productive efficiency. Sometime or other, hence, a payment problem inevitably becomes acute as it has become in India currently. Japan, in contrast, actively encouraged export promotion and all the government as well as the Bank of Japan policies were in tune with this dominant objective of strategic management.

The Political and Bureaucratic Pressures

An export-oriented strategy imposes a certain discipline not only on the lead bank and the enterprise but also on the government. All government policies in that case have to be in line with the export-oriented strategy. Once this discipline is lacking, a situation is created where politicians and bureaucrats can interfere with the functioning of the licensing system as well as the banking system with impunity either for their own gain or to please vested interests. And this is what happens in the Indian system. In Japan, there is less scope for corruption because of a competent bureaucracy with proven integrity and the *transparent and dominant objective of export performance*, which provides an effective and unequivocal yardstick of performance of the banks, the firms as well as the government and disciplines their strategies, policies and actions.

All these *differential* characteristics of the institutional and policy framework—differential with respect to Japan—have adversely affected the functioning of the lead bank systems. However, this institutional and policy framework is being liberalized since 1991; as a result, the lead bank systems may be able to function as effectively and efficiently as the Main Bank System in Japan during 1950 to 1970.[13] Of course, much would depend on the evolving policy environment and the guidance and incentives provided by the Central Bank and the Government.

Deregulation and Liberalization Measures: 1991 to 93

After the payments crisis in 1991, several measures have been taken to deregulate and liberalize the financial sector policies as well as the other trade, industry and foreign investment policies.[14]

Financial Sector Policies

Interest Rate: With effect from April 22, 1992, the rates on term deposits of all maturities of 46 days and over are made subject to a single prescription of not exceeding 13.0 percent per annum. Banks are now free to determine the maturity and deposit rates within this single ceiling rate of 13 percent per annum.

The lending rates by banks are now only subject to a *minimum* lending rate; the actual lending rates are left to the discretion of the banks except for the rates applicable to some of the priority sectors, for which *maximum* rates have been fixed—rates which presumably cover the banks' transaction costs, the risk and the financial costs.

All other interest rates are allowed to be determined by the market forces.

Capital Adequacy: All banks with international presence will have to achieve the norm of 8 percent as early as possible and in any case by March 31, 1994. Other banks will have to achieve a capital adequacy norm of 4 percent by March 31, 1993 and 8 percent by March 31, 1996. These norms relate to risk-adjusted assets.

Branch licensing: Under the liberalized branch licensing policy, only those banks which obtain the revised capital adequacy norms and prudential accounting standards have been given freedom to set up new branch offices and upgrade the extension counters into full fledged new branches without the prior approval of the Reserve Bank.

Entry of new banks: Provided they satisfy certain prudential norms, private sector is permitted to start new banks.

The Exchange Rate Policy

Effective March 1, 1992 a Liberalized Exchange Rate Management System (LERMS) has been introduced; this involves a rate flexibly determined by the Reserve Bank of India (applicable to certain transactions) and a market rate (for all other transactions)—a dual rate system. The spread between the market rate and the official rate has been remarkably stable. This system provided an opportunity for the development of market-determined transactions in foreign exchange as a preparatory arrangement for full convertibility on current account, established in early 1993.

Industrial Licensing

Since 1992, there has been a virtual abolition of the requirement of industrial licensing except for a short list of industries and abolition of the concept of monopoly involving limits on the assets of large industrial houses for permitting industrial investment. The number of industries reserved exclusively for the public sector has been curtailed and competition between the public and private sectors has been encouraged.

Import Licensing

The new policy substantially eliminates licensing, quantitative restrictions and other regulatory and discretionary controls. Exports and imports are allowed freely, subject only to a negative list of imports and exports. The restricted items of imports include mainly consumer goods which can be imported only against licenses. The tariff rates have also been lowered.

Direct Foreign Investment

Foreign direct investment up to 51 percent for foreign equity in 34 selected areas would now be subject to automatic approval. Other proposals are to be considered and approved on merit by the Secretariat for Industrial Approvals and more significantly, by the Foreign Investment Promotion Board specifically created to invite, negotiate and facilitate substantial investment by international companies that would provide access to high technology and world markets.

Portfolio Investment by Foreigners

In 1992, permission has been given to companies with a good track record to issue convertible debentures or equity to investors abroad, in order to enable them to tap investible funds available in international capital markets. Further, respectable foreign investors such as Pension Funds have also been allowed to invest in the Indian stock market with suitable mechanisms to ensure that this would not threaten the loss of management control (see Chapter 6 for the rationale of this measure).

Gold Imports

In 1992, general permission has been granted to nonresident Indians (either of Indian nationality or origin) to bring into India, as a part of their baggage, gold in any form up to 5 kilo grams, provided import duty is paid in foreign currency (see Chapter 6 for the logic of this measure).

Detailed information on the deregulation and liberalization measures is provided in the Reserve Bank of India Annual Reports—1991–92 and 1992–93

IV
CONCLUDING OBSERVATIONS

The lead bank systems—lead development bank, lead commercial bank and district lead bank—in India constitute financial innovations suited to the specific context of India; the first two systems are, in essence, variants of the main bank system in Japan and the universal bank system in the late-nineteenth century in Germany. With financial reforms initiated since 1991, a favorable environment would be created for the effective and efficient implementation of these financial innovations. However, such implementation would require appropriate guidance of the Reserve Bank of India. Further, several conditions need to be satisfied for the purpose.

1. First, the systems and their constituents should have a high degree of operational autonomy, which is all the more essential in countries with a democratic form of government. The competitive struggle for political leadership, which is the essence of a democratic form of government, requires of necessity that the effective range of political decisions should not be extended too far. If the effective range of

political decisions is not thus strictly limited, it is quite likely that in a democracy, with an increasing role of the state, decisions would turn out to be irrational even from the point of view of the basic development aims and objectives. Democracy does not require that every function of the state be subject to its political method. There are of course certain fields in which decisions have to be primarily political. These fields relate to the basic aims and objectives of development and the machinery for attaining them. However, once the aims and objectives have been specified and the machinery decided upon, the rest of the decision making process should be governed by purely business-like considerations with the role of the state restricted to that of a general supervisor.[15]

2. Second, even if the major part of the financial system is government-owned, its constituent units like the development banks should have adequate authority for experimentation and innovation relating to various financial instruments with a view to reducing the overall transaction costs and risk. This implies that within the framework of cooperation and coordination essential for attaining development objectives, there should be effective competitive pressures, and incentives to introduce financial innovations.

3. Third, sound functioning of the financial system is not possible without monetary and financial stability. To attain such macroeconomic stability should be the basic objective of the Reserve Bank of India and for the purpose, it should have the necessary independence from the government and should not be subject to political and bureaucratic pressures.[16]

4. Fourth, for performing the tasks and functions that have externalities or that affect all parts of the financial system, there should be *partnership relations* among the Reserve Bank, the development banks and the commercial and cooperative banks. Such relations would create a climate of mutual trust and confidence, eliminate all costs that arise from information asymmetry like the moral hazard problem and reduce transaction costs and risk relating to the operation and functioning of the system as a whole.

5. Finally, it is essential to forge a close and intimate relationship between the Reserve Bank and all types of banks in order to facilitate decisions relating to the system on the basis of information available to all of them. The problem is one of information and this cannot be obtained if there is an arm's length relationship between the Reserve Bank and the financial intermediaries.

In this context, what John Hicks has to say is very relevant. To quote:

> The financial intermediaries are listening points: The problem is one of transmission from them to the centre. It is not obvious that an arm's length system, using the 'price-mechanism' must always be the most efficient, or most 'economic' way of doing this job. It is not always the only way that is open for doing it. When the intermediaries are well established, the relations between them and the centre can be much closer...Centre must have power if it is to be effective. Whatever we think about monopoly and competition in the rest of the economic system, there are good reasons in this monetary sphere for not being afraid of some concentration.
>
> Whatever the links between the centre and the intermediaries, the collection of information, the information required, can never be perfect. The system will still be subject to shocks; things will happen which no one, who was in a position to take action, had foreseen. It is a system which is based upon arrangements for risk-taking in the face of an uncertain future; as such it is bound to be fragile. An arm's length system is particularly fragile. A serious blow to one part of it can have wide repercussions. Closer association, by making it easier to find a 'lender of last resort,' reduces the fragility.[17]

NOTES

1. See V.V. Bhatt, 'On improving the Effectiveness and Efficiency of the Financial System in India,' *Economic and Political Weekly* (volume XXVI, No. 41, October 12, 1991), and World Bank, *India: Financial Sector Report: Consolidation of the Financial System* (Washington D.C., 1990). See also V.V. Bhatt, 'On Restructuring the Monetary System', *Economic and Political Weekly* (March 1988), and V.V. Bhatt, 'On Restructuring the Financial System', *Economic and Political Weekly* (February 22, 1992).
2. V.V. Bhatt, *Development Perspectives*, ch. 10 (Oxford: Pergamon Press, 1980).
3. Asian Development Bank, *Profile of Financial Sector in India* (Manila, Philippines 1988). This whole section is based on the references cited in notes 1 and 3.
4. This account of the lead bank systems in India is based on the author's personal knowledge and involvement in developing these systems, when he was the general manager of IDBI, member of the Board of Directors of two commercial banks, one development bank, and the Unit Trust of India during 1969–72.
5. Reserve Bank of India, *Coordination Between Term Lending Institutions and Commercial Banks* (Bombay, 1976).
6. Jagdish Bhagwati, *Protectionism* (Cambridge, Mass: The MIT Press, 1988), pp. 98–102.

7. Reserve Bank of India, *Manual for Bank Supervision* (Bombay, 1990), pp. 114–17.
8. Asian Development Bank (n. 3 above), pp. 70–72.
9. Reserve Bank of India, '*Letter by Chief Officer, Department of Bank Operations And Development to All Scheduled Commercial Banks*' (Bombay, June 27, 1987).
10. See V.V. Bhatt, *Structure of Financial Institutions* (Bombay: Vora & Co. publishers 1972), Ch. 1.
11. See V.V. Bhatt, *Financial Institutions and Technical Consultancy Services: The Indian Experiment in Small Industry Promotion*, (Washington DC; World Bank, Economic Development Institute, Seminar Paper No. 24, 1981). Also in *Journal of Development Planning* (United Nations, No. 18, 1988).
12. World Bank, 1990 (n. 1 above).
13. 'Freeing India's Economy' *The Economist*, (London: May 23, 1992) and 'A Tiger Stirs' *The Economist*, (London: March 6–12, 1993), pp. 15-16.
14. *Annual Reports* 1991–92 and 1992–93, The Reserve Bank of India (Bombay: 1992 and 1993).
15. On delimiting the range of political decisions, See Joseph, A, Schumpeter, *Capitalism, Socialism and Democracy* (New York: Harper and Row, 1975), pp. 291–93.
16. See John Hicks, *Economic Perspectives* (Oxford: Oxford University Press, 1977), pp. 132–33.
17. See John Hicks, *A Market Theory of Money* (Oxford: Oxford University press, 1989). p. 110.

Chapter 5

Financial Institutions and Technology Policy

The financial system (including the government, when it acts as a financier) has a pervasive impact on the processes and patterns of resource mobilization, allocation and use. Quite logically, therefore, considerable attention is paid in the literature to its criteria for selection of projects for financing; the major emphasis has been on the 'right' system of relative (accounting) prices and social cost—benefit analytic techniques. However, the significant choices with regard to products, processes and machines are made at the project design stage. Once these choices are made the financial system has merely the option of accepting or rejecting the project; its criteria, cannot, however, affect the real choices to any meaningful extent. Even at the project design stage, the use of accounting prices can have a rationale only if complete information about the range of technology choice is available to the project designer.[1] It is not possible to have such information without an active and intelligent *search* and even *research*—in fact without an *institutionalized* technology policy.[2] Thus, project selection criteria would serve the intended purpose only if the field of technology choice possibilities is actively widened through an appropriate technology policy. It is the purpose of this chapter to indicate the major elements of such a technology policy and to emphasize the crucial role of the Technical Consultancy Service Centres (TCSCs) and the financial system in providing essential organic links between modern technology and domestic and foreign Technological Research Centers (TRCs) on the one hand, and the production system, on the other.

The broad outline of the technology policy is represented in Section I. The catalytic leadership function of the financial system in such a policy is emphasized in Section 2. How this function has been performed by banks in some countries is indicated in Section 3. The concluding observations are in the final section.

I
A BROAD OUTLINE OF A TECHNOLOGY POLICY

The less developed countries (LDCs) with all their handicaps of a late start have one critical advantage and that is related to the accumulated and growing scientific and technological knowledge. But to use this knowledge creatively for solving their own problems, they need to develop competence in the field of technology choice through an *institutionalized* technology policy. Sophisticated techniques of planning or project evaluation are not—cannot be—a substitute for such a technology policy; the former in fact have relevance *only* with such a policy.

Such a policy is essential because the present-day LDCs face a technology absorption and diffusion problem that is *qualitatively* different from that faced by the 19th-century developing countries like France, Germany and the Czarist Russia. Modern technology has long outgrown the stage when scientists learned from engineering and technological research, and hence has become immensely complex and knowledge-based, requiring high-level scientific and technological manpower for both its growth and operation. It is capital-, scale- and skill-intensive and, further, because of economic development and increasing real incomes, it is geared to the production of sophisticated goods and services intended to meet *simultaneously* a wide variety of functional, aesthetic, comfort and status needs and wants.[3]

Thus both technology and consumer products are oriented toward meeting the complex and dynamic want-pattern of the rich countries and are out of tune with the initial conditions, resource composition and the *basic functional want pattern* of the poor countries. Hence, the LDCs can take advantage of accumulated and growing knowledge *only* if they have the capacity to *search*, *select* and *creatively adapt* modern technology to their own environments and development objectives. Further, they have a problem of *upgrading* technology in their traditional sectors with a view to improving the living conditions of people with traditional skills. This problem cannot be identified by the technological systems of the developed countries; it has to be first formulated in concrete terms by the LDCs even to benefit from the knowledge accumulated so far.

Of course, the LDCs are in a position to obtain assistance from the TCSCs and the TRCs of the developed countries. But such help can be fruitful only if one knows the *problems* for which one is groping for solutions. This ability to ask questions and identify technology problems is essential to make correct technology choices. Further, in the case of small-medium enterprises, it would not be economically feasible to rely on foreign TCSCs. What, then, are the basic elements of a technology policy for the LDCs?

Obviously one has to start with the human problem of poverty and try to solve it through means (instruments) that are directly related to the problem. It is neither practical nor desirable to provide a *progressively rising* decent minimum of physical security to each family without providing it with work—that is, employment. So poverty can be removed only through full employment—employment of each individual and family at *progressively rising* levels of productivity.

Once one starts from this focal point, and given the natural resources, the problem becomes very *specific* and *concrete*: how to choose organizational forms and technology so as to fully employ the available and growing labor force and at the same time ensure each family initially a decent minimum level of living and later on a progressively rising minimum.

Obviously, wherever one wants to go, one has no alternative but to start from where one is. In this context, one has to start from the traditional sector with its skills, techniques and organization. In a large number of the LDCs, this sector employs about 80 percent of the labor force (60 percent in agriculture and related activities and 20 percent in traditional industry like rural transport and trade, food-processing, dairy and cattle breeding, forestry, poultry farming, piggeries, fisheries, organic manure, agricultural implements and household utensils and appliances); about 10 percent is employed in the modern sector and the remaining 10 percent is actually underemployed or unemployed. With the growth of population at the rate of about 2.5 percent per year, even if the modern sector grew at 20 percent per year, it would not be able to provide employment for the increase in labor force, let alone for the presently unemployed. Thus it is obvious that the traditional sector would have to absorb the currently unemployed as well as a part of the increase in the labor force.

Hence, the crucial problem is that of promoting the viable growth of the traditional sector and organically linking the modern sector growth with that of the traditional sector in a manner that supplements and reinforces the growth and the development of the latter. It is not possible to *supplant* the traditional skills and techniques by modern ones; they cannot solve the poverty problem.[4]

Therefore, in terms of technology choice there are two problems: (*a*) the problem of *upgrading* the traditional technology; and (*b*) the problem of *adapting and improving* modern technology in a manner that is consistent with the development objectives, changing institutional structures and natural resources. Without such *upgrading and adapting*, it is not possible to provide a *rising* minimum level of living for each family.

For both purposes, it is essential to identify the concrete ideas relating to the projects or project-complexes that have to be undertaken; the problem of technology choice can arise only after such initial identification. For both the sectors—the traditional and the modern—this identification process needs to be institutionalized, in say, Project Identification Centres (PICs).

The search for appropriate technology should begin with such *identified* project ideas. This function is of *critical significance* for both problems, i.e., of upgrading, and of adapting and improving. This is the design and engineering function that needs to be institutionalized in TCSCs.

It is the function of such a TCSC to design the machines, the processes and the products. This function requires knowledge of the initial conditions—of both the production and the organizational structures. It requires identification of current knowledge and the ways in which this knowledge can be applied; it requires identification of specific research problems and the ways in which they can be tackled within the country or abroad. Once one starts experimenting with the design of projects or project-complexes that are to be *implemented*—and this is how the design-engineering function is crucially linked with that of the PICs and the financial system—one has set in motion a process of *search* for relevant knowledge as well as relevant *research*: a cumulative process of innovation; a process which is self-reinforcing.

Thus as an integral part of development and technology policies, the LDCs need to develop the TCSCs with the capacity: (*a*) to identify technological choice problems; (*b*) to *search* for their solutions with the assistance, when necessary, of foreign TCSCs and domestic and foreign TRCs; (*c*) to adapt creatively the suggested solutions to actual project making; (*d*) to *upgrade* technology in the traditional sector (agriculture, and cottage and small industries); and (*e*) to identify technological research problems and thus link the TRCs with the production system. Thus, these centres can function as a vehicle for absorbing and diffusing the relevant modern technology, serving as an effective communication link with the foreign as well as the domestic sources of technology. At the same time, they can support and improve machine-building capacities by providing machine industries with designs as well as links with the evolving production structure. In the process, they could generate a wide variety of new project ideas in diverse fields.

Thus, such TCSCs are an essential link between modern technology and domestic and foreign TRCs on the one hand and the financial system and the production system on the other. Quite a number of countries (like Brazil, Mexico and India) have the TRCs but they function in a vacuum and are not in a position to tackle relevant problems of the production system; this has caused both an internal and an external brain-drain, and irrelevant research.[5] Some countries have tried to evolve TCSCs but have not been able to forge a link between them and the financial system and the production system with the result that such TCSCs remain still-born; some of the small industry service institutes in India and some other countries are of this type. Unless one starts from the *focal point of actual* project ideas—consistent with a country's development strategy—and hence from the production system and the financial system, the TCSCs too would function in a vacuum and would become obsolete.

Such TCSCs have to be *functionally* linked with the PICs, the financial system and the production system; without such an organic functional link, they would become obsolete and operationally irrelevant. In addition, they have to be organically linked with the TRCs; without this link, technological research would, again, become irrelevant. A research set-up—the TRCs—are essential; but such a set-up can derive its meaning and purpose only if it is related to the design-engineering function which is, in turn, intimately and vitally related to actual projects or project-complexes, which again have to be an integral part of a development strategy.

One sequence which organically relates one function to the other is: strategy → project ideas (PICs) → design and engineering (search for appropriate technology—TCSCs) → financial system → project implementation (production system) → new project ideas. The second organically related sequence is: strategy → project ideas (PICs) → design-engineering (TCSCs) → TRCs → design-engineering (TCSCs) → financial system → project implementation (production system) → new project ideas. The third such sequence is: design-engineering (TCSCs) → product, process and machine ideas → project ideas → design and engineering (TCSCs) → financial system → project implementation (production system) → new project ideas (see Figure 5.1). The important point to realize, however, is the central and crucial significance in these chains of the design and engineering function (the TCSCs). In the field of agriculture (high-yielding variety of seeds), there is some appreciation of the significance of these organically related functions; but in the other areas, this obvious and more or less self-evident function of technology policy is still not understood.

What is the role of the international community in general and of the international development institutions in particular in this field: (*a*) they can urge the LDCs to set up the PICs, the TCSCs, and the TRCs in the relevant fields, linked with the financial system and the production system, and assist them in the initial stages in a variety of ways; (*b*) for certain complex fields, they can set up regional or international TCSCs; (*c*) they can start on their own international or regional TRCs which should work primarily on research problems identified by the national and regional TCSCs and which should also function as clearing-houses for relevant information for the national TCSCs and the TRCs. It is only thus that national and international efforts can be effectively integrated for solving the urgent and immediate problems of poverty and socio-economic development.

II
THE CATALYTIC LEADERSHIP FUNCTION OF THE FINANCIAL SYSTEM

So far we have identified the technology problems and outlined the institutional structure and functions for a sound technology policy. The next question to be discussed is: which function or institution should play the catalytic leadership role so as to ensure the interaction among functions, specified in the technology policy outline. Since a project cannot be implemented without finance, the vital decision rests with the financial system (including the government when it acts as a financier). Hence the leadership function has to be assumed by the financial system; and this would be even more so when the financial system—like the development banks—has to play a promotional role in the development process.[6]

Currently, the financial system in a large number of the LDCs is trying to perform this function by inducing enterprises to make 'right' technology choices through its project selection criteria based on social cost-benefit analysis or economic evaluation of projects. However, since the financial system tries to evaluate an already formulated project, it obviously cannot affect technology choices, which are made at the project design and formulation stages. The project formulation task is performed, by and large, by the foreign TCSCs or their domestic counterparts for large enterprises. For the small to medium enterprises, the project formulation is based largely on the knowledge acquired by entrepreneurs from machine suppliers, large enterprises or past experience in the field; here again, the technology choice at one remove is in fact made by the foreign TCSCs or their domestic counterparts. The latter normally do not use accounting prices in their project design work and their choices are largely governed by their experience in the developed countries. This basic limitation of mere economic evaluation of projects is emphasized by Little and Mirrlees in a very illuminating way:

> In other words, a large number of economic choices will have been made already, either at the level of the initiating department, commission, or other decentralized public authority, or by the designing engineers...Now industrial engineers-good ones, anyway—are economists, but they are not usually the kind of economists who are trained to look at matters from the point of view of the economy as a whole. They will, or should, have profitability very much in mind. But they will, of course, assess profitability in the light of actual prices.
>
> The value of choosing from a list of projects according to a criterion using accounting prices, supposed to reflect real scarcities and benefits better than actual prices, is clearly greatly reduced if each such project has in effect been chosen from a long list of variants by a criterion (profitability) which uses actual prices. For instance, if it is desirable to put stress on employment by using low accounting prices for labor, then clearly *this stress should take effect at the level of project design and not merely at the level of final project selection*. Indeed, it may be at the former level that a low accounting price for labour would have its main effect...

> Of course, the sheer unfamiliarity will make for difficulty at first...where outside, especially foreign, firms of consultant engineers are involved, the difficulties may be greater. First, their psychological objections to accounting prices may be stronger as a result of private enterprise laissez-faire training, which does not sufficiently admit the possible divergence of social and private interest. Secondly, they generally have something to sell, which has usually been evolved in the light of actual prices. Designs are not all made afresh, from the bottom up, for the project on hand...
>
> Only very few western firms appear to have made any effort to adapt their designs to the different scarcities prevailing in developing countries...sometimes, indeed, the plan which western engineers design for a developing country is more 'modern',—i.e., capital intensive, potentially labor saving—than anything that exists in their own country. There are two obstacles to overcoming the problem. The first, and possibly more important, is often the lack of an informed and critical client, determined to get a plant which will be very profitable...
>
> For the reasons given, it may not be easy to get foreign engineers to adapt...However, it must be admitted, when everything in favor of accounting prices has been said, that communication between...departments etc: between departmental administrators and engineers and scientists; and between the local client and the foreign firms; is easier in terms of (predicted) actual prices...it is certainly best to keep the use of accounting prices as limited as possible (emphasis added).[7]

It must be emphasized, as Little and Mirrlees do, that it is not merely a question of the project designer using accounting prices for making technological choices. Even if he did use them, the range of choice is usually limited to actual alternatives already in use in the developed countries, especially with regard to the core processes and products.[8] Of course, this does not mean that there do not exist additional alternative core processes and products even within the range of modern technology. These alternatives, however, can be known only as a result of active search and creative adaptation of the various alternatives 'and in so doing, one ought to go beyond those best-practiced technologies on the shelf, giving open-minded consideration to discarded laboratory results, as well as to technologies now considered obsolete by today's major industrial concerns.'[9]

Foreign TCSCs or their domestic counterparts would not be inclined for obvious reasons to undertake such processes of search and creative adaptation of modern technology as well as the upgrading traditional technology. To induce them to do so would require 'an informed and critical client; determined to get a plant which will be very profitable'. This really means that the financial system (development banks) should actively support and/or help promote the TCSCs that have adequate technological competence to ask the right type of questions to all the possible sources of technology—the TCSCs, the TRCs and enterprises anywhere in the world—and evaluate the suggested solutions with regard to upgrading of traditional technology and creative adaptation of modern technology. The financial system without such domestic TCSCs would not be able to induce and enforce appropriate technological choices—the very purpose for which it is using economic evaluation techniques to select projects for financing.

This vital link between the financial system and the TCSCs is even more essential in a context where the development banks have to play promotional role in initiating a viable and widely diffused process of industrialization through the development of small and medium enterprises. This small and medium enterprise development is essential for several reasons:[10] to develop latent entrepreneurial and managerial ability on a wide functional and geographical basis; to create employment opportunities on a viable basis for whole families and particularly for workers without much training and literacy in rural and semi-urban areas (to save on overheads and distribution costs); to improve the distribution of wealth and income.

Such small enterprise development requires an institutional machinery (i.e., the TCSCs)—linked to the financial system (development banks)—for the identification of project ideas, preparation of feasibility studies, making appropriate technological choices, formulation of detailed projects with specification for machines, processes and products and providing assistance in project implementation and operation.[11]

The TCSCs can help the financial system in its promotional role as well as in appraising projects that the financial system would get directly from the project promoters. The centres should be autonomous; the financial system should support and/or help promote them but should not interfere in their functioning. Further, the financial system should not finance projects formulated by the TCSCs, without an independent evaluation in terms of its social cost-benefit criteria.

Such independent evaluation by the financial system serves a very essential function of appraising the soundness of the TCSCs themselves. The latter would have a compulsion to be up to date and alert; for, since the financial system personnel would have experience of appraising a wide variety of projects, they would be able to judge effectively the performance with regard to technology choice of the TCSCs. Many government operated TCSCs like the Indian Small Industry Service Institutes have failed in their main purpose because of the lack of such a vital link between them and the financial system.

Another point also needs to be emphasized. If the TCSCs are indeed successful in their functioning, they should be able to enhance the profitability of projects, which obtain their assistance; this is in fact their very purpose. If so, they should be self-supporting in their operations as well as their growth. Hence, they should charge reasonable fees to both the promoters as well as the financial system. Further, the capacity of the TCSCs to generate their own resources is a good index of their fruitfulness and efficiency.

III
THE LEADERSHIP ROLE OF THE FINANCIAL SYSTEM: SOME EXAMPLES

A catalytic leadership role of the financial system is not a very new phenomenon and it would be useful to indicate how some banks performed this function in different contexts.

This development banking task had been performed earlier during the 19th century in the then developing countries of Western Europe. Gerschenkron tells us of the 'truly momentous role of investment banking of the period for the economic history of France and of large portions of the Continent.' The relative shortage of both capital and entrepreneurial talent was made good by the creative response of the banking systems to the challenge of development. 'The continental practices in the field of industrial investment banking must be conceived as specific instruments of industrialization in a backward country', writes Gerschenkron.[12]

> In Germany, the various incompetencies of the individual entrepreneurs were offset by the device of splitting the entrepreneurial function: the German investment banks—a powerful invention, comparable in economic effect to that of the steam engine—were

> in their capital supplying functions a substitute for the insufficiency of the previously created wealth willingly placed at the disposal of entrepreneurs. But they were also a substitute for entrepreneurial deficiencies. From their central vantage points of control, the banks participated actively in shaping the major—and sometimes even not so major—decisions of the individual enterprises. It was they who very often mapped out a firm's path of growth, conceived far-sighted plans, decided on major technological and locational innovations, and arranged for mergers and capital increases (emphasis added).[13]

In those days, the banks could perform the tasks of identification, design and formulation of projects with the available design-engineering talents, supplemented when necessary by foreign talents. Now, with the much greater complexity of these tasks and with the imperative need for domestic technological capability to adapt, modify and improve both traditional and modern technology, the banking system cannot perform these tasks without establishing the TCSCs in the relevant fields.

The Swedish development banks seem to have perceived the chain relationship with regard to technological advance. High-voltage transmission, an automobile that combines passenger-car styling with the ruggedness needed for poor roads, an aircraft capable of landing and taking off on very short runways—these were some of the technological problems that were identified by bankers. As Drucker reminds us:

> Yet Swedish technological strategy had not been formulated by technologists. It seems to have come mostly from the industrial development bankers who head the country's three large banks. Not one of them is a scientist or an engineer; all of them, however, apparently understand the need for technological strategy that is appropriate to a small country where available resources have to be concentrated on filling gaps in a few areas rather than in providing the main advance. When World War II ended, Sweden was still largely a mining and lumbering economy. Now she has become, in terms of per capita output, Europe's leading industrial economy and has attained a standard of living second only to that of the United States.[14]

The role of the Industrial Bank of Japan (IBJ) has been discussed in Chapter 3; its role was similar to that of the various banks in Germany.

The Industrial Development Bank of India has clearly perceived the need, in the Indian context, of establishing; (*a*) relevant TCSCs for performing the various tasks related to project design work; and (*b*) their close and direct links with the banking system so as to enable the latter to perform its promotional role in stimulating a viable yet diffused process of industrialization in the backward parts of the country. As the Industrial Development Bank of India's report for 1971–1972 puts it:

> The Industrial Development Bank of India has been keenly aware of the limitations of financial and fiscal incentives in promoting industrial development in backward areas. It has been recognized that it would be essential to undertake considerable amount of project work for the purpose. This work comprises identification of project ideas, preparation of preliminary feasibility studies, search for managerial and entrepreneurial talents, preparation of detailed project reports, managerial, technical and financial assistance for project implementation, critical evaluation of projects from the national point of view and finally project supervision.[15]

Since 1970, the Industrial Development Bank of India has initiated action in this field by coordinating the functioning of the financial system and by linking this with such TCSCs as are established at its initiative. Given dynamic and imaginative leadership, these initiatives are pregnant with great possibilities;[16] unfortunately, such leadership has been lacking and as a result the IDBI's efforts in this direction have not given the expected results.

The Industrial Development Bank of India's role in creative adaptation of modern technology is also illustrated by a concrete case—the case of the Swaraj tractor.[17] For the small farms in India it was essential to have a low-horse power multipurpose tractor suited to their needs as well as resources. The multinational companies were producing tractors of 30 hp and above, using obsolete technology. Russian assistance was sought in 1965, but this implied a large foreign exchange cost and a large number of Russian experts. At any rate, the Russians suggested the purchase of 20hp tractors from Czechoslovakia. Mr. Suri, the Director-in-Charge of the Central Mechanical Engineering Research Institute, convinced the planners that India had the capacity to design, engineer and manufacture a 20 hp tractor suited to the specific Indian conditions. The Swaraj tractor was thus devised, a tractor which passed the test of the Tractor Testing and Training Station. Only two other tractors out of six had passed this test.

The Ministry of Agriculture and the public-sector Hindustan Machine Tools still favored Zeteor, a 20 hp tractor of Czech design, on the grounds that Zeteor was a production model, while Swaraj was still a prototype. The Hindustan Machine Tools decided to produce Zeteor on a turn-key contract with Czechoslovakia. The Swaraj tractor, thus, was left without a promoter.

Fortunately for the Swaraj, the Punjab Industrial Development Corporation became attracted by the idea at the persuasion of Mr. Suri and his team. The design-engineering tasks were offered to Mr. Suri (who was responsible for the tractor design), and his consulting firm, the technical personnel for the project being drawn from the Central Mechanical Engineering Research Institute staff who had worked on the design. The financing problem was solved at the initiative of the Industrial Development Bank of India, which appraised the project, was convinced of its viability and was attracted by the fact that the tractor was indigenuously designed and that its manufacture was based on skills, materials and equipment available in India. The Industrial Development Bank of India supported the project also on the grounds of the project's vital and organic links with small-scale ancillary industries, from which the Swaraj tractor project was to buy a substantial number of parts. This project has been successfully implemented and the firm has introduced already two new designs of tractors based on its own research and design work.

This project has relevance to the process of creative adaptation of modern technology. The success of this experiment was primarily due to the organic and sequential relationship among the following tasks and functions.

Identification of a project idea was the critical first stage. This was done by the Planning Commission in this case. The identification of available technological choices for this was the second; this was the function of a TCSC, in this case the Central Mechanical Engineering Research Institute. Identification of a research problem by a TCSC (in this case the Central Mechanical Engineering Research Institute) was the third stage. The research on this problem by a TRC (again the Central Mechanical Engineering Research Institute) and the transmission of the research result to the TCSC (M/S. Suri and Associates) was the fourth stage. The detailed project report by the TCSC to the project promoter (Punjab Industrial Development Corporation) and the financial system (Industrial Development Bank of India) was the fifth stage.

In this organic sequential relationship, the critical functions were performed by the TCSC and the financial system (Industrial Development Bank of India): the functions of identifying the relevant research problem, embodying the research results meaningfully into a concrete project and facilitating its implementation. Without the TCSC, neither the relevant research problem nor a concrete project would have been identified; and without the link between the TCSC and the financial system (Industrial Development Bank of India), the project would not have become operational. It appears from a priori reasoning as well as from this case study that the critical links in the process of creative adaptation of modern technology are the TCSC and the financial system; these two provide the essential links between the production system on the one hand, and the TRC and modern technology on the other. Without these two functional agencies, the production system and the technological research system are likely to evolve on parallel lines—as seems to have happened in a number of countries with TRCs.[18]

Figure 5.1
Functional Sequential Relationships

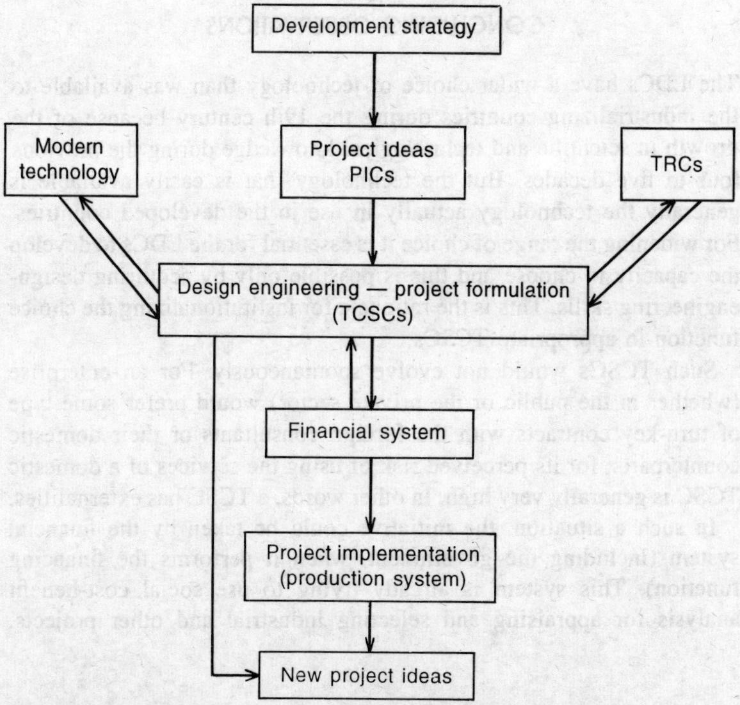

The vital significance of these links is again borne out by the Korean experience. Korea is one of the few countries which emphasized the relevance of a technology policy.[19] It started in 1966 with a TRC—Korea Institute of Science and Technology—which in some respects also performed the role of a TCSC. However, its major emphasis has been on technological research. This resulted in valuable research results. But, the Korea Institute of Science and Technology vis-à-vis its research function had not established the relevant links with the TCSC or the financial system. Its research effort, hence, lacked operational relevance.[20] This situation was rectified by the establishment in 1974 of a TCSC—the Korea Technology Advancement Corporation; this corporation also established links with the financial system through the Korea Development Finance Corporation and the Korea Credit Guarantee Fund. As a result, about 10 out of the 40 research results from the Korea Institute of Science and Technology have been actually embodied in concrete projects, some of which have been implemented by the Korea Technology Advancement Corporation itself.[21]

IV
CONCLUDING OBSERVATIONS

The LDCs have a wider choice of technology than was available to the industrializing countries during the 19th century because of the growth in scientific and technological knowledge during the previous four to five decades. But the technology that is easily available is generally the technology actually in use in the developed countries. For widening the range of choice it is essential for the LDCs to develop the capacity to choose and this is possible only by acquiring design-engineering skills. This is the rationale for institutionalizing the choice function in appropriate TCSCs.

Such TCSCs would not evolve spontaneously. For an enterprise (whether in the public or the private sector) would prefer some type of turn-key contracts with the foreign consultants or their domestic counterparts; for its perceived risk of using the services of a domestic TCSC is generally very high. In other words, a TCSC has externalities.

In such a situation, the initiative could be taken by the financial system (including the government, when it performs the financing function). This system is already trying to use social cost-benefit analysis for appraising and selecting industrial and other projects.

However, such ex post project evaluation cannot affect choices, which are inevitably made at the project design stage. To induce appropriate technological choices, the financial system needs to have a technological dimension to its project evaluation. It cannot do this without the help of the TCSCs. Once the financial system starts using the services of domestic TCSCs, the enterprises (public or private) too would be induced to do so. Thus the functions of the TCSCs and the financial system are organically related. These two provide the essential linkages between modern technology and the TRCs on the one hand and the production system on the other.

NOTES

1. V.V. Bhatt, 'On a Development Bank's Selection Criteria for Industrial Projects,' *Economic Development and Cultural Change*, Vol. 25, No. 4 (July 1977).
2. V.V. Bhatt, 'On Technology Policy and Its Institutional Frame,' *World Development*, Vol. 3, No. 9 (September 1975); also in World Bank Reprint Series: No. 29.
3. Ibid.
4. V.V. Bhatt, 'Development Problem, Strategy and Technology Choice: Sarvodaya and Socialists Approaches in India,' *Economic Development and Cultural Change* (Vol. 31, No. 1, October 1982).
5. On the concept of the internal brain drain and the technology problem in general, see the illuminating article by Paul Streeten: 'Technology Gaps Between Rich and Poor Countries,' *Scottish Journal of Political Economy*, Vol. 19, No. 3 (November 1972). Also, Jack Baranson, *North-South Transfer of Technology: What Realistic Alternatives are Available to the U.S.*? (US Department of State, December 1977); see also Charles Cooper, 'Science Policy and Technological Change in Underdeveloped Economies,' *World Development*, Vol. 2, No. 3 (March 1974).
6. V.V. Bhatt, 'Development Banking: Top Management Tasks and Structure,' *World Development*, Vol. 4, No. 6 (June 1976).
7. Ian M.D. Little and James A. Mirrlees, *Manual of Industrial Project Analysis in Developing Countries* (Paris: Development Center of the Organization for Economic Co-operation and Development, 1968), pp. 64–66.
8. V.V. Bhatt, 'Capital intensity of industries,' *Bulletin of the Oxford University*, Vol. 18, No. 2 (1956), pp. 179–94.
9. *Choice and Adaptation of Technology in Developing Countries* (Paris: Development Centre of the Organization for Economic Co-operation and Development, 1974), p. 81.
10. World Bank, *Development Finance Companies* (Washington: April 1976). To quote:

> One tendency has been to take a rather conservative view of their role. Such a view has led the DFCs to give more support to the stronger enterprises...Consequently, in its dealings with each DFC, the Bank should encourage the DFC to efforts that would increasingly make it *a catalyst for development* (p. 8, emphasis added).

11. World Bank, *Employment and Development of Small Enterprises* (Washington: February 1978). To quote:

> A satisfactory arrangement, in the World Bank's limited experience, is a technical assistance agency outside, but closely linked with, the financial intermediary for SSEs; the financial institution would thus act as a sponsor of technical assistance to its clients (actual or prospective) and of its clients to the technical assistance agency. The entity that provides or controls financing seems often to have the most leverage (or catalyst influence) on the other two parties (p. 40).

12. Alexander Gerschenkron, *Economic Backwardness in Historical Perspective* (Cambridge, Mass: Harvard University Press, 1962), p. 12.
13. Alexander Gerschenkron, *Continuity in History and other Essays* (Cambridge, Mass: Harvard University Press, 1968), p. 137.
14. Peter F. Drucker, *The Age of Discontinuity* (London: Pan Books, 1971), p. 71.
15. *Annual Report of the Industrial Development Bank of India*, 1971–72, (Bombay: August 1972).
16. V.V. Bhatt, 'Industrial Development Bank of India: A decade of Performance,' *Commerce*, Annual Number (January 1975); also in World Bank Reprint Series No. 18. See also V.V. Bhatt, 'Financial Institutions and Technical Consultancy Services,' *Journal of Development Planning* (United Nations, No. 18, 1988).
17. For details about this project, see V.V. Bhatt, 'Decision making in the public sector: case study of Swaraj tractor,' *Economic and Political Weekly*, Vol. 13, No. 21 (27 May 1978).
18. See Baranson (n. 5 above) and Cooper (n. 5 above). To quote Baranson on the experience in Brazil, Mexico, Colombia and Venezuela.

> These programs are generally associated with Latin American Universities and government-sponsored research institutes…These programs have met with varying degrees of success, but their scope has traditionally been limited to topics and areas of scientific investigation and exploratory research. Rarely have the programs concentrated on designing and engineering technologies with immediate and direct application to problems in industrialization (p. 14).

19. Hyung-Sup Choi, Adapting technology—the Korean case, in E. Rabinowitch and V. Rabinowitch (eds.), *Views of Science, Technology and Development* (Oxford: Pergamon Press, 1975).
20. Ka-Jong Lee, 'Technology Transfer and Developmental Strategies: The Role of Large Firms in Korea', Ph.D. thesis (University of Hawaii, August 1977), pp. 53–54.
21. Korea Technology Advancement Corporation, *K–TAC's Role in Commercialization of New Technology in Korea* (Seoul: 1978).

Chapter 6

On Participating in the International Capital Market

INTRODUCTION

Since 1970, international credit and capital market has grown in size and sophistication and provides considerable opportunities for the developing countries to operate in this market for the purpose of meeting their growing requirements for external resources as well as for the optimum management of their external assets and liabilities. Further, it enlarges the scope of export possibilities in the field of financial services particularly for the Asian countries like India. Thus, it is essential for the developing countries to participate actively in this market. However, for such participation to be possible, they need to evolve an institutional and policy framework that is appropriate for establishing their creditworthiness, organically linking their domestic market with the international market, integrating their domestic financial markets and developing the necessary institutionalized expertise and technology. Moreover, to take advantage of export possibilities with regard to financial services as well as other types of service products, they need to be active participants in the process of multilateral negotiations relating to trade in services in the Uruguay Round of trade negotiations. Only thus will they be able to evolve a services compact that suits their needs and capacities.

The rationale for participation as well as the domestic institutional and policy frameworks, essential for the purpose, are presented in this chapter with particular reference to India. However, this is just for the sake of illustration; what is said about India applies to other developing countries of her type as well.

India is one of the few countries in the group of the less developed countries (LDCs) that has the potential for developing the needed institutionalized expertise and technology for active participation in the international market. Further, there is a certain immediacy as well as urgency for her to do so in order to reduce the foreign exchange cost of operating in this market as well as to enlarge the scope of her export effort. For such active participation, it is essential for her to adapt her macroeconomic policy framework and institutional capacity to the evolving nature and characteristics of the international market.

Such is the broad theme of this chapter. The nature and characteristics of the evolving international capital market are tersely presented in Section I. The immediacy as well as the urgency for participation in this market is the theme of Section II, while Section III and IV deal with the pre-requisites for such participation in the sphere of institutional and policy framework. Some concluding observations are made in the final section.

I
NATURE AND CHARACTERISTICS

The international capital market that has been evolving since the late fifties and early sixties after a state of suspended animation during the inter-war years is characterized by the interrelated and interlinked phenomena of internationalization, globalization, integration and innovations.[1]

Internationalization

This market is international in the sense that it is not subject to the regulation and control of any national authority. The Euro-market is in this respect similar to the informal credit markets in several developing countries—the markets that are out of reach of the national regulating agencies. The former is relevant for large participants—large corporations, public entities and sovereign governments—while the latter for the small enterprises of all types. However, both these markets are characterized by relatively low transaction costs for borrowers partly because of their freedom from regulation.

Globalization

The globalization aspect refers to the interlinkage that is establ among national markets as a result of progressive removal of exchange controls on capital flows and liberalization of the various financial centers in the developed countries together with the revolution in information gathering, processing and transmission made possible because of technological developments in the fields of computer and telecommunications (both described pithily as computronics). This phenomenon has widened and deepened the scope of the international market as financial institutions are now able to offer 24–hour sales and trading capability in debt and equity instruments. It is now possible to make global offerings of debt and equity, which widens the scope of the market, and the market now provides opportunities for swap deals relating to currency and/or interest rate—the opportunities that deepens the scope of the market.

This interlinkage of national markets has evolved particularly after the mid-seventies into an international market in financial instruments, denominated in several key currencies. International transactions were predominantly in sterling during 1870 to 1914 and in the U.S. dollars in the sixties and the early seventies; the international market since then is a multi-key currency market and it is this phenomenon which has made it possible to evolve the currency swap markets after 1982—an evolution which was pioneered by the World Bank in 1983.[2]

The interlinking of national markets—the phenomenon of globalization—has led to the convergence of interest rates in different national markets. In Euro-markets, covered interest rate parity holds almost instantaneously. More significantly, interest rate changes—nominal and real—orginating in one major financial center are being quickly transmitted to the other financial centers, despite the floating of the major key currencies. There has been thus a growing interdependence among major financial centers and this has reduced the scope for national monetary policies that are out of line with those in the other centers. Further, capital flows have become a dominant causal factor at least in the short run in the determination of interest rates and exchange rates; and this can lead to misallocation of resources among various productive sectors as a result of price signals not consistent with comparative cost patterns. To minimize the adverse effects of speculative capital flows, it has now become essential to have international coordination of macroeconomic policies in major countries, particularly relating to interest rate and exchange rate policies, through an international institution like the International Monetary Fund.

Integration

The integration of money, banking and securities markets as a result of progressive deregulation—that is, the removal of legal restrictions on interest rates and the functional scope of various financial institutions particularly since 1979—has linked the national financial markets, created a competitive environment, and given rise to the phenomenon known as securitization. The large borrowers—and in particular the multinational corporations—find it profitable now to borrow directly from the securities market at a cost lower than the cost of borrowing directly from the international banks. This development has blurred the distinction between investment banks and the commercial banks and both are evolving into universal banks, which provide all types of financial services, a sort of a department store type of banking.[3] This development has widened the market for financial services because of the integration of bank and nonbank financial intermediaries; the borrowers tap now not only the resources of the banks but also the resources of the other financial intermediaries. Even the international banks are now raising resources from the securities market through securitization of their assets as well as by issuing their own securities. The market has also deepened because of the securitization of assets, which otherwise would have been dormant—for example, the assets in the form of houses or loans.

To take advantage of the globalization and integration phenomena, there has been a progressive proliferation of banks worldwide—an institutional internationalization of banks.[4] Banks have continued rapidly to increase their branches and representative offices abroad. Furthermore, foreign banks have continued to expand their share of the total bank business. International business has also been growing in importance for the banks.

These developments in the international capital market have increased competition among financial institutions. As a result, the cost of borrowing, for example, for large corporations has declined and the net yield (net of risk and transaction costs) to primary lenders or investors has increased, while the fees and margins of banks have diminished.

Innovations

The widening and deepening of the market and the growing intensity of competition among financial institutions have induced several financial innovations or technical changes. As Adam Smith[5] observed a long time ago, the size of the market and technical change (or division of labor) are interrelated phenomena; the greater the size of the market, the greater the scope for technical change; the greater the technical change, the greater is the size of the market. And so it has happened in the international financial markets. These innovations[6] or new financial instruments have widened the choice with regard to instruments for both the savers and the investors and borrowers. Investors now can choose instruments with characteristics (relating to yield, liquidity, risk and transaction costs) that they prefer, and similarly borrowers too have a wider choice with regard to instruments with different cost-risk combinations.

The basic rationale for these innovations relates to the reduction of subjective risk by wide diffusion and sharing of risk. The perception of risk is different for different market participants because of asymmetry of information, different capacity to absorb and process the information and the differing attitudes towards risk;[7] these innovations tend to shift risk to willing risk takers— willing partly because their perception of risk or subjective risk is lower than those who want to shift the risk. This process of diffusing, sharing and shifting of risk—largely as a result of the phenomenon of securitization—has its dangers; it creates uncertainty with regard to the location, extent and pricing of the risk and as a result a sort of inertia or lethargy in properly appraising the risk involved in the light of potentially available information.[8] This may lead to instability and vulnerability of the international financial system as a whole because of the inter-locking assets and liabilities of various financial institutions. Further, expectations tend to be based on what Keynes calls, 'average opinion thinks about average opinion' or what Pigou calls, 'errors of optimism and pessimism,' resulting in inherent instability of credit as Keynes christened it.[9] Adequate prudential regulation of the national as well as the international financial system with lender of last resort provision is, thus, essential for the stability of the system as a whole. This is the rationale for an institution like the international central bank.[10] The requirement for prudential regulation is already recognized by the national authorities and an international agreement with regard to capital adequacy requirement for financial institutions is a pointer to what needs to be done at an international level. After this necessary digression to pinpoint the vulnerability of the unregulated international market, let us now revert to the nature of financial innovations that have been introduced in the international financial markets.

In the seventies, the OPEC preferred to keep their surpluses arising from the oil price shock—quadrupling of oil prices in 1973, which quintupled in 1979—as Euro-dollar deposits with international banks. At the same time, there was instability in the interest rates in the various financial centers. These two events gave rise to the innovation of syndicated bank loans at variable interest rates. These loans were primarily made to the oil-importing developing countries and the lack of proper risk appraisal by the international banks as well as the borrowing developing countries ultimately led to the debt crisis of 1982 and after—a crisis which still remains to be resolved.

The other important innovations were introduced after 1982. By that time, the payment imbalances were arising largely among developed industrial countries. The surplus countries like Japan and West Germany preferred to invest in securities, and in the borrowing countries—mainly the U.S.A.—the borrowers preferred to borrow by issuing securities of various maturities. This conjuncture led to the securitization process and the major innovations tried to deal with the risks arising from the volatility of interest rates and exchange rates, resulting from the breakdown after 1973 of the Bretton Woods system of fixed exchange rates, and the structural payment imbalances among the developed countries. These are also the innovations which are relevant for the developing countries that are creditworthy.

The first such innovation is the Note Issuance Facility (NIF) or its variants like the Revolving Underwriting Facility (RUF) or the Euro-Commercial Paper (ECP). A RUF is a facility in which a borrower issues, on a revolving basis, bearer notes which are sold to investors, who may or may not include banks, either by a placing agent or under a tender mechanism. This issuance of notes may or may not be underwritten for a medium-term period by a group of underwriting banks. The ECP was developed by adopting the technique customary in the U.S. commercial paper market, whereby short-term paper of variable maturities is issued to one or more dealers on an uncommitted basis, whose task it is to place it with the banks and other investors.

The main advantage is one of cost. The borrower essentially benefits from short-term interest rates and a smaller margin on the rate because the investor is only taking on a short-term risk. A small underwriting fee to the underwriter, who will have only a contingent risk, converts it into a medium-term facility. The particular advantage to creditworthy LDCs, like some of the Asian countries, is that as the borrower's credit standing improves, the margin on its paper decreases, whereas with a syndicated loan the borrower would be fixed into a margin for the life of the loan. The other advantage to a developing country is that, as the investors are a separate group, it can diversify the funding source away from those banks who have traditionally been lenders to the country—which is obviously very important if the country has substantial financial needs. Lastly, as notes under a RUF are issued regularly and partly to nonbank investors, a borrower's name would become established in a market which is effectively a bridge between the banking and capital markets, making it possible ultimately to tap the capital market by way of Floating Rate Notes and Euro-bonds.

Though so far the NIFs have been arranged overwhelmingly for developed countries, a number of developing countries, notably South Korea, Singapore, India and Indonesia, have begun to arrange the NIFs, mostly for small amounts. First RUF for an Indian borrower was undertaken by the London branch of the State Bank of India at the end of 1984 which was then refinanced in 1986 partially by way of a Euro-commercial paper program—again a first for an Indian borrower. This experience enhanced India's creditworthiness; though the first paper was traded at the margin of a few basic points above LIBOR, it was then placed with investors at rates below LIBOR.[11] The first issuance of Euro-commercial paper (ECP) from India has been by the Industrial Credit and Investment Corporation of India (ICICI) in 1987.

While the advantages of the securitized market obviously apply to developing countries, who generate enough bank and investor interest, it also has, in a different form through some methods, a limited application to other countries. These methods may be called *credit enhancement schemes*.[12] In essence, the security—a bond or a note—issued by a borrower would have to be structured in a way that makes the risk acceptable to international investors. One way to enhance creditworthiness would be through collateralizing the debt instrument. Such credit support may take the form of direct collateralization by the assignment of certain foreign currency revenues to back principal and interest payments on a bond. Commodity indexed bonds or bonds linked with export performance or performance of specific projects are also instances of such schemes. Credit enhancement can take other forms such as the comfort to investors of having the World Bank in a co-financing role or a guarantee from a mutilateral agency.

Credit enhancement can be used not only to allow countries of lesser creditworthiness to tap private capital sources but can also be used by other developing countries, including India, to meet other objectives. Collateral, partial or whole, can for example be used to lengthen the maturity of a borrowing beyond the normal term of market financing. Alternatively, if the collateral were in a foreign currency or linked to a foreign currency, it could be a useful hedge against the risk of a devaluation of the domestic currency. These methods of credit enhancement can, of course, be used on non-securitized financings equally well.

Such innovations, however, can be introduced only if the developing countries become active participants in the international market. The innovations so far introduced have not been motivated by the special needs of the developing countries. The reasons are: developing countries have not been significant participants in the market and secondly most financial institutions are inherently conservative and therefore tend to introduce innovations mainly in their dealings with the most creditworthy borrowers—which developing countries have not been for some time.

The most interesting innovation as a result of globalization relevant to the developing countries is the development of the swap market in both currency and interest rate swaps. A swap, as the market understands the term currently, is a medium- or long-term arrangement between two parties in which each party commits to service the debt obligation of the other. This has been the most radical or revolutionary innovation that has been introduced in the international market in recent years.[13] As a result, borrowers are no longer restricted only to those markets in which their name is acceptable or where their credit standing is the highest but which do not provide the currency and type of debt they require. A borrower can tap the market for borrowing, where he is most creditworthy and hence can get the most favourable terms and then trade or exchange this debt obligation with the most creditworthy borrower in another market, where his own credit standing is low but which is still preferred by him for business reasons. This in fact is the application of the comparative cost principle to capital transactions. For example, a developing country, traditionally excluded from the fixed rate dollar bond market, can raise a syndicated floating rate dollar-or-sterling-loan and swap it into fixed rate dollars. Such swap techniques are not linked to new transactions only. Indeed, to a considerable extent, the swap market does not distinguish between primary and secondary swap transactions and swaps can be arranged in such a way as to match identically the payment date on existing borrowing, that is, for the purpose of the management of existing debt with a view to reducing the risk arising from exchange rate and interest rate changes.

The Industrial Development Bank of India (IDBI) and the Export Import Bank of India (EXIM BANK), for example, have taken advantage of this swap market. So far, the IDBI has entered into four currency cum interest swap transactions and the EXIM BANK has entered into two such deals. (These two along with the ICICI and the State Bank of India (SBI) have resorted to external borrowing from the international market as have some public sector firms like Air India, which also took advantage of one swap transaction to reduce its debt obligation.) Some other Asian countries like South Korea have also tapped this market.

Unfortunately, swaps are generally confined to the more creditworthy developing countries like some Asian countries particularly as swap counterparties tend to be large corporations as well as banks who are not in a position to take on the third world risk. Certainly, the role of multilateral institutions who may stand up as swap counterparties would be useful and institutions like the World Bank and Asian Development Bank could assume this role. It is the World Bank which pioneered swap transactions in 1983 and it has considerable experience of dealing in the international market as well as taking advantage of financial innovation;[14] it is hence in a position to offer advisory services to the developing countries and suggest methods and techniques of credit enhancement for participating in the international market.

II
THE RATIONALE FOR PARTICIPATION

The developing countries like India would have to rely increasingly on the international market for several reasons:

(*a*) to obtain external resources essential for accelerating their pace of development; (*b*) to manage external debt with a view to reducing debt service obligations; (*c*) to manage international reserves; and (*d*) to take advantage of import substitution and export possibilities relating to financial services.

External Resources

The average annual growth rate of GDP for developing countries as a group has declined from 6.1 percent during 1965 to 80 to 3.8 percent during 1980 to 86 partly as a result of a negative resource inflow from abroad. They need net external resources at least equal to 3 percent of their GDP to regain the pre–1973 momentum of development. The opportunities for concessional borrowing from multilateral and official agencies are quite limited because of the fiscal, payments and growth problems facing the developed countries. Thus the developing countries have to take recourse to borrowing from the international market.

For India, the average annual growth rate has increased to about 5 percent since 1980 from 3.7 percent during 1965 to 80. However, this growth rate is inadequate for appreciably raising the living standards, removal of poverty and securing reasonable levels of employment. The opportunity of obtaining concessional assistance have been diminishing in importance since 1975; her non-concessional debt as a result has been rising from about 6.5 percent of total external debt to about 27 percent or more currently and is estimated to rise to more than 50 percent in the next few years.

External Debt Management

The external debt of all developing countries has increased from about 13 percent of GNP in 1970 to more than 35 percent currently and debt service as a percentage of exports of goods and services has risen from about 10 percent in 1970 to about 20 percent or more by 1993. For India, the total external debt as a percentage of the GNP has been more or less stable though private debt as a percentage of the GNP has risen from about 0.2 percent in 1970 to more than 1.1 percent by 1993; the debt service as a percentage of the exports of goods and services, too, has been more or less stable in the range of 24 to 27 percent during 1970 to 1993.

The debt service obligations change as a result of the volatility of interest rates and exchange rates. However, the risk arising from such changes can be reduced by effective and efficient management of debt.

Such opportunity has been created in the international market since 1982 as a result of the innovation of currency-interest rate swaps. It is not possible to avail of this opportunity without actively participating in the international financial markets. For highly indebted countries, the debt to GNP ratio is very high (about 45 percent) and the debt service ratio too is quite high (about 30 percent). For Sub-Saharan countries, the debt to GNP ratio is even higher at 57 to 58 percent and the debt service ratio is about 20 percent. For these countries, the reduction of both these ratios is essential for attaining reasonable rates of growth. For the Sub-Saharan countries, debt relief in various forms is already being considered; it is possible to do so as most of their debt is to official agencies.

However, most of the debt of the highly indebted countries particularly in Latin America is owed to the private sector; for these countries, some radical solution to this problem is imperative. This debt is being securitized and sold at a discount in the international market; but the advantage of this discount is not available to the debtors. It may be possible to devise some mechanism to pass on the discount to the debtors. The International Monetary Fund (IMF), for example, can buy this debt at a discount in the market and pass on this discount to the debtors. In such a case, the discounted debt obligation of the debtors would be to the IMF. The latter can create a type of trust fund to finance the purchase of debt and can recover this debt from the indebted countries over a period of time. The advantage of the IMF as an intermediary is that it is in a position to negotiate with the debtor countries and monitor the change in the macroeconomic and institutional policy framework—the changes which are essential for promoting growth and development and establishing creditworthiness in the international market.[15] The evolving international market could create suitable financial instruments for these types of transactions. However, for this to be possible, the developing countries should have the capacity of exploring the possibility of and introducing such innovative financial instruments as may be necessary.

The Management of Foreign Exchange Reserves

The developing countries as a group have gross foreign exchange reserves equal to about 3.5 months of import coverage; for India, these reserves constitute about 4 months import coverage. The international market provides opportunities of investing these reserves and changing the composition of such investment so as to obtain a satisfactory yield on such investment and reduce the risk arising from interest rate and exchange rate changes.

Import Substitution and Export Possibilities

For some countries like South Korea and India, which have a sound well developed financial system and adequate technical and professional manpower, there is a potential that can be developed, through institutionalized expertise and financial technology, for acquiring the capacity to provide financial services to domestic borrowers, intending to have operations in the international market, as well as to export such services to the other developing countries. These services are generally skill-intensive and much less capital-intensive than some of the manufactured products. Developing the capacity for providing such services on the basis of their dynamic comparative advantage would strengthen their payment position by saving on foreign exchange cost relating to their transactions in the international market (import substitution advantage) as well as by earnings from the export of such services. This potential somehow has not been exploited; the necessary institutional and policy changes, hence, have not been identified and implemented. For their effective and efficient participation in the international market, it is essential to seize all opportunities for the actualization of this potential.

III
PRE-REQUISITES FOR PARTICIPATION

Participation in the international capital market is possible only if certain preconditions or pre-requisites are satisfied through an appropriate institutional and policy framework. This framework has to be such as to: (*a*) establish and maintain creditworthiness; (*b*) bring about progressive integration of the domestic and international markets; and (*c*) promote competitive impulses and pressures for improving the effectiveness and efficiency of domestic financial markets in an environment of financial stability ensured through strategic and prudent regulation of the financial system.

These are interrelated and interlinked policy measures and it is not possible to take action on one front without at the same time relating it to the other two. How to evolve such an institutional and policy framework requires detailed study and research in the context of a given country. At this stage, what is attempted in this and the next section is merely a tentative broad outline of such a framework.

Establishing and Maintaining Creditworthiness

Creditworthiness, as the market understands it, depends generally on certain characteristics of the growth process. One is that external debt should be growing at a rate lower than the growth rate of national income and the other is that exports should grow at a rate higher than the rate of increase of debt servicing obligations. Thus, the higher the growth rate of income and exports, the greater would be the opportunity of external borrowing; and the larger the external borrowing—if productively and efficiently invested—the higher would be the growth rate of income and exports.

Productivity or efficiency of investment is thus the most critical factor. The institutional and policy frameworks, however, should be such as to create a favorable environment for entrepreneurial functioning and competitive pressures and incentives for increasing investment and improving productive efficiency. The price system for this purpose has to be as little distorted as possible; otherwise the decision signals would turn out to be misleading. Further, administrative controls or regulations or interventions, when essential for the purpose of accelerating the pace of development, should be minimum, of strategic significance, selective, purposive and time bound, and should be, what Bhagwati calls 'prescriptive' rather than 'proscriptive'.[16] The Far Eastern governments, by and large, issue prescriptions rather than proscriptions...whereas countries such as India do the opposite. The governments of 'dos' generally produce economic performance superior to that produced by governments of 'don'ts'.[17] The former foster and promote entrepreneurial impulses, while the latter stifle them; the former establish a symbiotic relationship with the private entrepreneurs, while the latter induce adversarial response and unproductive wasteful expenditure to overcome or to take advantage of restrictive measures without a positive rationale.

To be creditworthy is not enough. A country has to establish its creditworthiness in the market by its continuous presence in order to seize opportunities as they arise of borrowing as well as management of external assets and liabilities. It may be advantageous to borrow, even when external resources are not required, when one's payments position is strong and growth experience good; one may obtain most favorable terms in such a situation and the additional resources so obtained can be used for pre-payment of debt incurred earlier on less favorable terms.

Further, in such a situation, it may become possible to introduce credit enhancing innovative financial instruments, that tailor debt service obligations to one's ability to repay. Such transactions or operations need to be undertaken in all the major financial centers and in particular in the Asian centers like Tokyo, because of what Linder calls the emergence or arrival of the Pacific Century[18] in place of the earlier American Century and still earlier, the British one or Pax Britannica of the nineteenth century.

For borrowing for financing infrastructure projects, the cost of borrowing from the international market can be reduced if such borrowing can be arranged along with assistance from multilateral international institutions like the World Bank. Such cofinancing arrangements can enhance one's creditworthiness in the market and thus make it possible to borrow on favorable terms.

Integration

Such operations are not feasible without some degree of integration of the domestic markets with the international market—a purposive integration that induces the required capital inflow, while at the same time fosters and promotes the growth of the domestic financial markets. To promote such integration, it is essential to develop investment banking expertise and computer and telecommunication facilities for rapid gathering, processing and transmittal of information essential for decision making. It may not be possible for the domestic banks initially to undertake guarantee or underwriting obligations or to lead manage loans or issue of securities. However, it is possible and essential to develop the expertise and capacity to offer advice and assistance to the domestic as well as the foreign clients, particularly in the developing countries. The domestic banks are likely to have better information and understanding of the domestic and the external resource requirement of domestic firms—public or private—as well as of the domestic financial markets and the opportunities they offer. Hence, they would be in a better position to offer advice to and formulate suitable proposals for the domestic firms, thus reducing the foreign exchange cost of external transactions. And once this capacity is developed, such advice and assistance can be given to the other developing countries as well, thus exporting financial services on the basis of their dynamic comparative advantage.

Several Indian banks—commercial as well as development—have developed merchant banking expertise for offering advice to the Indian firms with respect to their operations in the Indian markets. And the banking system has several branches abroad in the major financial centers. Thus, it is not difficult for Indian banks to develop the capacity and the expertise of operating actively in the international market as some of them like the State Bank of India are already doing to some extent. What is now required is a deliberate strategy for the purpose.

Only four banks—the State Bank of India, the Bank of Baroda, the Bank of India and the Indian Overseas Bank—have a significant presence abroad in terms of their branches. The State Bank of India has 23 branches; the Bank of Baroda has 50, the Bank of India has 25 and the Indian Overseas Bank has 11—accounting in all for 109 branches out of a total of 122 branches for the entire Indian banking system. These are the banks that have the institutional basis for operating in the international market, provided they develop the required expertise at the head office as well as in their branches. They need to have a strategy of using purposively their branches abroad for operations in the international market. So far, the top management of these banks have had no strategy with regard to their branches abroad and there was no proper guidance and assistance from the head offices to these branches with regard to their operations—largely because of lack of expertise and experience at the level of top management with regard to the international market. This is also due to the obsessive involvement of the banking system, including the Reserve Bank of India, with the regulation of interest rates and credit allocation in India without much appreciation of the international context.[19]

It may be necessary for these banks to have a strong link with some international banks for evolving partnership relationships with regard to their operations in the international market. In that case, the international banks can lead manage issues of securities or syndicated loans with or without guarantee or underwriting obligations, while the Indian partners could concentrate on the background work relating to formulation of proposals for client firms or institutions. Such a relationship should ensure equitable sharing of fees and margins between the two partners. Since some of the prominent international banks have branches in India, it should not be difficult to forge such relationships.

Attracting Foreign Investors to the Indian Market

India, like some other countries such as South Korea, has already evolved some financial instruments and institutions to attract foreign investors. The Unit Trust of India (UTI) started in 1986 the INDIA FUND in Guernsey and the India Growth Fund Inc in the U.S.A. in 1988 in collaboration with Merril Lynch to induce foreign investors and particularly nonresident Indians (NRIs) to invest in the securities market of India. Further, India has attractive deposit schemes and other schemes for portfolio and direct investment in India for the NRIs. All these instruments are primarily developed to attract capital inflow from the NRIs and that is quite a good tactical move. The NRIs are quite familiar with India, have emotional and other links and a strong desire to be fully informed about the developments and also to contribute toward her development—particularly if that is also profitable for them. Further, once these instruments become established and well known as a result of the NRIs participation, it may not be difficult to attract other foreign individuals and institutions to invest in these instruments. With the experience gained so far, it may be desirable to offer these facilities for investment to all foreign individuals and institutions. (Recently, reputable foreign investors such as pension funds have been allowed to invest in the Indian stock market—see Chapter 3.) In this effort, the branches of foreign banks in India can be very useful. They have been involved in attracting the NRI investment and because of their experience, familiarity and links with the major financial centers, they are in a position to induce foreign investors other than the NRIs to invest in India in the instruments currently aimed at only the NRIs.

These foreign banks have been useful also as catalysts in generating competitive impulses even in the segmented financial markets of India. Though their business in India represents only about 3 percent of the total for the banking system, about 24 foreign banks have 150 branches and are quite active in introducing financial innovations. The Standard Chartered Bank is proposing to start a stock broking firm; the Grindlays Bank is trying to diversify and enter the fields of venture capital fund, leasing and mutual fund; and the Citibank has already started a computer software subsidiary that now ranks third in the business of

Indian exports in this field. The banks like the Citibank and the Hong Kong Bank have introduced innovations like the Automatic Teller Machine and electronic gadgets that enable customers to perform banking business round the clock. The Citibank has now set the pace in terms of showing what a foreign bank can do in the field of retail banking; it has introduced new ideas relating to personal loans, service on telephone etc. The Bank of America is going upmarket offering the services of personal banking officers to clients who are known in the business as high networth individuals. As the Chairman of the State Bank of India perceptively observed: the new edge to the competition from the foreign banks 'has made us less complacent.'[20] It has been a wise decision of the Indian authorities to let these foreign banks operate in India; they are a window to the outside world, an instrument for adapting foreign innovations to the Indian environment and also for integrating the Indian markets with the markets abroad. They have provided a fresh breeze of competition in the highly administered system of Indian banking; their presence is an opportunity that can be exploited for forging vital links with the international market.

The other link which needs to be established is with the Emerging Markets Growth Fund (EMGF), sponsored by the International Finance Corporation (IFC) to purchase securities of developing countries' companies listed on the foreign as well as the domestic stock exchanges. The EMGF is investing in nine emerging stock markets; they include: in Asia—India, the Republic of Korea, Malaysia, the Philippines and Thailand; and in Latin America—Argentina, Brazil, Chile and Mexico. Other countries currently under consideration include Jordan, Nepal and Turkey.[21] The securities of companies, in which EMGF is interested in investing in the domestic market, can be later on listed in the markets of the major financial centers; the EMGF approval of such securities would enhance their attractiveness to foreign investors in the foreign markets.

Of course, it would be essential to reduce the transaction cost to the foreign investors of dealing in securities of the Indian firms by streamlining the legal and other administrative procedures. The attractiveness of Indian securities for foreign investors can be enhanced by deliberate and purposive elimination of transaction costs and risk, arising from functionless political and bureaucratic procedures or interventions, and reduction of other such costs and risk by innovative ways of handling such transactions with minimum delay, and adequate and timely provision of the required information.

Integration and Interest Rate Policy

Integration of domestic with the international market implies that interest rates should be related fairly closely to the interest rates in the major financial centers. Since the developing countries would like to stimulate capital inflows and discourage capital outflows, domestic interest rates or yields, adjusted for expected exchange rate changes, on deposits and bonds should be higher than those prevailing abroad. At the same time, to discourage excessive borrowing from abroad, the domestic interest rates or the cost of borrowing should be lower than the cost of borrowing abroad, adjusted for expected exchange rate changes. Such an interest rate policy can be implemented only if there are pressures and incentives for the domestic banks and the financial markets to improve their efficiency of operations by reducing the transaction costs for both lenders and investors and borrowers, and an exchange rate policy that is consistent with and adequately coordinated with the domestic interest rate policies.

The domestic interest rate policies have also some relationship with the differential relating to the domestic and the foreign gold prices. The foreign investors and particularly the NRIs may prefer to invest in gold by purchasing gold abroad and selling it in India when the profit margins on such transactions are quite high. It appears from available evidence that the NRIs are selling foreign exchange to the gold smugglers for rupees at a premium of about 20 to 25 percent above the official exchange rate. The latter export gold illegally to India because of about 50 percent differential between the domestic and the international gold prices. Thus, the attraction of financial instruments for some NRIs is much less than for the illegal transactions in the currency markets.

If the NRIs and the foreign tourists are permitted to bring gold to India with an import duty of 20 to 25 percent on the value of gold, it is quite likely that the differential in the international and domestic prices of gold would be narrowed. And this for two reasons: (*a*) because of the freedom to import gold in India, the supply price of gold may become lower than what it is now; currently there is a risk attached to gold smuggling; (*b*) further, with such import of gold, the demand for gold with an investment motive may decline as the expectation of higher domestic prices may be dampened.

If the price differential is narrowed, the NRIs currently selling foreign exchange to smugglers may be attracted by the other financial instruments, thus increasing the inflow of resources through official banking channels. Even if the price differential were not narrowed, the situation would be better than what it is now. The government's expenditure incurred to prevent gold smuggling would considerably diminish, the government's revenues would increase as a result of the import duty on gold, and with a free market for gold, there would be possibilities for the Reserve Bank of India to use gold as an instrument for its open market operations, as well as for strengthening its gold reserves. Such gold imports may also facilitate larger exports of gold ornaments and jewellery, in which because of traditional skills, India has a comparative advantage. And the NRIs may, in that case, import them from India. Further, the black market in foreign exchange may shrink and there may result a closer alignment between the official and the black market exchange rates of the rupee.

Gold is a commodity unlike any other in the sense that it is durable, not subject to wear and tear, and internationally acceptable like any other convertible currency. Further, in India, for traditional reasons—the sanctity attached to gold, its value as a reserve asset and its use in ornaments—the demand for gold is likely to increase, despite high prices, at least at half the rate of growth of population. It is for these reasons that in spite of stringent gold control, illegal gold imports have continued for several years.

From the country's point of view, the private gold stocks can be mobilized in emergencies like a breakdown of the international monetary and financial system or a war, and used as foreign exchange. Any way, the suggested policy measure is worth trying out for some years to find out its consequences, particularly as it does not involve any use of India's official foreign exchange earnings or reserves.

Recently, in the 1992 Budget, the NRIs have been permitted to bring gold in any form up to 5000 grams (or 5 kilograms) as a part of their baggage on payment of import duty in foreign exchange (Rs. 220 per 10 grams). It is necessary to analyze the impact of this measure on the black market for foreign exchange, the smuggling of gold as well as other commodities.

IV
LIBERALIZATION OF THE DOMESTIC FINANCIAL MARKETS

For gaining access to the international market as well as for improving the investment and productive efficiency in India, it is essential to reduce transaction costs and risk relating to financial instruments, through financial innovations that provide a wider choice of instruments to the savers and the investors as well as to the borrowers. For this purpose, there has to be freedom from functionless legal and administrative restrictions on the functioning of the financial markets and deliberate creation of a policy environment favorable for generating competitive impulses and for entrepreneurial functioning.

Competitive Impulses

The restrictions on the functional scope of financial institutions need to be progressively relaxed for creating a competitive environment. As is happening in the major financial centers, the commercial banks should be permitted to engage in investment banking activities, which are, as emphasized earlier, essential for operating in the international market. Several banks have now entered the field of merchant banking, mutual funds, leasing, housing finance, etc. and they need to extend their activities to investment banking also.

The entry of commercial banks in this field is essential for another reason also. As is happening in the international market, the major corporate borrowers in India too are increasingly relying on the securitized markets for their resources. The banks are likely to lose this profitable market and if they are to be financially viable, they need to diversify their activities into fields like investment banking that make it possible for them to earn fees from their domestic as well as foreign clients.

Such competitive and entrepreneurial impulses cannot be generated unless the top management of financial institutions has freedom from ad hoc interference from the government and other administrative controls and restrictions that prevent them from operating in an entrepreneurial manner. The fixity of tenure, at least for five years, for the top management of these institutions is imperative if they are to function as innovative entrepreneurs. Currently, the entrepreneurial talents of the top management have scope only in a vertical direction, that is, in accommodating the whims and caprices of the politicians and the bureaucrats rather than in the horizontal direction of improving their services to their customers. This has to change.[22]

Strengthening the Money and Capital Markets

Several measures have been taken recently to promote and strengthen the securities markets in India. The Discount and Finance House of

India (DFHI) has already started its operations relating to short-term financial instruments. The Credit Rating Information Services of India Ltd. (CRISIL) has been established to rate companies as well as securities listed on the capital market. A national market has effectively been created by an electronic link-up between the five major stock exchanges in India, which simultaneously transmits price information and other data to all exchanges. The Stock Holding Corporation of India (SCHI) has been formed by the financial institutions in order to provide clearing house facilities to promote speedier transfer of securities. This corporation acts as a central clearing agency for registering the transfers of securities and reduces considerably the timelag in effecting transfers. The Securities and Exchange Board of India (SEBI), similar to the Securities and Exchange Commission of the U.S.A., has been set up to promote orderly and healthy growth of the securities market. All these developments seek to attract and protect investor interest by provision of better and fuller information with regard to the companies whose securities are listed in the national stock exchanges.

However, unless the financial institutions are permitted to operate as brokers, dealers, underwriters and investors in the money and capital markets, the growth and development of these markets may be inhibited. Various types of banks should be permitted to assume such functions. In that case, it may become possible to evolve a market in short-term instruments by converting the present inter-corporate deposits into a negotiable commercial paper, making company deposits into a tradeable certificate of deposit, and bills of exchange into what are known in the international market as the NIFs. The markets for these instruments and the treasury bills need to be integrated with the active participation in these markets by the financial institutions including the UTI, the Life Insurance Corporation of India (LIC) and the Employees' Provident Fund (EPF); for this to be possible, restrictions on their investment portfolio need to be relaxed. The commercial and development banks, if they assume investment banking functions, could strengthen these markets in various ways. These markets can also be widened and deepened by securitizing dormant assets like house mortgages and the like. The commercial and development banks too can securitize some of their assets as a measure of raising more resources for their functioning.

The promotion or strengthening of the market for short-term instruments through refinancing or rediscounting facilities with the Reserve

Bank of India or the Industrial Development Bank of India is not an effective or efficient method for the purpose; such facilities should be used sparingly and only as a last resort. They become necessary only when the financial markets are fragmented along with the interest rate structure because of administrative regulations. The viable method of strengthening these markets is through an appropriate interest rate policy.

The Structure of Interest Rates

The fragmentation of financial markets has arisen partly because of the irrationality in the administered structure of interest rates. This structure does not reflect the differential transaction costs and the risk attached to various instruments, and this gives incorrect signals to investors and savers, lenders and borrowers, and prevents integration of the financial markets as well as adaptation of appropriate financial innovations. The lack of integration is further aggravated through fiscal measures like exemption from the tax on interest income from some instruments.

This structure thus needs to be rationalized. It may be necessary to have some administered rates but they need to be flexible so as to reflect the changing economic situation. However, even to know the levels at which such interest rates should be fixed and changed in the light of the developing situation, it is essential to have market determined interest rates, particularly related to the negotiable tradeable instruments. On this logic, interest rates on bank deposits and government securities should be flexibly administered, while the financial markets and institutions should be free to determine the other rates, including the interest rates on loans.[23]

It may be necessary to direct credit to certain so called priority sectors; but these sectors, to be priority sectors, must be very few like small farmers, small enterprises of all types, and exports. As is done currently, credit to these sectors should be fixed as some proportion of deposits; but it is not necessary to fix administratively the interest rates on advances or loans. Fixing both the price and the quantity would affect the viability of the banks if they strictly adhere to the directives; if they do not, they will be induced to raise the cost of borrowing by levying noninterest charges to such borrowers, thus adversely affecting the very sectors that are given priority status. Credit allocation to such sectors through directives without fixing interest rates on loans would induce the banks to introduce such innovations as reduce transaction costs and risk to both the lenders and the borrowers, and thus improve the effectiveness and the efficiency of the banking system; at present, there is no such incentive and the financial viability of the banks is already undermined.

Exemption of interest income on some instruments from taxation does not appear to be the right instrument for raising the rate of financial saving; it merely provides artificial incentive for reallocating saving toward the favored instruments. For stimulating saving in terms of financial assets, it would be much more effective to exempt net saving—that is, increase in financial assets minus change in financial liabilities—from taxation. This would raise the net return on all financial instruments and discourage consumption, without fragmenting the financial markets. Such a modified expenditure tax can replace several separate taxes if the following tax base is adopted: (income from all sources + capital gains + gifts received)—[(increase in financial assets—change in financial liabilities) + gifts given to others + expenditure on one house meant for one's own use]

Such a tax would replace several separate taxes like income tax, capital gains tax, gifts tax and inheritance tax, thus simplifying the tax system, and at the same time stimulating financial saving.[24]

Prudent Regulation and Supervision

Liberalizing financial markets from the functionless administrative controls, regulations and directives does not mean that there should be no regulation and supervision of these markets. In fact, financial markets are fragile and susceptible to what Pigou calls errors of optimism and pessimism and in addition, unsound financial practices—like cheating, fraud and unwise hasty ill-informed decisions—have large cumulative and self-reinforcing external diseconomies as they affect the entire financial system and, through it the productive sectors.

For this purpose, the institutional infrastructure is already in place. The Reserve Bank of India has this responsibility vis-à-vis the banking system; the Industrial Development Bank vis-à-vis the development banks; and the newly created Securities and Exchange Board of India vis-à-vis the securities markets. These institutions need to be strengthened in the light of the emerging needs that may arise as a result of liberalization.

V
CONCLUDING OBSERVATIONS

The international capital market as it has been evolving provides an opportunity for developing countries like India to attract the required capital inflow for accelerating their pace of development, manage their foreign exchange assets and liabilities to their advantage and develop export capabilities in the field of financial services. Active participation in this market would not only improve their access to the market but also indicate the institutional and policy frameworks essential for developing effective and efficient domestic financial markets. Of course, since participation does imply a progressive integration of the domestic markets with the international market, it would make the domestic markets vulnerable to the vicissitudes of the international market. But as the Chinese say: by opening your windows you of course get flies along with fresh air; but if you don't open the windows, you will not get flies but at the same time, no fresh air either.

The possibilities of such participation would be enhanced if the developing countries like India take a constructive stand with regard to the multilateral negotiations in respect of trade in services under the Uruguay Round. Such active participation in negotiations would result into multilateral rules in the sphere of trade in services and safeguards for the developing countries, subject of course to eventual and negotiated erosion with 'graduation,' perhaps even slower paced than as now being discussed for goods.[25]

This would open out opportunities for export of services like financial services and computer software, that are skill intensive and with regard to which countries like India have a potential dynamic comparative advantage. Further, the increased competition would also tend to improve the domestic financial system, thus stimulating greater productive and investment efficiency in the productive sectors.

Confrontation and rhetoric for special and differential treatment in the matter of trade as well as trade in services, or for an international economic order arouse only hostility and are self-defeating. In fact as it has happened in the area of trade in goods, that would give greater discretionary powers to the administrative authorities in the developed countries; without an agreed and negotiated system of multilateral rules, the international system would provide opportunities for governments of the economically strong countries to dominate in one way or another (witness the Voluntary Export Restrictions—VERs—and the Voluntary Import Expansions—VIEs) the weaker ones.[26] It is to the advantage of the developing countries to have an international system based on multilateral rules rather than political and economic power. And to have such a rule based system, it is essential—nay, vital—for the developing countries to participate actively and intelligently in the negotiations for trade in goods as well as for trade in services. Intelligent participation in negotiations would also indicate to the developing countries the areas in which the domestic institutional and policy frameworks need change and improvement. Hostility and confrontation are possible with ignorance; cooperative ventures require intelligence and diligence.

NOTES

1. For an excellent detailed review of the evolution and recent trends in the international capital market see, Bank for International Settlements (BIS), *Recent Innovations in International Banking* (Basle: April 1986) and Maxwell Watson, et al, *International Capital Markets* (Washington, D.C.: International Monetary Fund, January 1988).
2. Hakan Lonaeus, 'How the Bank Finances Its Operations,' *Finance and Development*, Vol. 25, Number 3 (September 1988).
3. R. W. Goldsmith, *Some Reflections on the Past, Present and Future of Financial Institutions*, Mimeograph (1974).
4. Alexandre Lamfalussy, 'Structural Changes in the International Financial Markets,' *International Journal of Development Banking*, Vol. 4, Number 1 (January 1986).
5. Adam Smith, *The Wealth of Nations*, edited by Andrew Skinner (London: Penguin Books, 1970). See also Allen Young, 'Increasing Returns and Economic Progress,' *The Economic Journal*, Vol. 38, Number 152 (December 1928); and Nicholas Kaldor, 'The Irrelevance of Equilibrium Economics,' *The Economic Journal*, Vol. 82, Number 328 (December 1972).
6. On the logic of financial innovations, see V. V. Bhatt, 'On Financial Innovations and Credit Market Evolution,' *Economic and Political Weekly*, Vol. 22, Number 22 (May 30, 1987).
7. On the essential subjectiveness of risk perception, see Tony Lawson, 'Probability and Uncertainty in Economic Analysis,' *Journal of Post Keynesian Economics*, Vol. 11, No. 1 (Fall 1988).
8. Percy S. Mistry, 'Globalisation of Financial Markets: Implications for Asian Developing Countries,' *International Journal of Development Banking*, Vol. 5, No. 2 (July 1987).
9. John Maynard Keynes, *A Treatise on Money*, Vol. I (London: MacMillan and Co., 1930), p. 27.
10. John Hicks, *Critical Essays in Monetary Theory* (Oxford: Oxford University Press, 1967), pp. 172–73.
11. Eric Roll, *International Capital and Credit Markets and Developing Countries,' State Bank of India Monthly Review*, Vol. 36, No. 6 (June 1987).

12. Ibid.
13. A. J. David, 'The Banking Revolution—Banks and Industry,' *State Bank of India Monthly Review*, Vol. 36, No. 2 (February 1987).
14. Hakan Lonaeus, 'How the Bank Finances Its Operations,' (n. 2 above).
15. Dr. Arjun Sengupta, a former executive director of the IMF, has made a very viable and feasible proposal more or less on these lines. See Arjun Sengupta, 'A Proposal for a Debt-adjustment Facility in the IMF,' *The World Economy*, Vol. 11, No. 2 (June 1988).
16. Jagdish Bhagwati, *Protectionism* (Cambridge, Mass. The MIT Press, 1988) pp. 98–102.
17. Ibid, p. 98.
18. Staffan Burenstam Linder, *The Pacific Century* (Standford University Press, 1986).
19. S. K. Verghese, 'Developments in International Banking and Prospects of Indian Banks' Overseas Business,' *Economic and Political Weekly*, Vol. 23, No. 18 (April 30, 1988).
20. T. N. Ninnan, 'Foreign Banks Profitable Presence,' *India Today*, Vol. 13, No. 14 (July 16–31, 1988).
21. 'Foreign Portfolio Investment for Development: An IFC Initiative,' *Finance and Development*, Vol. 23, No. 2 (June 1986).
22. V. V. Bhatt, 'On Restructuring the Monetary System,' *Economic and Political Weekly*, Vol. 23, No. 8 (March 19, 1988).
23. V. V. Bhatt, Ibid, and V. V. Bhatt, 'Resource Mobilization in Developing Countries: Financial Institutions and Policies,' *Economic and Political Weekly*, Vol. 21, Nos. 25 and 26 (Issue 21–28, 1986).
24. V. V. Bhatt, *Development Perspectives* (Oxford: Pergamon Press, 1980), Ch. 15.
25. Jagdish N. Bhagwati, 'Trade in Services and the Multilateral Trade Negotiations,' *The World Bank Economic Review*, Vol. 1, No. 4 (September 1987), pp. 567–68.
26. Ibid and Ian M. Little, *Economic Development* (New York, Basic Books Inc. 1982), pp. 374–375.

Chapter 7

Relevance of a Development-Oriented Banking System for Developing and Transforming Economies

Introduction

The mainstream economic theory—the neoclassical theoretical apparatus—ignores the role of institutions in the development process. 'In the analysis of economic performance through time, it contained two erroneous assumptions: (*i*) that institutions do not matter; and (*ii*) that time does not matter.... Institutions form the incentive structure of a society, and the political and economic institutions, in consequence, are the underlying determinants of economic performance.' Hence, 'Neoclassical theory is simply an inappropriate tool to analyse and prescribe policies that will induce development'.[1]

One vital institution that it ignores is the financial system, which determines not only the way in which resources are mobilized and allocated but also the effectiveness and efficiency with which they are invested and used. It is ironic that the neoclassical economists have ignored this role of the financial system, even after Schumpeter had pointedly drawn attention to its role in financing innovations, which determine the pace and pattern of development, on the basis of both theoretical and historical considerations.[2]

Recently Morishima, himself a neoclassical economist, has drawn attention to the vital role of the financial system—and in particular the role of the banking system—in financing innovations, and suggested the manner in which the neoclassical theoretical apparatus should be altered to take account of the strategic factors that have in fact shaped the historical process of development—the factors which economic historians have emphasized.[3] For example, Gerschenkron has emphasized the role of universal banks in shaping the industrialization process in Western European countries during the late nineteenth century as discussed in Chapter 2. The Japanese experience has been similar in the post-war period; the main bank system, as shown in Chapter 3, played a crucial role in accelerating the pace of development during 1950 to 1973 in Japan. And *given the constraints*, imposed by an unfavorable institutional and policy framework, the lead bank systems in India did play a significant role in India's development during 1970–90, as indicated in Chapter 4.

Such historical experience as well as theoretical considerations suggest that the pace and pattern of development in the backward developing countries and the transforming economies (of Eastern and Central Europe, the Successor States of the USSR and China and Vietnam) will be shaped by the financial system they evolve. For the present, the financial system is quite weak in the developing countries[4] and the emerging market economies are still in the process of initiating financial development, suited to a market economy.[5]

The objective of this chapter is to indicate the direction in which the financial system will evolve in these countries in the light of the problems they face and the historical experiences of other countries, as analyzed in the earlier chapters. Of course, such evolution cannot take place unless the institutional and policy framework is development-oriented. Assuming that the governments are strongly committed to quicken the pace of development, this chapter suggests that the evolving pattern of the financial system would be in important respects similar to the development-oriented banking systems of Germany, Japan, and India; the latter's historical experience thus would have great relevance for the developing and transforming economies.

Both sets of countries face certain common problems: restructuring of State Owned Enterprises (SOEs) either before or after privatization and promotion of new private enterprises. Such restructuring of SOEs and promotion of new private enterprises would require substantial external finance through the financial system.

If the financial system is to be viable and effective, it cannot afford to provide such finance without ensuring the profitability of such enterprises through effective monitoring devices. The question then is: What type of financial system could perform this function effectively and efficiently? Subsequent discussion of this theme relates to both developing and transforming economies; however, since the problems are more acute in the transforming economies, the latter receive particular attention.

I
FEASIBLE SEQUENTIAL EVOLUTION OF THE FINANCIAL SYSTEM

Two broad types of financial systems have evolved: the market-oriented or arm's length system in the UK and the USA and the bank-oriented or control-oriented system in Western Europe (in particular in Germany) and post-war Japan.[6] As Gerschenkron has shown, the latecomers in the industrialization process have evolved the bank-oriented system because of the limited saving capacity of households (due to what Marx called lack of primitive accumulation through trade) and the large requirements of external finance of new industrial enterprises without a previous track record. Even in Czarist Russia, during the early part of the twentieth century, the system that was evolving was similar to the universal banking system of Germany.[7]

Of course, neither of these two systems is pure; each has an element of the other. In the UK and the USA, both banks and capital markets have co-existed, while in continental Europe and post-war Japan, the capital markets have evolved *after* the development of the banking system, which in a way assisted this evolution. The basic difference between the two systems, however, relates to the corporate—or enterprise—governance function; the capital market performs this function in the market-based system, while the banks have historically performed this function in the bank-oriented system. Since external long-term finance was provided by the banks, they had to perform the monitoring functions—ex-ante, interim and ex-post—effectively for their own soundness and viability.

It may be noted that securities markets cannot evolve without a sound banking system.[8] It is the banks which provide liquidity that maintain confidence in the payments system, which in turn facilitate trade in commodities and in financial assets. Further, the brokers and market makers or dealers have to rely on credit from the banks for maintaining liquid markets in securities. And quite often, even investors—individuals or institutions—have to rely on bank credit for purchasing securities. Thus development of a sound banking system is a pre-requisite for the evolution of the securities markets.

In the initial stages of the development of a market economy in the transitional as well as developing economies, it does not seem feasible or likely that the market-based system of external finance and corporate governance would emerge for the following reasons:[9]

1. The basic motives of the households to save in most of these countries would be related to transaction and precautionary motives, as their capacity to save is limited and hence they cannot afford to invest in risky market instruments. The current interest in equities is due to hyperinflation and negative interest rates on deposits in banks—as happened in Japan during 1945–50—and this speculative bubble would burst soon, once macro-economic stability is ensured. Such collapse of the stock market occurred in Japan after 1949.
2. It becomes possible for enterprises to issue market instruments like equity and bonds when they are well established and have a track record, on the basis of which the investors can form their judgment about the riskiness of their market instruments. In these countries, entrepreneurs and enterprises have inevitably to be new as new industries develop and it is not possible for the market—*even if it exists*—to evaluate the risk relating to their investments. Further, the existing enterprises—whether state-owned or privatized—have to be reconstructed or rehabilitated and hence risk attached to them cannot be evaluated by the investors.
3. The equity markets in these countries are at a rudimentary stage, are volatile, thin, illiquid and speculative. The capital markets would develop when enterprises mature: institutional investors, like pension and provident funds, and insurance companies, and credit-rating agencies and legal and regulatory framework for full disclosure of information and investor protection evolve: and a certain class of individuals with a capacity to save in excess of what is required for transaction and precautionary purposes emerge. These conditions at present are not met in these countries. Further, the market-oriented system is not geared to meet the financial requirements of small and medium enterprises, and the new entrepreneurs and enterprises.

Premature attempts at developing a market-based system would result in speculative bubbles, cheating and fraud, and when the market crashes, as it would, investor confidence would be shaken, thus inhibiting the gradual and systematic evolution of the market.[10]

Though in the transitional period, it may not be possible to raise new capital or resources by commercialized enterprises—SOEs or privatized—it would be essential to make a beginning in evolving a sound legal, regulatory and judicial infrastructure for facilitating and even stimulating the evolution of the securities market. An equity market would be needed even during the transition period to make it possible for investors—whether individuals or investment funds—to reshuffle or change their portfolio obtained by either initial purchase of shares in a privatized enterprise or as a result of the massive voucher privatization schemes as in Russia or in the Czech Republic. Apart from that, after macro-economic stability is established, there may be some enterprises (including new private enterprises with or without foreign collaboration) which are profitable or potentially profitable, and after commercialization, they may be able to raise resources—through equity or bonds—from the domestic as well as foreign investors.

To begin with, it would be essential to commercialize all large SOEs so as to enable them to have a distinct legal status with their own Boards of Directors; this would also be necessary to prevent spontaneous privatization as has happened in all countries, including China. Once this is done, it may be possible for them to sell their equity at an opportune time—possibly after they are restructured. East Germany's success in privatization was to some extent partly due to *immediate* commercialization and restructuring of enterprises before they were sold largely to West German firms on certain conditions by a legal public organization with clear objectives, to be attained in a given time frame.[11]

Enterprises—SOEs or private—*initially* would not be able to raise resources from the market; however, it would be necessary for the government (if it is not to rely on central bank financing, as it should not) to raise resources from the market to finance its fiscal deficits (on capital account) incurred for financing infrastructure investment.[12] So a market in government bonds would have to emerge soon; however, this market cannot evolve without the active support and participation of the banks.

Thus even for the evolution of securities markets (including government bond market), the development of a sound competitive banking system has to have the first priority.[13]

II
RATIONALE FOR A DEVELOPMENT-ORIENTED BANKING SYSTEM

Conceptually, one can distinguish between two types of banking systems—arm's length and control-oriented. In the arm's length banking, the banker need not monitor the enterprise he finances as he lends money only on the basis of collateral or security—right over the physical assets of the enterprise in the event of enterprise failure to repay the loan in time. However, no banker can rely only on collateral; it would be too costly for a banker to be perpetually engaged in the business of selling physical assets. He does need to appraise the enterprise and its management, partly through repeated short-term transactions to avoid the risk of adverse selection; he thus has to engage in some type of ex-ante and interim monitoring. He may not like to liquidate the enterprise even when it faces temporary financial distress as the legal procedures are too cumbersome and costly, and in addition the enterprise may be potentially and from the long-run point of view quite viable. The banker may like to assist the enterprise through technical and financial assistance. Thus, there could hardly be a pure type of arm's length banking.

Such banking is not feasible anyway in the transitional as well as the developing economies for two reasons: first, because of ill-defined property rights and lack of machinery for enforcement of contracts, there is unlikely to be a market for enterprise physical assets.[14] Second, and much more important from the bank's point of view, is the question of moral hazard—the enterprise may be much too risky and/or may be unwilling to repay the loan. Further, in these countries, the restructuring finance required may be quite large and, as discussed earlier, the enterprise would not be able to raise this finance from the capital market, not only because of the underdevelopment of the market, but also because the outside investors may not have enough trust and confidence in the capacity as well as the willingness of the enterprise to provide adequate yield on its securities; this distrust and lack of confidence would naturally prevail as the majority of privatized enterprises—commercialized as well as non-commercialized—are controlled by the insiders: managers in Russia and the Czech Republic, and managers and workers in Poland and Hungary. Even the SOEs in all countries, including China, have come to be controlled by insiders with greater enterprise autonomy and control over retained earnings; in this case, the moral hazard problems would be even more acute, as the managers do not own the assets of the SOEs.[15]

Hence, all types of enterprises would have to depend on the banks for their working capital as well as investment finance. No profit-oriented and viable bank would provide such finance without adequate and effective monitoring and in particular without the right to supervise, and if need be to change the management or even to liquidate the enterprise in the event of poor performance. The adverse selection and moral hazard problems arising from asymmetry of information would have to be tackled by effective ex-ante, interim and ex-post monitoring.[16] This monitoring to be effective has to be based on mutual trust and confidence arising out of a partnership relationship between the bank and the enterprise. Would such a relationship emerge in these countries?

Most of the SOEs and privatized enterprises had and have a relationship with the state banks, which have a good deal of information about them as well as personal contacts with the managers.[17] So the problem of adverse selection may not arise. Further, the chances of its occurrence can be reduced by effective ex-ante monitoring—a critical appraisal of the enterprise, its investment proposals and its management capacity. The enterprise would have to cooperate as it has no alternative sources of finance, while restructuring investment is essential for improved profitability. There are two additional reasons why mutual trust and confidence may be established. First, if the enterprise is assured of a long-term relationship with the bank such that the bank would be prepared to share some risk in the event of temporary financial distress or liquidity constraints, it would have an incentive to provide full information through formal as well as informal channels. Second, if the enterprise is assured of adequate finance, if need be through the capacity of the bank to arrange syndicated loans in participation with the other banks, it would have an additional incentive not to cheat or mislead the bank.

The bank may be willing to forge such a long-term relationship if it is satisfied that the enterprise management is responsible and trustworthy; for, in a competitive environment, the bank has an incentive to enlarge its business, particularly with reliable and dependable borrowers. Further, the bank may agree to share some risk with the enterprise if it is assured of participation in enterprise governance (through interim monitoring) and a contingent right to get involved in the management of the enterprise (by changing the management and/or imposing such financial or technical restructuring of the enterprise as may be necessary).

UWE, BRISTOL LIBRARY SERVICES

These conditions are all the more necessary if the bank has to arrange syndicated loans in participation with the other banks; for the other banks would trust, shall we say, the lead bank only if they have confidence in its monitoring capacity. The incentive of the participant banks is that they would be able to expand their business without incurring monitoring costs. Thus a system of reciprocal delegated monitoring may emerge as a result of the inherent compulsion of the situation in which both banks and enterprises have to function.[18]

Such an evolution of the banking system is essential to tackle the twin problems of external financing and corporate governance. Later a stage may emerge when some large enterprises may be so profitable and viable so as to raise their required resources from the capital market at a cheaper cost than the banks and without the necessity of monitoring by the banks. In fact the banks themselves can help this process as they did in Japan and in Germany in the later part of the nineteenth and early part of the twentieth century; their incentive would be the fee-earning business of these enterprises and their deposits.[19]

In this process, the investment funds or mutual funds would have their true function to perform. In the early stages, these funds would not be able to raise resources from the market. They would have simply ownership rights—and that too not large enough to perform any significant role of corporate governance. Their interests would be identical to those of the banks and quite likely, as seems to be happening, they may emerge as subsidiaries of the banks—thus increasing the share of equity owned by the banks indirectly up to whatever limit is legally admissible.[20] Thus the banks' equity stake in the enterprises would also provide an incentive to them to evolve effective monitoring capacity.

Once the enterprises mature and some large profitable enterprises emerge, the banks would be able to assist them in raising resources from the market through the instrumentality of the mutual funds; in effect this would mean merely shifting of assets from the banks to the mutual funds.

If these economies have to emerge as successful developing market economies, it appears that the likely evolution of the financial system would be in the direction indicated in the broad outline earlier. The political economy constraints may keep this evolution from taking a zigzag course with some ups and downs.[21] However, given political stability and establishment of macroeconomic stability, the specific history and circumstances of the economies are such that their growth prospects would depend on this type of evolution of the financial system.[22] It should be the objective of the governments to establish such an institutional and policy framework as may facilitate this type of evolution of the financial system.

III
ROLE OF DEVELOPMENT BANKS

The privatization process in all countries has been somewhat gradual and chaotic; and several large enterprises have still to be privatized in all the countries. Even in East Germany where the process has been swift, there are about 100 large enterprises, which still remain to be privatized. Even if the process gains momentum now—the indications are not very promising as even in Poland the mass privatization plan has to be shelved for the time being—it appears that some large enterprises of strategic or critical significance may not be privatized. These are also the enterprises which are loss making and finance their losses, because of the hard budget constraint, through the banking system, even in China.

These economies cannot afford to have permanently loss-making enterprises if they have to acquire a growth momentum. Hence, it is essential to restructure—including splitting—these enterprises in a planned manner. Such restructuring would have a long gestation lag and would require financing on a long-term basis at subsidized interest rates. It would be much better to provide such long-term loans than to provide subsidies through the government budget. What then should be the mechanism for the process of restructuring and financing these enterprises?

In several countries, including Japan, the mechanism has been a development bank; in Japan, the Industrial Development Bank and the Japan Development Bank have successfully performed such a role.[23] In these countries, too, it would be easier and much more effective and efficient to establish development banks for the purpose than to rely on ineffective government ministries or departments, which have probably given up any measure of corporate governance role, particularly after the demise of any effective central planning.[24]

Scarce technical and financial expertise—including such assistance as many be available from institutions like the World Bank and foreign countries—should be concentrated in these development banks to equip them to formulate plans of restructuring with the assistance of, where necessary, outside consultants or experts. These development banks should provide long-term financing only on condition that the enterprises implement the restructuring plans. These banks should acquire, by law, all powers of monitoring the enterprises during the process of their restructuring.

These banks could, at a later stage, also provide assistance to other banks, particularly with respect to appraisal of investment projects, and also participate with them in giving loans to privatized and new private enterprises on a syndicated basis.

These development banks should raise their resources through issuing bonds which should be subscribed by the other banks; these other banks would have an incentive to buy such bonds if they are considered to be eligible securities by the central bank for the liquid-asset requirement that it may impose on the normal commercial banks as well as for temporary access by the banks to central bank assistance. It was thus that the Industrial Bank of Japan obtained its resources as well as the Japan Development Bank. The banks also would have an additional incentive to buy these bonds if the development banks give them the business of providing working capital assistance through short-term loans to the assisted SOEs.

The initiative to establish such development banks has of necessity to be taken by the governments.

IV
INSTITUTIONAL AND POLICY FRAMEWORK

The emergence of a market economy would, of necessity, be an evolutionary process. Such evolution, however, would depend critically on the role of the state in establishing an appropriate governance structure for the economy as a whole.[25] The role of the state historically has been related to the relative backwardness of a country; the greater the relative backwardness, the greater has been the role of the state in shaping the economic environment and making it favorable for the emergence of private entrepreneurs and the introduction of innovations.[26] Market economy does not imply *laissez-faire laissez-passer*. Apart from the establishment of rule of law—private property rights, enforcement of contracts, and legal, regulatory and judicial infrastructure—the central role of the state has to relate to the development of a sound effective and efficient financial system, as the financial system, and in particular the payments settlement and clearing system, has externalities as they affect the functioning of the entire economic system.[27]

Regulatory Framework for the Financial System and Resource Allocation

For the evolution of the financial system in the direction indicated earlier, the central bank along with the Ministry of Finance would have to play a strategic role.

Central Bank Autonomy

To play this role effectively, the central bank should have operational autonomy to perform its functions of initiating a process of financial development, safeguarding the stability and soundness of the system and maintaining macro-economic stability. In particular, in the present context of the transitional and the developing economies, the central bank would have to perform the following functions:

1. Removal of the Debt Overhang: The banks have no particular incentives for improving their effectiveness and efficiency as long as they are experiencing losses as a result of non-performing loans. This debt overhang will have to be removed in some such manner as Japan did after the war—the creation of old and new accounts; the liquidation of old accounts by offsetting losses against reduction of equity and retained earnings, once the system has started operating on sound lines; and recapitalization of banks at that stage.[28] At the same time, it is essential to ensure that such losses do not occur in the future, and this can be ensured only if the enterprises are restructured and their profitability is improved through the provision of external finance and a sound enterprise governance structure established through the monitoring function of the banking system.

   If a central bank takes a leading role in the restructuring of banks, it will acquire sufficient knowledge about the functioning of these banks and that will enable it to later regulate them effectively through its own monitoring function, necessary for providing liquidity to the banks in times of financial distress as well as for ensuring credit allocation on sound lines. In Japan the central bank performed such a role and in fact encouraged actively the evolution of a syndicated loan system as an integral part of the main bank system.[29]

2. Ensuring Profit-Oriented Functioning of Banks: Since the banking system is a vital part of the market economy, the central bank would have to create an incentive structure that ensures the financial viability of the system. In particular, it would have to perform three functions: regulation of interest rates (as in Japan) on deposits and lending in such a way as to ensure profitability of the banks; effective prudential regulation and supervision of the banking system by setting standards for capital adequacy, asset classification, accounting and auditing, reserve and liquidity requirements, etc.; and acquiring the sanction to enforce such regulation and controls by making access to its resources by the banks conditional on the soundness of their performance. Further, it will have to ensure competitive functioning of the banking system but prevent too much competition (which may be destructive of the viability of the system) by restricting entry of new banks beyond a point. Its own effectiveness in supervising the banks would be adversely affected if there are too many banks.[30]
3. Maintenance of the Stability of the System: The central bank should be in a position to enforce financial discipline not only with regard to the banks but also with regard to the government. For such discipline, there should not be *automatic* access to its resources either by the government or the banks; its credit creation should be related to improving the effectiveness and efficiency of the banking system in resource mobilization and allocation, and improving the productive and investment efficiency of state and private enterprises; and maintaining macroeconomic stability.[31]

Policy Orientation Towards Promoting Exports and Viable Import Substitution

It would be easier to evaluate the performance of enterprises by the banks as well as the government and central bank, if the performance criterion is related to exports and viable import substitution. In the process of restructuring the state enterprises and establishment of new private enterprises, the appraisal criteria by the banks and the government should relate to the international competitiveness of the enterprise concerned. This criterion provides a *transparent unequivocal yardstick for the measurement of performance* of industries and firms—a yardstick much more reliable than any sophisticated cost-benefit analysis. It is this yardstick which would enable the government to determine its effective policies for incentives as well as penalties. Such a yardstick disciplines government, firms and banks in formulating their plans and policies; no other disciplining factor can be as effective as export performance; further, such a yardstick makes the task of *enterprise governance by the banks* much more effective and much less amenable to moral hazard problems than any other yardstick.[32]

Macroeconomic Stability Essential for the Evolution of the Financial System

Any financial system has to operate in an environment of uncertainty as all financial or credit transactions relate to the future, which is uncertain. Hence, it is essential not to aggravate this inevitable uncertainty by policies that may endanger macroeconomic stability. In an inflationary environment, it is difficult to appraise and evaluate costs and benefits of financial transactions and ensure the sound functioning and evolution of the financial system.

To maintain such stability, it is necessary to have fiscal balance without resorting to central bank finance. The government should thus ensure a surplus in its current account; that is, should have such tax and expenditure policies as to result in government saving, necessary for partly financing government investment in infrastructure. Any deficit on its capital account as a result of its investments, that are complimentary and supportive of the private sector, should be financed only by issuing bonds to the public rather than by resorting to central bank credit.[33]

The stabilization and structural adjustment policies, further, should be growth-promoting. The unregulated and unstructured trade and price liberalization in the East European countries and Russia actually aggravated instability and resulted in large fiscal deficits, directly or indirectly financed by central bank credit. The resulting hyperinflation led to declines in outputs and incomes and social distress.[34] While China and Vietnam pursued growth-promoting measures, their gradual and structured liberalization policies created an environment favorable for growth, and thus also favorable for further reform measures.[35]

The sudden, sharp and swift liberalization measures in Russia and Eastern Europe were dictated by political economy considerations; with the collapse of the central governance structure of central planning and lack of consensus with regard to the structural fabric of the economies, it perhaps became necessary to take the measures that they did in order to make the process of transition to a market economy irreversible. However, this has created a situation that may lead to social discontent, strengthening the vested interests that oppose the establishment of a market economy.[36]

V
CONCLUDING OBSERVATIONS

Privatization, in itself, does not guarantee great economic performance. It has to be accompanied by measures that establish political and economic institutions that govern the incentive structures of households, firms, and banks in a market economy.[37] This problem has not arisen in East Germany because of the unification with West Germany; the latter's institutional structure has become relevant and effective for East Germany.[38] China and Vietnam[39] are gradually shaping the institutions of a market economy, while still retaining the central governance structure, which enables them to evolve gradually and effectively the institutions of a market economy. This process has become somewhat chaotic and unregulated in Russia and Eastern Europe; hence, the evolution of market economy institutions may take more time. The backward developing countries have to strengthen their institutions; they are quite weak at present.

Further, mere privatization is not a substitute for restructuring the state enterprises so as to make them internationally competitive. Such restructuring as well as the emergence of new private enterprises is not possible without external financing. Under their specific circumstances, this external financing will have to be obtained from the banking system; however, a profit-oriented banking system would not provide the required long-term external finance without strict monitoring—in particular without ex-ante and ex-post monitoring, which provides the mechanism for enterprise governance. Thus, the process of privatization and restructuring is vitally related to the evolution of the banking system that can provide external finance along with enterprise governance structure, *applicable to all enterprises, whatever their ownership pattern*. This is unlike the capital market, which provides governance structures or mechanisms only for publicly held large corporate enterprises, whose shares are actively traded in the market.

Thus, the major policy direction in these countries should be towards developing an effective banking system that can simultaneously tackle the twin problems of external finance as well as enterprise governance for all types of enterprises.

Similar problems were faced by Japan and Germany after the war. The main bank system in Japan was the response to the challenge of providing external finance along with external enterprise governance to enterprises that were largely controlled by managers (insider control as in the ex-socialist countries) and required large external resources for restructuring and expansion.[40]

West Germany faced similar problems, which were tackled by its universal banks. 'The banks helped to rebuild German industry...after 1948. Firms rely extensively on loan, as against equity, finance and the banks exercise an important monitoring role through their representation on the Supervisory Board...the role of banks tends to counter "short-termism", and provides a mechanism for reorganizing management in good time, when a company starts running into trouble.'[41]

The main functions of external finance and enterprise governance were also performed by the banks during the industrial spurt in Germany during the late nineteenth century:

> ...the Universal Bank, which in Germany, along with most of the countries on the continent, became the dominant form of banking. The difference between banks of the Credit Mobilier type and commercial banks in the advanced industrial country of the time (England) was absolute. Between the English banks essentially designed to serve as a source of short-term capital and a bank designed to finance the long-term investment needs of the economy, there was a complete gulf. The German banks, which may be taken as a paragon of the type of Universal Bank, successfully combined the basic idea of the Credit Mobilier with the short-term activities of commercial banks.... But the German banks, and with them the Austrian and Italian banks, established the closest possible relations with industrial enterprises. A German bank, as the saying went, accompanied an industrial enterprise from the cradle to the grave, from establishment to liquidation through all the vicissitudes of its

existence. Through the device of formally short-term but in reality long-term current account credits and through development of the institution of supervisory boards to the position of most powerful organs within corporate organizations, the banks acquired a formidable degree of ascendancy over industrial enterprises, which extended far beyond the sphere of financial control into that of entrepreneurial and management decisions.... The Continental practice in the field of industrial investment banking must be conceived as specific instruments of industrialization in a backward country.[42]

Thus, historical experiences as well as the specific constraints and context of the exsocialist countries and the backward developing countries indicate that they would evolve a bank-oriented financial system to tackle the problems of external finance and enterprise governance, at any rate, during the initial stages of their evolution towards a sound market economy. Further, such a system, particularly in respect of ex-post monitoring appears to be superior in performance than the market-based takeover or bankruptcy mechanisms. 'There are good reasons to choose the German rather than the British style of capital markets: substantial bank involvement both in long-term lending and management of industrial companies, discouragement of hostile takeovers. In practice, the effectiveness of German banks as monitors of company performance...and the apparent ineffectiveness of the British takeover mechanism in eliminating poor performance and creating post-merger efficiency gains...makes the German system unambiguously superior.'[43] Similar is the case with the Japanese main bank system.[44]

NOTES

1. See Douglass C. North, 'Economic Performance Through Time', *The American Economic Review*, Vol. 84, No. 3 (June 1994).
2. See Joseph A. Schumpeter, *The Theory of Economic Development* (Cambridge, Mass: Harvard University Press, 1934) and Joseph A. Schumpeter, *Business Cycles*, Volume I and II (New York: McGraw-Hill Book Company, 1939).
3. See Michio Morishima, *Capital and Credit: A New Formulation of General Equilibrium Theory* (Cambridge: Cambridge University Press, 1992).
4. For the weaknesses in the financial systems of the developing countries, see World Bank, *World Bank Development Report 1989: Financial Systems and Development* (Washington, DC: World Bank, 1989).

5. For the passive financial systems in ex-socialist countries and emerging market economies, see Gerard Capiro, David Folkerts-Landau, and Timothy D. Law, (eds.), *Building Sound Finance in Emerging Market Economies* (Washington, DC: International Monetary Fund and World Bank, 1994).
6. For this terminology, see Erik Berglof, *Corporate Governance in Transition Economies: The Theory and its Implications* (Washington, DC: World Bank Economic Development Institute, 1994).
7. See Alexander Gerschenkron, *Economic Backwardness in Historical Perspective* (Cambridge: Harvard University Press, 1962).
8. See Hans. J. Blommestein and Michael G. Spencer, 'The Role of Financial Institutions in the Transition to a Market Economy', in *Building Sound Finance in Emerging Market Economies*, ed. Gerard Caprio, David Folkerts-Landau and Timothy D. Lane (Washington: World Bank and IMF, 1994).
9. Ibid.; see also V.V. Bhatt, 'Japan: Main Bank System and India: Lead Bank System', *International Journal of Development Banking*, Vol. 12, No. 1 (January 1994). See also Chapter 3 of this book.
10. The recent collapse of the largest Russian Investment Company—MMM—indicates the fate of premature attempts at developing capital markets. See 'Russia's Crumbling Financial Pyramid', *The Economist* (30 July-5 August 1994), pp. 67–69. See also 'China's Stock Markets: Erupting', *The Economist* (6–12 August 1994), pp. 60–61.
11. This process was somewhat similar to that in Japan; see Chapter 3 in this book; see also Ernst-Ludwig von Thadden, *Centralised Decentralisation: Corporate Governance in the East German Economic Transition* (Washington, DC: World Bank Economic Development Institute, 1994).
12. Governments will have to invest in restructuring SOEs as well as in infrastructure projects. Hence there would be fiscal deficits. What is essential is to have a surplus in current account—that is government saving to finance investment. The capital account deficit, arising out of investment expenditures, would be necessary but should be financed by issuing bonds to the public and not by resort to central bank credit. See in this connection Michael Bruno, 'Stabilization and Reform in Eastern Europe', in *The Transition in Eastern Europe*, Volume 1, ed. Olivier Jean Blanchard, Kenneth A. Foot and Jeffrey D. Sachs (Chicago: The University of Chicago Press, 1994).
13. See Hans J. Blommstein et al. (n. 8 above).
14. See Erik Berglof (n. 6 above).
15. See Yingyi Qian, *Reforming Corporate Governance and Finance in China* (Washington, DC: World Bank Economic Development Institute, 1994).
16. See Chapter 3.
17. See John M. Litwack, *Corporate Governance, Banks and Fiscal Reform in Russia* (Washington, DC: World Bank Economic Development Institute, 1994).
18. See Chapters 3 and 4.
19. For such a role of the main banks in Japan see Chapter 3. For the role of universal banks in the late nineteenth century in Germany see Joseph A. Schumpeter, *Business Cycles*, Volume 1 (New York: McGraw Hill Book Company Inc., 1939), pp. 348–49. To quote: 'While elsewhere, this use of short-term credit, created *ad hoc*, led to a situation in which it was up to the entrepreneurs to look (unless receipts were coming in quickly) for some method of funding and thus consolidating their position,

these 'industrial' or 'promoting' banks provided machinery to do this themselves. They took care of the necessary issues of stocks and bonds, thus helping the enterprise to redeem its short debt and providing it with additional means. In order to effect this, they were ready to take those stocks or bonds for their own account not only if they were unable to place them, but also in the ordinary course of their business routine. They thus were able to await developments before making an offer to the public and even, in many cases, to keep a parcel for good. When eventually they placed the securities acquired, they again financed the private investors so that, temporarily at least, the transaction often meant no more than a shift in assets' (pp. 348–49). See also W.P. Kennedy, *Industrial Structure, Capital Markets, and the Origin of British Economic Decline* (Cambridge: Cambridge University Press, 1987).
20. See Erik Berglof (n. 6 above) and John M. Litwack (n. 17 above).
21. See Gerard Roland, *Political Economy Issues of Ownership Transformation in Eastern Europe* (Washington, DC: World Bank Economic Development Institute, 1994).
22. The behavior of banks seems to have already changed in the direction of profit-oriented functioning. See in this connection, Peter Dittus, *Corporate Governance in Central Europe: The Role of Banks* (Bank of International Settlements, 1993). Recently 20 private banks have been identified by the first World Bank project as the strongest in Russia's fledgling finance sector. Under that project, the 20 banks—located in nine cities across the country—are being paired with international banks in the West to sharpen their lending and accounting skills. The World Bank is also providing resources, along with the European Bank for Reconstruction and Development, to these banks to enable them to provide long-term loans to privatized enterprises, which require such assistance for their restructuring projects. See *World Bank News*, Vol. XIII, No. 25 (23 June 1994).
23. See in this connection, Frank Packer, *The Role of Long-Term Credit Banks within the Main Bank System* (Washington: World Bank Economic Development Institute, Working Paper Number 94–06, 1994) and Japan Development Bank, *Policy-Based Finance: The Experience of Post-War Japan* (Tokyo: Japan Development Bank, 1993).
24. For the role of development banks, see Chapter 2.
25. For the vital role of such governance structure for the economy as a whole, see World Bank, *Governance: The World Bank Experience* (Washington: World Bank, 1994). To quote: '...governance is how power is exercised in the management of a country's economic and social resources for development.' See also the forthcoming volume on Japanese Civil Service and Development by the World Bank Economic Development Institute.
26. See Alexander Gerschenkron (n. 7 above).
27. See Gerard Caprio, Jr. and Lawrence H. Summers, *Finance and its Reform: Beyond Laissez Faire* (Washington: World Bank Policy Research Working Paper, No. 1171, 1993).
28. See Chapter 3. See also Sanjay Dhar and Marcelo Selowsky, 'Dealing with the Bad Debt Problem in Transition Economies', *Finance and Development*, Vol. 31, No. 2 (June 1994).
29. See Chapter 3.

30. See Gerard Caprio, Jr. and Lawrence Summers (n. 27 above) and Chapter 3 in this book.
31. See Michael Bruno (n. 12 above).
32. See in this connection, World Bank, *East Asian Miracle* (Washington, DC: World Bank, 1993). In the East Asian countries, the state policies tilted in favor of export promotion. And this played a strategic role in development in several ways. First, it provided the means for equipment and technology imports. Second, it provided an effective channel for the acquisition of knowledge relating to technology, multinational firms, international markets and marketing technologies; this was one of the significant factors contributing to acquisition of technological knowledge and thus had externality of critical importance. Third, it provided a *transparent unequivocal yardstick* for the measurement of performance of industries and firms—a yardstick much more reliable than any sophisticated cost-benefit analysis. It is this yardstick which enabled the government to determine its policies for incentives and subsidies as well as penalties. Fourth, it created an environment that *minimized* corruption and rent-seeking activities. And finally, it disciplined government as well as firms and banks in formulating their plans and policies; no other disciplining factors could have been as effective as export performance.

    The book also emphasizes that liberalization of imports should not precede export success and that liberalization of the financial sector should not imply relaxation of interest rate controls or entry restrictions; a sound bank-oriented financial system with adequate prudential regulatory mechanisms with sanctions has an externality that should not be endangered by premature attempts at liberalization. This is an important lesson for the emerging market economies from the experiences of the East Asian countries. In this connection, see also, Juro Teranishi and Yutaka Kosai (eds.), *The Japanese Experience of Economic Reforms* (London: Macmillan Press, 1993). See also Chapter 2 in this book.
33. See Michael Bruno (n. 12 above).
34. Ibid.; and Ronald I. McKinnon, 'Financial Growth and Macroeconomic Stability in China: 1978–1992: Implications for Russia and Other Transitional Economies', *Journal of Comparative Economics*, Vol. 18, No. 3 (June 1994); See also Chapter 3 in this book.
35. Ibid.; and David Dollar, 'Macroeconomic Management and the Transition to Market in Vietnam', *Journal of Comparative Economics*, Vol. 18, No. 3 (June 1994).
36. See Gerard Roland (n. 21 above).
37. See Douglass C. North, 'Economic Performance Through Time', *American Economic Review*, Vol. 84, No. 3 (June 1994). To quote: 'Privatization is not a panacea for solving poor economic performance.... Institutions form the incentive structure of a society, and the political and economic institutions, in consequence, are the underlying determinants of economic performance. Time as it relates to economic and social change is the dimension in which the learning process of human beings shapes the way institutions evolve.... It is adaptive rather than allocative efficiency which is the key to long-run growth.'
38. See Ernst-Ludwig von Thadden (n. 11 above).
39. See Yingyi Qian (n. 15 above) and David Dollar (n. 35 above).
40. See Chapter 3 in this book. See also Masahiko Aoki and Hugh Patrick (eds.), *Japanese Finance and the Main Bank System* (Oxford: Oxford University Press, 1994).

41. See G. Hallett, 'West Germany', *Government and Economics in the Post-War World*, eds. A. Graham with A. Seldon (London: Routledge, 1990), pp. 83–84.
42. See Alexander Gerschenkron (n. 7 above), pp. 270–271.
43. N.F.R. Crafts, 'Productivity Growth Reconsidered', *Economic Policy*, 15 (1992), pp. 387–414.
44. See Paul Sheard, 'The Main Bank System and Corporate Monitoring and Control in Japan', *Journal of Economic Behaviour and Organization* (1989). See also 'Bankruptcy', *The Economist* (25–31 July, 1–7 August 1992).

Statistical Appendices

A. Appendix to Chapter 3

Statistical Appendix Relating to the Main Bank System

Appendix A
Statistical Tables

Table 1:	Classification of Listed Japanese Firms into Main Bank Groupings
Table 2:	Analysis of Listed Japanese Firms According to Rank of Main Bank as Shareholder in 1980 and as a Source of Borrowings in 1971
Table 3:	Analysis of Outside Directors of Listed Japanese Firms 1980
Table 4:	Main Bank Indicators: The Long—Term Credit Banks Compared with Other Banks
Table 5:	Statistics of Estimated Sample
Table 6:	Diversification of Bank Trading and Its Effect on Terms of Loan
Table 7:	Size and Structure of Large Japanese Banks by Business
Table 8:	The Percentage of Outstanding Loans for Plant and Equipment Investment in Selected Industries by Bank Category
Table 9:	Cross-Holding Ratios 1962 to 1974

Table 1
Classification of Listed Japanese Firms into Main-Bank Groupings.*

			Proportion of Total Assets	
Name of Grouping	*Number of Firms*	*Relative Frequency (%)*	*Relative Frequency (%)*	*Cumulative Frequency (%)*
Mitsui	105	12.0	18.0	
Mitsubishi	117	13.4	13.7	
Sumitomo	108	12.4	14.4	
Fuyo (Fuji)	105	12.0	10.3	
Sanwa	51	5.8	7.6	
Daiichi Kangin	71	8.1	917	73.7
Affiliation with one of above in state of flux	33	3.8	2.7	76.4
Seven other city banks	70	8.0	4.5	80.9
Industrial Bank of Japan	51	5.8	10.5	91.4
Long-Term Credit Bank	16	1.8	0.4	91.8
Other Financial Institutions	33	3.8	1.0	92.8
Affiliated with Non-Financial Firm	52	6.0	1.9	94.7
Affiliation Unknown	61	7.0	5.3	100.0
Total	873	100.0	100.0	

* For the 873 non-financial firms listed on the Tokyo Stock Exchange (First Section) in 1982. Group affiliation was determined on the basis of shareholdings, borrowings, representation on boards of directors, and historical associations.
Source: Keizai chosa kyokai, 1983: *Keiretsu no kenkyu: daiichibu jojo kigyohen*, pp. 1–22. Reproduced from Sheard (1989).

Table 2
Analysis of Listed Japanese Firms according to Rank of Main Bank as Shareholder in 1980 and as Source of Borrowings in 1971

	Breakdown of Listed Firms			
	Rank of Main Bank as Shareholder, 1980		*Rank of Main Bank as Source Borrowings, 1971*	
Rank	*No. of Firms*	*Relative Frequency (%)*	*No. of Firms*	*Relative Frequency (%)*
1	124	16.4	489	67.3
2	172	22.7	125	17.2
3	113	14.9	47	6.5
4	84	11.1	17	2.3
5	52	6.9	14	1.9
6	34	4.5	7	1.0
7	20	2.6	10	1.4
8	13	1.7	7	1.0
9	15	2.0	2	0.3
10 or more	131[a]	17.3	9	1.2
Total	758[b]	100.0	727[c]	100.0

[a] Includes 86 not among top twenty shareholders.
[b] Forty-four of the 809 firms examined had no borrowings in 1981, and for seven relevant information was not obtainable.
[c] Sixty-nine of the 809 firms examined had no borrowings in either or both 1980 and 1971, and for another thirteen information was not obtainable.
Source: Compiled from Keizai chosa kyokai, 1973: *Keiretsu no kenkyu: daiichibu jojo kigyohen*; Kigyo keiretsu soran, 1981: *Kigyo keiretsu soran*. Reproduced from Sheard (1989).

Table 3
Analysis of Outside Directors of Listed Japanese Firms, 1980 [a]

	Breakdown of Firms According to Number of Directors Formerly or Concurrently from:			
Number of Directors	*Outside the Firm*	*Largest Shareholder*	*Largest Source of Borrowings (Main Bank)*	*Civil Service or Government*
1	96 (11.9)	156 (19.3)	252 (33.1)	145 (17.9)
2	102 (12.6)	90 (11.1)	89 (11.7)	48 (5.3)
3	89 (11.0)	52 (6.4)	26 (3.4)	29 (3.6)
4	95 (11.7)	27 (3.3)	5 (0.7)	20 (2.5)
5	82 (10.1)	19 (2.3)	3 (0.4)	14 (1.7)
6	67 (8.3)	24 (3.0)		7 (1.7)
7	48 (5.9)	18 (2.2)		2 (0.2)
8	43 (5.3)	13 (1.6)		2 (0.2)
9	36 (4.4)	10 (1.2)		1 (0.1)
10	28 (3.5)	5 (0.6)		2 (0.2)
11	14 (1.7)	6 (0.7)		1 (0.1)
12	8 (1.0)	3 (0.4)		1 (0.1)
13	6 (0.7)	2 (0.2)		
14	6 (0.7)	2 (0.2)		
15	4 (0.5)			
16	3 (0.4)			
17	2 (0.2)			
18	1 (0.1)			
19	2 (0.2)	1 (0.1)		
None	77 (9.5)	381 (47.1)	386 (50.7)	537 (66.4)
Total	809 (100.0)	809 (100.0)	761[b] (100.0)	809 (100.0)

[a] All firms were listed on the Tokyo Stock Exchange (First Section) in 1980.

[b] Forty-three firms had no borrowings in 1980, and for five firms the largest source of borrowings could not be identified.

Source: Compiled from Kigyo keiretsu soran, 1981: *Kigyo keiretsu soran*. Reproduced from Sheard (1989).

Table 4

Main Bank Indicators: The Long-Term Credit Banks Compared with Other Banks

	1967 (1st Section Tokyo)			*1990 (1st Section Tokyo)*			*1990 (1st & 2nd Section: Tokyo)*	
	No. of Cos. to which lead Lender	*No. of Cos. to which Second Director*	*of which President/ Chairman*	*No. of Cos. to which Lead Lender*	*No. of Cos. to which Second Director*	*of which President/ Chairman*	*No. of Companies for which Leading Bank Shareholder (Over 3%)*	*No. of Companies for which Second Bank Shareholder (over 3%)*
Mitsubishi	87	61	4	134	91	8	83	129
Sumitomo	78	42	4	113	50	7	77	106
Mitsui	78	31	2	102	40	0	48	89
Fuji	73	55	10	126	87	6	116	137
IBJ	70	48	8	70	75	17	85	106
DKB	61	58	11	95	103	10	127	127
Sanwa	52	34	3	62	56	4	102	132
LTCB	20	4	0	18	22	6	22	69
Tokai	17	13	1	29	30	2	88	102
Daiwa	9	16	1	16	25	2	47	82
Saitama	8	0	0	11	13	2	27	31
Kyowa	6	12	0	12	19	0	24	56
Taiyo-Kobe	5	7	1	15	26	3	49	80
NCB	4	3	0	5	6	0	5	36
Bo Tokyo	2	7	1	8	27	3	8	12
Hok. Taku.	1	8	0	5	10	1	16	21

Source: Keiretsu no Kenkyu, 1968, 1991; Kigyo Keiretsu Soran, 1991, 1992.

Notes: Following the conventions of keiretsu no kenkyu, the loans of all financial institutions in the six major bank groups (and the Tokai group) have been aggregated to determine the largest lender. Companies which are seconded directors are calculated for the city banks individually. DKB and Taiyo-Kobe figures for 1967 are the sum of the pairs of pre-merger banks. Shareholding numbers for Mitsui and Taiyo-Kobe are from 1989.

Reproduced from Frank Packer, The Role of Long-Term Credit Banks within the Japanese Main Bank System, (Mimeo., 1993).

Table 5

Statistics of Estimated Sample

Characteristics and Terms of Loan	*Units*	*Total Sample (except for 100 percent)*			*Under the Average Dependence*			*Over the Average Dependence*			*100 Percent Dependence*		
		A	S	N	A	S	N	A	S	N	A	S	N
Nominal Rate of Interest	%	6.43	0.85	2,159	6.36	0.83	1,133	6.52	0.86	1,026	6.58	0.87	727
Ratio of Compensating Balances	%	47.2	34.2	2,171	49.0	34.7	1,135	45.2	33.5	1,036	62.1	46.4	702
Degree of Main Bank Dependence	%	57.3	19.8	2,337	41.8	11.1	1,218	74.1	11.9	1,119	100.0	0	830
Turnover	Million Yen	1,356	1,140	2,337	1,516	1,197	1,218	1,181	1,048	1,119	969	1,509	803
Rate of Current Profit to Turnover	%	2.4	4.3	2,143	2.4	4.2	1,120	2.5	4.4	1,023	3.3	5.2	717
Ratio of Net–Worth to Total Capital	%	10.8	8.0	1,767	10.6	7.8	946	11.1	8.2	821	11.9	8.3	488

Source: Small Business Finance Corporation, Business Survey on Small and Medium-Sized Firms, September 1984.

Notes:1. Firms are divided into four sub-groups depending on their degree of main bank dependence. The average degree of main bank dependence 57.3 per cent is for the total sample except for 100 per cent dependence.

2. Some firms, which have their turnover less than 10 million yen or more than 5000 million yen, are excluded from the above samples. Reproduced from Horiuchi (1992).

Table 6

Diversification of Bank Trading and its Effects on Terms of Loan

Characteristics of Terms of Loan	*Units*	*One Bank Trading*	*Two Banks Trading*	*Three Banks Trading*	*Four Banks Trading*
Nominal Rate of Interest	%	6.38	6.45	6.31	6.07
Ratio of Compensating Balances	%	42.8	36.3	38.0	38.6
Degree of Main Bank Dependence	%	100.0	74.3	58.8	45.9
Turnover	100 Million Yen	12.1	14.5	17.8	28.7
Rate of Current Profit to Turnover	%	2.8	3.1	2.6	2.6
Ratio of Net-Worth to Total Capital	%	12.0	12.8	12.8	11.6
Number of Firms		117	149	194	391

Source: Same as in Table 5.

Notes: 1. Samples are restricted by the same conditions as of Table 5. The four groups are those of firms with trade relationships with banks in both loan and deposit markets.

Reproduced from Horiuchi (1992).

Table 7
Size and Structure of Some Large Japanese Banks by Business

Banks	*Total No. of Borrowing Firms*	*Ranking by This Total Number*	*Share of Borrowing Firms with Main Bank Relationship in Total (%)*
City Bank			
Dai-Ichi Kangyo Bank	24,479	1	31.2
Mitsubishi Bank	20,922	2	32.7
Long-Term Credit Bank			
Industrial Bank of Japan	3,035	17	19.7
Long-Term Credit Bank of Japan	2,060	28	7.8
Regional Bank			
Yokohama Bank	3,707	15	28.4
Shizuoka Bank	3,037	16	44.6
Second Regional Bank			
Nagoya Bank	2,011	29	20.0
Hyogo Bank	1,454	46	19.4
Trust and Banking Corporation (TBC)			
Mitsubishi TBC	2,288	22	7.7
Mitsui TBC	2,228	24	9.3

Source: Shukan Diamond (ed.), 'Tokubetsu Chosa: Kono Ginko no za Ayaushi' (Special Report: Some Banks Declining Shukan Diamond, vol. 76 (March 5, 1988). Reproduced from Horiuchi (1990).

Table 8

The Percentage of Outstanding Loans for Plant and Equipment Investment in Selected Industries by Bank Category

	1956			*1966*			*1974*			*1988*		
	Long-Term Credit Banks	*JDB*	*City Banks*	*Long-Term Credit Banks*	*JDB*	*City Banks*	*Long-Term Credit Banks*	*JDB*	*City Banks*	*Long-Term Credit Banks*	*JDB*	*City Banks*
Machinery	64.7%	14.5%	6.8%	42.9%	5.9%	5.0%	36.7%	5.5%	18.4%	12.0%	5.6%	28.6%
Chemicals	56.2%	14.9%	10.7%	41.5%	10.3%	14.4%	38.0%	7.3%	18.6%	26.2%	14.1%	26.7%
Textiles	47.8%	14.9%	21.2%	46.7%	5.6%	7.6%	35.1%	7.1%	18.1%	7.7%	3.1%	25.8%
Mining	42.1%	49.6%	1.4%	20.0%	71.4%	2.0%	26.7%	34.5%	12.9%	12.1%	8.5%	13.1%
Steel	63.7%	22.5%	4.2%	43.9%	2.6%	9.5%	39.7%	3.4%	15.8%	28.6%	10.5%	15.2%
Shipping	22.5%	47.6%	24.7%	3.5%	70.8%	9.8%	17.7%	59.7%	12.4%	9.8%	39.2%	14.5%
Electric Power	29.2%	46.3%	12.2%	28.1%	44.7%	6.1%	32.1%	28.2%	11.1%	25.6%	35.3%	10.4%
All Loans for P&E Investment	37.5%	33.1%	16.8%	36.1%	17.4%	15.2%	29.1%	11.3%	30.2%	8.9%	6.0%	32.9%

Source: Industrial Bank of Japan 75 Year History for years 1956, 1968, 1974; the Bank of Japan Economic Statistics Annual and Nikkei telecom for 1988.

Note: The category of machinery includes general industrial machinery, electric machine tools, transportation machinery (including automobiles and ships), and precision machinery.

Reproduced from Packer (1993). see Table 4.

Table 9
Cross-holding Ratios, 1962 to 1974

	Mitsubishi	*Mitsui*	*Sumitomo*	*Fuyo*	*Daiichi K.*	*Sanwa*
1962.9	17.30	8.80	20.13	10.49	10.14	7.58
1966.9	16.81	10.52	18.43	11.17	10.85	9.07
1970.9	20.71	14.14	21.83	15.26	17.19	11.18
1974.9	26.57	17.37	24.71	19.10	16.90	13.01

Source: Itoh, Misumi, and Ichimura (1990). Reproduced from Ito (1992), p. 191.

B. Appendix to Chapter 4

Statistical Appendix: India—Structure and Efficiency of the Financial System

Appendix B
Statistical Tables

Table 1: Indicators of Financial Development
Table 2: Structure of Household Sector's Saving
Table 3: Structure of the Financial System—Gross Financial Assets of Financial Institutions
Table 4: Institutional Structure of Selected Financial Systems: Assets as Percentage of Total Gross Assets of the Financial System
Table 5: Selected Securities Markets: 1987
Table 6: Network of Financial Institutions
Table 7: Public Sector Banks: Income and Expenditure
Table 8: Indicators of the Quality of the Portfolio of Banks
Table 9: The Industrial Credit and Investment Corporation of India (ICICI) Spreads
Table 10: ICICI: Loan Recovery Performance
Table 11: Performance of Selected Projects/Companies Financed by the ICICI during 1981–87
Table 12: Performance of Indicators of Selected Companies
Table 13: Income Expenditure: Korea Development Bank and Korea Long Term Credit Bank
Table 14: Performance of Selected Projects Financed by the Korea Development Bank during 1976–85

Table 1
Indicators of Financial Development

Indicators	*1965–66*	*1969*	*1981–82*	*1989–90*	*1990–91*
1. Financial Interrelations Ratio (Net increase in Financial Assets to Net Capital Formation)	0.98	—	1.86	2.50	—
2. Financial Assets of the Financial System/GDP (Percent)	—	—	62	94	
3. Aggregate Deposits of Banks/GNP (Percent)	—	—	25.7	35.3	36.8
4. Household Sector's Saving in the Form of Financial Assets/NDP (Percent)	5.5	—	9.7	12.6	12.2
5. Rural Deposits/Total Deposits (Percent)	—	3.1	—	15.0	15.3
6. Rural Bank Branches/ Total Bank Branches	—	22.5	—	58.1	58.4
7. Population per Bank Branch	—	65,000	19,000	11,600	11,000

Source: Reserve Bank of India, *Report on Currency and Finance 1989–90*: and Annual Report 1990–91: V. V. Bhatt. *Development Perspectives* (Pergamon Press, Oxford, 1980) Chapter 10; Reserve Bank of India Bulletins January, 1991 & January 1992.

Table 2
Structure of Household Sector's Saving (Percent of Net Domestic Product)

Saving	*1981–82* *11.8*	*1985–86* *12.2*	*1989–90* *15.5*	*1990–91* *15.5*
1. Physical Assets	5.2	4.4	5.6	5.8
2. Financial Assets	9.4	10.7	12.6	12.2
3. Financial Liabilities	2.8	2.9	2.7	2.5
4. Net Financial Assets (2–3)	6.6	7.8	9.9	9.7
5. Net Financial Saving/Total Saving (Percent)	56	64	64	63

Source: Reserve Bank of India, *Report on Currency and Finance*, 1989–90 and *Annual Report*, 1990–91.

Table 3
Structure of the Financial System—Gross Financial Assets of Financial Institutions

	1981		1989	
	(Percent of Total Assets)	*(Percent of GDP)*	*(Percent of Total Assets)*	*(Percent of GDP)*
A. Banking System	69	43	60	56
i) Reserve Bank of India	14	9	12	11
ii) Banks	55	34	48	45
B. Specialised Financial Institutions	11	7	17	16
C. Social Security Institutions: (Insurance, Pension & Provident Fund)	19	12	23	22
D. Financial System Total Assets	100	62	100	94

Source: Estimates Based on data given in Reserve Bank of India, *Annual Report 1989–90 and Report on Currency and Finance, 1989–90.*

Table 4
Institutional Structure of Selected Financial Systems: Assets as a Percentage of Total Gross Assets of the Financial System

	Developed Countries (Average: 1985)	*Advanced Developing Countries (Average: 1985)*	*South Korea (1984)*	*India (1989)*
1. Central Bank	5	24	12	12
2. Deposit Banks	57	59	50	48
3. Specialised lending institutions*	14	11	33	17
4. Contractual saving institutions	24	6	5	23

* Includes collective investment institutions.
Source: World Bank, *World Development Report, 1989* and Sources cited in Table A-3.

Table 5
Selected Securities Markets: 1987

		A *Mature Markets*				*B* *Emerging Markets*			
		USA	UK	Japan	Canada	India	Brazil	Korea	Thailand
1.	Number of stock exchanges	12	6	7	5	19	9	1	1
2.	Number of listings	6,727	2,015	2,019	1,146	2,390	592	626	175
3.	Market capitalisation (US$ billion)	3,506	827	4,393	291	27	44	141	26
4.	Share of individuals in the ownership of the value of corporate securities (percent)	53	35	31		37			

Source: The Industrial Finance Corporation, *Emerging Markets Data Base*: Reserve Bank of India Bulletin Feb. 1983: *The World Guide to the World Securities Markets* and The Centre for Monitoring Indian Economy: *Basic Statistics Relating to the India Economy*, Vol. I August 1991.

Table 6
Network of Financial Institutions

	1971	1990
1. Reserve Bank of India (RBI) (Central Bank)		
2. Commercial Banks		
Number	87	198
Branches	12,000	580,940
of which:		
(a) Rural Banks		
Number		196
Branches		14,247
(b) Foreign Banks		
Number		21
Branches		136
3. Cooperative Banks		
		(Number)
(a) State Cooperative Banks		28
(b) Central Cooperative Banks		354
(c) State/Central Land Development Banks		19
(d) Primary Agricultural Credit Societies		87,000
(e) Primary Cooperative Banks		1,331
4. Term Lending Institutions		
A. All India		
(a) Industrial Development Bank of India (Apex Development Bank) (IDBI)		
(b) Industrial Credit and Investment Corporation of India (ICICI)		
(c) Industrial Finance Corporation of India (IFCI)		
(d) Industrial Reconstruction Bank of India (IRBI)		
(e) National Bank for Agriculture and Rural Development (NABARD)		
(f) Agricultural Finance Corporation (AFC)		
(g) Export-Import Bank of India (Exim Bank)		
(h) Small Industries Development Bank of India (SIDBI)		
(i) National Housing Bank (NHB)		
(j) Housing Development Finance Corporation Ltd. (HDFC)		
(k) Housing and Urban Development Corporation Ltd. (HUDCO)		
(l) Infrastructure Leasing and Financial Services Ltd. (ILAFS)		
(m) Risk Capital and Technology Finance Corporation Ltd. (RCTFC)		
(n) Tourism Finance Corporation of India Ltd. (TFCI)		
(o) The Technology Development and Information Company of India Ltd. (TDICI)		
B. State Level Institutions		
(a) State Financial Corporations (SFCs) Number		18
(b) State Industrial Development Corporations (SIDCs) Number		26

5. Social Security and Investment Institutions	
(a) Life Insurance Corporation of India (LIC)	
(b) General Insurances Corporation of India (GIC)	
(c) Employees Provident Fund (EPF)	
(d) Mutual Funds	
Number (excluding UTI)	7

Table 7
Public Sector Banks: Income and Expenditure
(percent of total assets)

	1987	*1990*
1. Interest income	7.23	8.50
2. Other Income	0.67	0.82
3. Total income	7.90	9.32
4. Cost of Funds	5.46	6.48
5. Gross spread (3–4)	2.42	2.84
6. Administrative cost	2.31	2.68
7. Provision for risk or actual defaults	NA	NA
	—	—
8. Administrative cost plus risk	2.31	2.68
9. Gross profits (5–8)	0.11	0.16
10. Capital and reserves as a percentage of total advances	3.67	4.64
11. Non-performing advances as a percentage of total advances*		10–15

* Estimated on the basis of the quality of portfolio relating to agricultural and industrial advances. See Table 8.

Source: (1) Estimates based on data given in Indian Banks' Association, Financial Analysis of Banks, 1987, Volume I and (2) Reserve Bank of India, Report on Currency and Finance, 1987–88, 1989–90 and 1990–91

Table 8
Indicators of the Quality of the Portfolio of Banks

	1986	*1987*	*1988*	*1990*
Recovery performance of direct agricultural advances: Percentage of recoveries to demand	56.5	57.1	56.8	—
Loans outstanding to sick small scale industry as a proportion of total loans to small scale industry (percent)	—	17.7	17.6	15.6
Loans outstanding to sick non-SSI industry as a proportion of total loans to Non-SSI industry (percent)	—	—	12.0	11.9
Loans to all sick units as a percentage of total bank advances	—	9.4	9.7	9.2
Loans to all sick units as a percentage of bank advances to industry	—	18.1	18.2	17.4

Source: Estimates based on data given in the Reserve Bank of India, *Report on Trend and Progress of Banking in India, 1989–90.*
Note: A 'sick' industrial company, under the Sick Industrial Companies Act 1985, is one that has been registered for at least 7 years, has accumulated losses equal to or exceeding the sum of its paid-up capital and free reserves, and has suffered cash losses (before providing for depreciation) in both the current and preceding financial years.

Table 9
The Industrial Credit and Investment Corporation of India (ICICI) Spreads
(percent of total assets)

	1981	*1985*	*1988–89*
1. Gross yield	11.01	12.66	12.55
2. Cost of funds	7.67	8.30	9.03
3. Gross spread (1–2)	3.33	4.36	3.52
4. Risk*	0.87	1.64	1.79
5. Administrative cost	0.43	0.34	0.33
6. Risk plus administrative cost (4+5)	1.30	1.98	2.12
7. Profits (3–6)	2.03	2.38	1.40

* Risk is defined as gross risk before write-backs. (Provision for Risk)
Source: World Bank., *Staff Appraisal Report: India, Industrial Finance and Technical Assistance Project* (Washington: World Bank, March 7, 1988)

Table 10
ICICI: Loan Recovery Performance

	1982	*1985*	*1987–88*
1. Ratio of repayment of principal to repayment due (percent) (collection ratio)	73.3	73.0	74.4
2. Collection ratio after rescheduling (percent)	82.5	81.5	81.8
3. Arrears/total outstanding loans (percent)	2.4	2.6	3.1
4. Arrears after rescheduling/total outstanding loans (percent)	1.4	1.7	2.1

Source: World Bank., *Staff Appraisal Report: India, Industrial Finance and Technical Assistance Project* (Washington: World Bank, March 7, 1988)

Table 11
Performance of Selected Projects/Companies Financed by the ICICI during 1981–87

	Sample Size (Number of Projects)	*Projects Completed in Time (Percent)*		*Projects with Delays up to 12 Months (Percent)*	*Projects with Delays over 12 Months (Percent)*
Time over run					
(i)	113	47		37	16
(ii)	242	45		38	17
Cost over run		*Projects with cost over run (percent)*		*Aggregate cost over run (percent)*	*Average cost over run for affected projects (percent)*
(i)	113	41		19	30
(ii)	242	42		13	25
Profitability	*Sample size (Number of projects)*	*Projects with anticipated return of 12% or more (percent)*	*Projects making profits (percent)*	*Projects incurring losses (percent)*	*Projects yet to be completed (percent)*
(i)	53	45	59	41	–
(ii)	88	47	49	28	23
		Number of companies			
	Sample size	*Over 20%*		*10–19%*	*0.3–9%*
Exports to sales ratio	26	3		7	16

Source: World Bank, *Staff Appraisal Report: India, Industrial Finance and Technical Assistance Project.* (Washington: World Bank, March 7, 1988)

Table 12

Performance Indicators of Selected Companies

	Number of Companies in the Sample			*Number of Profit Making Companies (Percentage of 1)*			*Return on Capital Employed (Percent)*			*Gross Profits to Sale (Percent)*		
	1			*2*			*3*			*4*		
	81–82	*84–85*	*87–88*	*81–82*	*84–85*	*87–88*	*81–82*	*84–85*	*87–88*	*81–82*	*84–85*	*87–88*
1. RBI sample (i)	621	621	621	—	—	—	17.9	13.4	10.5	10.3	9.2	8.6
(ii)	720	1,867	621	—	—	—	11.2	8.7	8.3	9.3	8.3	8.6
2. IDBI sample 401	401	401	70	76	76	16.7	13.8	10.0	10.2	9.1	9.8	
3. ICICI sample 417	417	417	84	79	82	17.7	15.3	13.3	10.6	10.1	9.6	
4. Data base of capitaline series	—	542	824	—	81	77	—	5.55	3.51	—	6.35	7.26
5. Sample of Centre for Monitoring Indian Economy	—	—	—	—	—	—	—	9.8	8.3	—	7.6	7.2
6. Public sector companies (CMIE sample)	—	—	—	—	—	—	—	5.7	5.4	—	7.9	7.4
7. Average yield on ordinary shares	—	—	—	—	—	—	5.88	3.21	4.32	—	—	—
8. Government of India securities running yield	—	—	—	—	—	—	—	7.67	8.52	—	—	—

Source: Securities and Exchange Board of India, 1990. *State of the Capital Market—1989–90* and the Centre for Monitoring Indian Economy, *Basic Statistics Relating to the Indian Economy*, August 1990.

Table 13
Income Expenditure: Korea Development Bank and Korea Long-Term Credit Bank
(percent of total assets)

The Development Bank	*The Korea Development Bank*		*The Korea Long-Term Credit Bank*
	1985	*1987*	*1989*
1. Gross yield	8.80	8.50	8.30
2. Cost of funds	7.50	7.30	5.90
3. Gross spread (1–2)	1.30	1.20	2.40
4. Administrative cost	0.60	0.59	0.96
5. Default risk provision	0.36	0.53	0.30
6. Administrative cost plus risk (4+5)	0.96	1.12	1.26
7. Gross profits (3–6)	0.34	0.08	1.14

Sources: World Bank, *Staff Appraisal Report: Korea Development Bank* (Washington, DC: World Bank, 1989) and Annual Report of Korea Long Term Credit Bank (Seoul: 1990).

Table 14
Performance of Selected Projects Financed by the Korea Development Bank during 1976–85

	Sample Size	Projects Completed Ahead of Schedule (Percent)	Projects Completed in Time (Percent)	Project with Delayed Completion (Percent)
Time over run (i)	164	0.6	49	50.4
Cost over run		*Projects with cost saving (Percent)*	*Projects with cost overrun (Percent)*	*Project with anticipated costs (Percent)*
		72	26	2
Financial performance		*Projects with anticipated or more than anticipated return*	*Projects with below projected return*	*Projects with losses*
		44%	40%	16%
	Sample size (number of projects)	*Projects with higher than 15% exports to sales ratio (Percent)*	*Projects with below 15% exports to sales ratio (Percent)*	
	156	90	10	

Sources: World Bank, *Staff Appraisal Report: Korea Development Bank* (Washington, DC: World Bank, 1989) and Annual Report of Korea Long Term Credit Bank (Seoul: 1990).

Index

agricultural finance, 109–10, 111–12
Agricultural Finance Corporation, 212
Air India, 157
arm's length system, 177, 180
Asian Development Bank, 157
assets, disposal of, 76, 88; and loans, 17–18; real, 17; specialization in one type of, 19
asset deflation, 74
Automatic Teller Machine, 165

Bank of America, 165
Bank of Baroda, 163
Bank of Japan, 66, 68, 76, 78, 94, 96, 97, 98, 125
Bank of India, 163
bank-oriented system, 177, 190
bankruptcy laws, 100, 190
Bhagwati, J., 58, 117, 161
bond market, 54, 72, 89, 103, 179
borrowers, primary, 19
borrowing, 15, 16, 20
Botswana Development Corporation (BDC), 42, 47, 50, 55
brain-drain, 136
branch licensing policy, 126
Bretton Woods system, 22, 154
business ethics, common code of, 16–17

capital adequacy norms, 126, 154
capital gains tax, 171
capital finance, 112, 117
capital flows, exchange controls on, 151
capital markets, 11–12, 51, 54–57, 89, 110–11, 168–70; expansion of, 19–20; international, 128, 149–74
capital structure of firms, reconstruction of, 94
cash flow analysis, 19
central bank, international, 153
Central Bank, and need for autonomy, 34, 38; and need for a development orientation, 33; and promotion of financial innovations, 33; regulatory and promotional functions of, 34, 39
Central Mechanical Engineering Research Institute, 143–44
Citibank, 164–65
city banks, 24–29, 82, 85, 97
cofinancing arrangements, 162
collateral, 17, 18, 68, 69, 72, 73, 113, 118, 155–56, 180
collective guarantees, 17
commercial banks, case study of a, 24–32; in cooperation with development banks, 86–87; as dominating the financial system, 108–9; and investment banking, 12, 20, 100, 152, 168; lack of coordination with lead bank, 117; and lack of operational autonomy, 123; as part of financial network, 192; as subscriber to bonds of development banks, 53; and technology, 19
commission to bank agents, 31–32
competition, domestic, 125; international, 125; non-price, 78–79; price, 79, 96

competitive spirit, 55, 56
computronics, 151, 162
consortium finance, arrangements, 120; promotion of, 109, 118
control-oriented financial system, 177, 180; *see also* bank-oriented system
core bank relationship, 83
corporate bond market, deregulation of, 90–91
Corporation Reconstruction and Reconstructing Law, 70
credit allocation, 22, 23, 96–97, 100–101, 122, 163, 170–71; controls, 119–20, 124
Credit Authorization Scheme (CAS), 118–20
credit contract, 16
credit creation, 122–23
credit enhancement schemes, 155–56, 157, 162
credit instability, 34, 38
credit market, evolution of, 9, 150; informal, 21, 23; interlinking with labour market, 17; structure of, 35
Credit Mobilier concept, 10, 41, 42, 43, 62, 66, 67, 85–86, 101, 103, 189
credit money, innovation of, 18
Credit Rating and Information Services of India Ltd. (CRISIL), 54, 169
credit rationing, 35
credit transaction, 14–15, 51; interlinking with trade transactions, 17
creditworthiness, 149
crop insurance schemes, 23; absence of, 30
cross shareholding, 185; mechanisms, 75, 82, 83, 84, 88–89
currency rate swaps, 20, 22, 53, 151, 156–57, 159

Dai-Ichi Kangyo Bank, 82, 197, 200, 203, 205
dealers, 16, 169; established formal, and new technologies, 21; informal market, 19, 21
dealers' market, expansion of, 16
debt crisis of 1982, 154
debt service obligations, 158–59, 161–62
decentralized decision making, 29
delegated monitoring function, 71–72, 74, 76, 84, 103, 182
department store banking, 20
Deposit Insurance and Credit Guarantee Corporation, 108
deposits and lending, linking of, 30
deposit mobilization performance, 26, 78, 96–97
depositors, gifts to, 79
Depository Institutions Deregulation and Monetary Act, 1980, 90
deregulation, 11, 126–28, 152
design-engineering, 135–37, 138–39, 142, 143, 146
Design Engineering Consultancy Services, 57
Designated Bank System, 68
Designated Financial Institution System for Munitions Company Financing, 80
development banks, lead development bank function of, 113; and a competitive environment, 55, 60; coordination of, 112–13; and the creation of new markets, 47, 60; and financial innovations, 49, 60; and investment finance, 117; need for a plurality of, 55, 86–87; and operational autonomy, 56, 58, 60, 86, 129; and performance of public enterprises, 55–57; and promotion of specialized institutions, 54–55; and resource mobilization, 53–54, 55; and the role of the state, 58–60
development of mines, the role of the state in, 60
Discount and Finance House of India (DFHI), 54, 108, 168–69
division of labour, 14, 40, 153
Dodge stabilization plan, 70, 94, 96
door-to-door solicitation, 79

economies of scale, 18, 20, 21
economies of scope, 20, 72

economies of specialization, 20
education, and the role of the state, 58
Emerging Markets Growth Fund (EMGF), 165
Employees Provident Fund (EPF), 169, 213
enterprise, spirit of, 43
entrepreneurial assistance, 50, 60, 111, 112
entrepreneurial development programmes, 50–51
entrepreneurial exploitation, opportunities for, 58
equity share markets, 54, 69, 72, 103, 178–79
establishment expenses of city banks, 25
Euro-Commercial Paper (ECP), 154–55
Euro-market, 21–22, 91, 150
Euro-dollar market, 20, 91
ex-ante monitoring, 72–73, 84–85, 101, 103, 177, 180, 181, 188
ex-post monitoring, 85, 99, 101, 103, 177, 181, 188, 190
exchange rates, 22; policy, 127
export credit, 110
Export–Import Bank (EXIM), 110, 157, 212
export promotion, 12, 40–41, 59, 92–94, 97, 115, 125, 186–87
external assets, management of, 149
external debt management, 157, 158–59
externality, 33

Farmers' Protection Deposit Scheme, 30
financial innovations, 49–54, 129, 153–57, 168
financial instruments, diversity of, 20
fiscal deficits, 122–23
foreign banks, expansion of, 152; role of, 12, 164–65
foreign exchange, black market in, 166–67
foreign exchange cost, 150, 160, 162
Foreign Exchange and Foreign Trades Control Law, 90
foreign exchange license, 124
foreign exchange market, management of, 108
foreign exchange requirements, 57
foreign exchange reserves, management of, 158, 159–60, 172
foreign exchange transactions, 72
foreign direct investment policies, 126, 127
foreign investment, 164–65
Foreign Investment Promotion Board, 127
foreign portfolio capital, 51, 62
Fuji Steel, 85
Fukuda, S., 81
full convertibility on current account, 127
futures, 20

Gandhi, Mahatma, 27
General Insurance Corporation of India (GIC), 52, 53, 101, 110, 112, 213
gensaki, 90
German Universal Banks, 44, 45–46, 47, 50, 52, 56, 59–60, 62, 85, 103, 189
Gerschenkron, A., 60, 86, 100, 141–42, 176, 177
gifts tax, 171
gold, import duty on, 166–67
gold imports, 128
gold prices, domestic and foreign, 166–67
gold smuggling, 166–67
government intervention, 33–34, 101, 102, 122, 128–29
Grindlays Bank, 164

Hicks, John, 130
high-yielding varieties of seeds, 137
Hindustan Machine Tools, 144
Hong Kong Bank, 165
Horiuchi, A., 81
Horiuchi, T., 81, 83
Hoshi, T., 87
households, limited saving capacity of, 177, 178–79
Housing Development Finance Corporation (HDFC), 54, 212

Housing and Urban Development Corporation Ltd., 212
housing finance, 110, 168

Ikegaio Tekko, 85
import of capital goods and technology, 41
import duty, 128
import license, 124; licensing, 102, 127
import protection, 93
import substitution, 12, 59, 92–94, 97, 115, 125, 158, 160, 186–87
income tax, 171
INDIA FUND, 164
India Growth Fund Inc, 164
Indian Overseas Bank, 163
Indian Small Industries Service Institutes, 141
individualized financial transactions, 16
Industrial Bank of Japan, 10–11, 41–42, 44, 47, 50, 51–54, 56, 66, 68, 73, 81, 82, 84, 85–86, 93, 98, 101, 103, 142, 183, 184, 197, 200, 203
Industrial Credit and Investment Corporation of India (ICICI), 10, 42, 49, 51, 52, 53, 54, 56, 86, 109, 112–13, 115–16, 155, 157, 212, 215, 216
Industrial Development Bank of India (IDBI), 10, 42, 45, 49–56, 58, 85–86, 109, 110, 112–13, 142–45, 157, 170, 171, 212
Industrial Development Finance Institutions (DFI), 109
industrial enterprises, international competitiveness of, 59, 60
Industrial Finance Corporation of India (IFCI), 52, 86, 109, 112–13, 212
Industrial and Mining Development Bank of Iran, 10, 42, 47, 50–51, 52, 53, 55
industrial growth, 40
industrial licensing, 127
Industrial Reconstruction Bank of India (IRBI), 109, 212
industrialization, and the role of the state, 41–42, 46, 58; and technology change, 61
inflation, 122–23
informal market transactions, 111
information gathering, 20; costs of, 27, 30
Infrastructure Leasing and Financial Services Ltd., 212
inheritance tax, 171
innovations, cost and risk reducing, 22; introduction of, 9; and policy interventions, 22–23
input dealers, as a source of credit, 111
insurance, 18; deposit, 23; risk, 74
intercorporate shareholders, 88; *see also* cross shareholding
Inter Institutional Group (IIG), 52
Inter-Institutional Meeting (IIM), 112–14, 119
interest rates, 22, 79, 89, 96, 98, 109, 110, 122, 123, 126, 158; arbitrage, 90; convergence of, 151; policy, 166–67; regulation of, 163, 186; removal of restrictions on, 152; structure of, 170–71
interest rates ceiling, 22–23
interest rate swaps, 20, 22, 33, 151, 156–57, 159
interim monitoring, 85, 101, 83, 177, 180, 181
interlocking shareholding, 89
intermediaries, 16
international debt crisis, 34, 38
International Finance Corporation, 165
International Monetary Fund, 38, 152, 159
intervention, public or government, 33–34, 101, 102, 122, 128–29
investment banking, 12, 51–52, 54, 62, 100, 141, 152, 162, 168, 169
investment banks, 10, 20
investment financing, 112–13, 117
investment license, 124
Investor's Agency Department, 32–33

Japan Airlines, 85
Japan Centre for Economic Research, 83

Japan Development Bank, 84, 85, 183, 184
Japan Housing Loan Inc, 54
joint stock company with limited liability, 18

Keynes, J.M., 24, 33, 153
Korea Credit Guarantee Fund, 145
Korea Development Finance Company (KDFC), 10, 42, 45, 48–49, 51, 52, 54, 145
Korea Institute of Science and Technology, 45, 49, 145
Korea Investment and Finance Corporation (KIFC), 54–55
Korea Investment and Securities Co. Ltd., 55
Korea Long Term Credit Bank, 10, 11, 52, 53, 54, 101, 116, 218
Korea Technology Advancement Corporation, 145
Korean Development Bank, 85–86, 101, 115–16, 218, 219
Kyoto Institute of Economic Research, 83

Land Development Banks (LDBs), 111, 212
lead bank, and branch expansion programme, 121–22; and district development, 120–22; functions of, 113–14, 118–20; lack of coordination with commercial banks, 117; origin of, 117–18
lead bank system, 11, 61, 67, 106–7, 111
leasing, 54, 164, 168
legal framework, to reinforce trust and confidence, 20–21
legal bankruptcy, 75–76
lending, 15, 16
liberalization policies, 11, 125, 126–28, 167–71
Liberalized Exchange Rate Management System (LERMS), 127
licensing system, 124–25
life insurance companies, nationalization of, 110
Life Insurance Corporation of India (LIC), 52, 53, 101, 110, 112, 169, 213
Linder, S.B., 162
liquidation, 71, 79, 85, 89, 116, 180, 181, 189
Little, I.M.D.,138–39
loans, securitization of, 20
loan and deposit markets, 71, 72, 74, 79, 90–91, 96
loan recovery performance, 116, 122, 215
loan syndicates, 68, 181–82
long-term credit, 18, 51, 53, 54, 62, 68, 98, 114–15; banks, 85, 93
Long-Term Credit Bank of Japan, 82, 197, 200, 203
Long-Term Credit Bank of Korea, 85–86
long-term deposit, 31
lottery deposits, 79
low-income groups, mobilizing resources from, 10

main banks, and autonomy, 103, 124; as bearer of losses, 76; and core banks, 83; and entrepreneur and project appraisal, 72–73, 77, 84; and evaluation of new technology, 73; government role in, 66–67; impact of liberalization on, 89–92; as monitor of performance, 71, 74–75, 79, 84, 88; origin of, 67–70; reciprocal relationship between, 82–83
main bank system, 10–11, 19, 61, 66–105, 106–7, 112, 114, 125, 128
management changes, 71, 75, 79, 88, 100, 114, 181
management contracts, 57
management, and judgement capability, 45
managerial assistance, 60, 71, 111, 112, 116, 118, 143
market for negotiable certificates of deposits, 90
markets, protected domestic, 46–47

market for repurchases, 90; *see also* gensaki
market-oriented financial system, 177, 178; *see also* arm's length system
market size, increase in, 40–41, 49–50
Marx, Karl, 13, 177
mechanisms for information gathering, need for, 74–75
medium-term credit, 111
merchant banking, 52, 108, 163, 168
mergers, 46, 48, 71, 75, 76, 79, 85, 88, 100, 142
merger and acquisition (M&A) activity, 89
Merril Lynch, 164
military production, financing of, 68
Mirrlees, J.A. 138–39
Mitsubishi Bank, 82, 203
Mitsubishi group, 74, 88, 197, 200, 205
monetary stability, 21
money market, 110–11, 168–70
Money Market Deposit Accounts, 90
money market instruments, 54
money market mutual funds (MMMFs), 90
money lenders as source of credit, 111
monitoring devices, 74
monopoly, concept of, 127
mortgage loans, 110
multi-bank relationship of firms, 82, 99
multi-key currency market, 151
multinational corporations, 152
multiple banking system, 118, 119

National Bank for Agriculture and Rural Development (NABARD), 109–10, 212
National Development Banks, 56, 192
National Housing Bank (NHB), 110, 212
nationalization of banks, 24, 25, 33, 102, 108, 121
new banks, entry of, 126
New Japan Steel, 85
Nippon Yakin Kogdyo, 85
Nissan, 85
Nittoku Metal Industry, 85
norms to evaluate performance, 56, 57
note issuance facilities (NIFs), 20, 154–55, 169

options, 20
OPEC, 154

Packer, F., 81, 85
partnership relationship, between bank and firm, 71–89, 91–92, 181; between national and international banks, 163–64; between Reserve Bank of India and constituent banks, 129
payment settlement accounts, 71, 81, 84, 91
Pension Funds, 128
Perreire brothers, 10
personal guarantee, 16
Pigmy Deposit Scheme, 27, 30–32
Planning Commission, 144
portfolio investment by foreigners, 128
Post Office Savings Bank, 108–9
post-war debt in Japan, 69–70
poverty, removal of, 134–37
'prescriptive' controls, 58, 117, 161
price structure, rationalization of, 92
Primary Agricultural Cooperative Credit Societies (PACs), 111, 212
priority production system (PPS), 94–95
project appraisal, 44–45, 55–56, 77, 84, 85, 87, 93, 101, 103, 113–14, 116, 122–23, 124, 140, 146
project evaluation, 19, 116, 133, 143
project formulation, 57, 78, 138
Project Identification Centres (PICs), 135–37
project selection criteria, 132, 138, 140–41, 146
project supervision, 45, 77, 87, 101, 103, 114, 116, 122–23, 124, 143
projects, profitability of, 138, 141
'proscriptive' controls, 58, 117, 161
provident funds, 178
Punjab Industrial Development Corporation, 144

Reconstruction Finance Corporation (RFC), 94, 96

rediscounting, bills, 52, 111, 169–70
refinancing, 52, 108, 109, 110, 155, 169–70
Regional Rural Banks (RRBs), 110, 111
rehabilitation and rescue, 74, 75–76, 78, 85, 87, 89, 99–100, 103, 114, 116, 118
relatives, as source of credit, 111
Reserve Bank of India, and control over commercial banks, 123–24; and the exchange rate, 127; financial assets of, 210; funding of NABARD, 109–10; as India's Central Bank, 107–8 and the institutional infrastructure, 171; and nationalization, 30, 33; and the financial network, 212–13; and post-sanction scrutiny, 120 and refinancing and rediscounting facilities, 169–70; and reintroduction of participation certificates, 111; and setting up of institutions, 54; and Syndicate Bank, 32–33
resource mobilization, 112, 121–22, 132, 186
retail banking, 165
Revolving Underwriting Facility (RUF), 154–55
risk, borrowers', 14, 18, 22, 23; borrowers' subjective, 15; credit, 118, 119; default, 25, 78, 97, 116; lenders', 14–15, 18, 19, 20, 23, 113; lenders' subjective, 15, 16, 18, 19; spreading of, 18
risk appraisal, 19
risk diffusion, 52–54, 153
risk premium, 50–51
risk reduction, 15, 16, 17, 22, 52–54, 73, 77, 78, 79, 96–97, 102, 103, 113, 118–19, 129, 153, 157, 165, 167, 170–71
risk sharing, 75, 93–94, 113, 153, 181
risk transference, 51

safe custody, 54
Saint Simonians, 43
Sanwa group, 88, 197, 200, 205
Schumpeter, J.A., 9, 13, 175
Sechaba Investment Trust and Stockbrokers Botswana Ltd., 55
Secretariat for Industrial Approvals, 127
securities, 17, 18, 19, 20, 31, 110, 154, 155, 162, 163, 165, 169, 177, 180; *see also* collateral
'securities democratization' movement, 70
Securities and Exchange Board of India (SEBI), 169, 171
securities markets, 18, 51, 152, 177, 179
securities transactions, 54
securitization, process of, 51, 152, 153, 154
security-cum-equity type of innovation, 18
Sheard, P., 81, 85, 87
short-term credit, 17, 18, 45, 50, 51, 53, 54, 68, 71, 111
short-term open markets, 90
short-term transactions, 71, 180
'single window' concept, 118
Small Business Finance Corporation, 81
small enterprises, credit guarantee schemes for, 23; development of, 140; financing of, 10, 22, 24–27, 33, 111, 170; role of banks in, 24–27, 29, 30–33, 121–22, 123; technical assistance for, 10, 27, 29
Small Industries Development Bank of India, 212
Small Scale Industry Bank, 109
Smith, Adam, 14, 40, 46, 153
special purpose savings, facilities for, 79
Standard Chartered Bank, 164
State Bank of India, 25, 155, 157, 163, 165
State Cooperative Banks, 110, 212
State Enterprises, restructuring and privatization of, 102
State Finance Corporations (SFCs), 109, 112, 212

State Industrial Development Corporations (SIDCs), 109, 112, 212
State Owned Enterprises (SOEs), restructuring of, 176, 179, 180, 181, 184
Structural Adjustment and Stabilization, 102
structural payment imbalances, 22, 154
swaps, 156, 157
Swaraj tractor, 143
Syndicate Agricultural Foundation, 32
Syndicate Bank, establishment of, 25; and loans to small enterprises, 25–26; nationalization of, 24, 25, 30; operational autonomy of, 24; productivity of, 28–29; promotion policy of, 28; recruitment policy of, 27–28; reduction of wage costs, 32; transaction and administrative costs of, 26

takeover, 75, 76, 88, 100, 190
tariff exemptions, 93
tariff rates, lowering of, 127
tax exemptions, 79, 170–71
tax incentives, 93
technical assistance, 50, 60, 71, 87, 89, 111, 112, 116, 118, 143, 180
technical change, 14
technical consultancy services centres (TCSCs), 48, 57, 132–37, 140–46
Technical Consulting Organization (TCO), 11, 49, 51, 122
technological change, and growth in industrial output, 40
Technological Research Centres (TRCs), 132, 134, 136, 137, 140, 144
technology, absorption and diffusion of, 133, 136; adaption of, 133, 135–36, 139, 140, 142, 143–44; need for upgradation of, 133, 135–36, 140
technology choices, 57, 84, 93, 132–33, 141, 144, 146
Technology Development and Information Corporation of India (TDICI), 49, 54, 212
technology import license, 124
technology policy, institutionalized, 133; need for an appropriate, 11, 57, 132; and the role of the state, 58
Tehran Stock Exchange, 55
Teranishi, J., 95
Tourism Finance Corporation of India Ltd., 212
Toyo Kogyo, 88
trade, multilateral negotiations relating to, 149, 172–73
traditional sectors, and employment, 134; need to promote growth of, 134–35
transaction costs, 14–15, 18–26, 30, 33, 49–50, 54, 59, 73, 77, 79, 89, 96–97, 102, 113–14, 118–19, 150, 165, 167, 170–71
transfer register facilities, 54
trustee administration, 72

Unit Trust of India (UTI), 33, 52, 53, 101, 109, 111–12, 164, 169, 213
universal banking system, 10, 18–19, 66, 67, 128
universal banks, 11, 18, 41, 44, 85, 86, 100, 108, 152
Uruguay Round of trade negotiations, 149, 172

venture capital investments, introduction of, 54, 164
Voluntary Export Restrictions (VERs), 172
Voluntary Import Expansions (VIEs), 173

wage and salary reduction, 71
World Bank, 12, 41, 61, 151, 156, 157, 162, 183

Yamaichi securities, 85
Yawata, 85

Zaibatsu ties, 106
Zeteor tractor, 144